DRUMMER'S WIDOW

JOANNA FITZPATRICK

La Drôme Press

Also by Joanna FitzPatrick

Katherine Mansfield

(1888-1923)

THE DRUMMER'S WIDOW

LD

First published by La Drôme Press
Carmel Valley, California

Library of Congress Control Number: 2014907542
FitzPatrick, Joanna
The Drummer's Widow / Joanna FitzPatrick
ISBN: 978-0-9916549-0-1
ISBN: 978-0-9916549-1-8 (eBook)
1. Grief—Fiction. 2. Women writers—Fiction. 3. Widowhood—Fiction. 4. Music business—Fiction. 5. Abusive relationships—Fiction. I. Title

Cover Design: Susan Bancroft & Patricia Hamilton
Cover photograph: J. FitzPatrick
Author photograph: Ed McCann

This book is dedicated to those who have grieved
over the loss of their loved ones;
and to the terminally ill and their caregivers
who have found the hope and the courage to
move forward in spite of it all.

I.

A chair is still a chair, even when there's no one sittin' there
But a chair is not a house and a house is not a home
When there's no one there to hold you tight
And no one there you can kiss goodnight.

Now and then I call your name
And suddenly your face appears
But it's just a crazy game
When it ends, it ends in tears.

A House Is Not a Home
Lyrics by Burt Bacharach & Hal David

1

Marisa flipped on a light switch, and a thousand watts of overhead track lights flooded the dining room table in her downtown New York loft. She spread out a folder of unpaid bills: ambulance charges, mortuary services, doctor bills, and credit card and bank statements that she'd been shoving in a drawer. Then she sat and waited for the buzzer to ring, which it did exactly on the hour, awaking the cuckoo clock who screeched ten times.

Now on her own, she met Andrew Sachs in the entry and took his coat. He had been their accountant for more years than she cared to count and he had helped her with the closing of Jules's bank accounts and the transfer of funds over to her name. But for all the years he'd come to their home to do their taxes, she'd never had to meet him without Jules who buffered Andrew's caustic remarks about their ad hoc accounting.

Andrew accepted a glass of water before he sat down at the dining room table and pulled out a notepad and pencil from his fat briefcase.

Marisa watched him frown and shake his head as he picked up and put down the unpaid bills. Yes, it was all there, she thought. A tragic novel that Andrew only read as figures that didn't add up. He took off his horn-rimmed glasses and put them in their case before he looked up at her. "You're going to have to sell your loft."

Her back stiffened. "What? How can you say that after looking over those papers for five minutes?"

"Remember, Marisa, I've been doing your taxes for years and I'm well aware of your finances." He took in the cluttered walls of art posters and dusty shelves of memorabilia from years of world tours. "You know," he said, "a change would really do you good. Why not move to a cozy, uncluttered modern apartment?"

She was about to interrupt him and say that cozy-modern was an oxymoron but was distracted by Jules, who she imagined settling into his chair across the room, leaving her to deal with Andrew who rambled on. "Or what about an active senior facility where a hundred or so people all live in their own apartments? With meals served in a congenial dining room, there'd be no need to cook. You could eat with the other guests who would all be people your age. Wouldn't that be nice? No stress over whether you remembered to turn off the stove. I happen to know of a very good one, if you're interested." He stopped and smiled across the table at Marisa, who gripped her cell phone.

"Wouldn't you like that?"

"No, I wouldn't like that. Why do I have to sell my loft?"

"Isn't it obvious?" He glanced down at the stack of bills. "You can't afford to live here on your own. Jules might have been a very respected musician, but he didn't leave you a pension. You can't live on his Social Security check. It just isn't enough."

"But what about the royalties from his recordings and books? And the income I make from editing manuscripts for publishing houses? I know I've fallen behind but I don't need that much to live on."

"Marisa, listen to me. Please. The royalties don't amount to much and not only do you have debts to pay off, but also the maintenance in your building has increased. And the monthly costs of living in a downtown loft ... just look." He grabbed a few bills and flung them down. "It's all right here in black and white."

"I don't see in black and white, Andrew. Never did and I'm not going to start now." She stood up and gathered the papers back into an accordion folder.

"Look, Marisa, I'm just trying to help. You're living beyond what you can afford. You and Jules always did, but now he's gone and you can't maintain this place on your own. Manhattan's real estate market has peaked, and if you don't sell soon you're going to take a big loss when you finally do."

She stopped herself from saying, "Or do you mean I've peaked?" Instead, she thanked him for coming over (she was sure she'd receive a bill in the mail shortly) and handed him the folder. He hastily packed his briefcase and said he'd be in touch.

She sank down into the couch across from Jules's chair.

"Well, my dear, what did you think of that?"

He's only trying to help. You shouldn't be so tough on him.

"Me? What about him wanting to move me into an old people's home? Andrew Sachs isn't going to decide how I live. Since you're not here, I can make my own decisions. It's one of the many benefits of widowhood."

She pulled her phone out of the pocket of his old vest that she wore on chilly evenings and added to her Notes: Put ad in Craigslist for tenants.

"I know," she said. "I don't like the idea any better than you do. But Andrew's right about some things. Let's face it, I need income."

She went over to her desk and tapped S-E-R-E-N-D-I-P-I-T-Y. *Serendipity* had been her daughter Camille's idea, and she had set the blog up before she returned to California. Marisa had argued against it. "Why on earth would anyone want to read what I write?"

"C'mon, Mom, don't be so hard on yourself. Just write down whatever you feel strongly about and readers will show up. Besides, you need a project. You spend way too much time talking to Dad's empty chair."

Camille was partially right. Though the blog didn't keep her from still talking to Jules, it helped to fill her lonely days with new, though virtual, friends. She not only wrote detailed reviews of pertinent books on grief and widowhood, but also consoling notes to those who asked for her advice, even meeting in a chat room.

Marisa put on headphones to block out the street noise below and, accompanied by Eric Satie's sympathetic melodies she read a comment from username *indespair* who was asking her to suggest a book that would encourage him to break through his chronic grief.

She recommended *A Widow's Story* by Joyce Carol Oates who wrote her experience of grief after her husband died and her life collapsed. Marisa had found Oates's plaintive wail, "I've made myself sick by widowhood, and I am sick of it; the prospect of another few weeks of this, let alone years, is overwhelming," a useful mantra when she needed to shake herself out of self pity.

"You can't grieve forever," she wrote *indespair* though wondered herself if it was possible that someday she, like Oates before her, would "yield to the recognition that this is my life now."

At the dining table, after Marisa poured her son Miles a second glass of his favorite grape, Pinot Noir, she told him about her meeting with the accountant. He listened, leaning back in his chair, rocking back and forth, even after she finished.

It was his way, like his father, to mull things over before saying anything. She always thought they both did it to irritate her because she never could stand waiting a long time for a response. She crossed her arms and stared at Miles, trying hard not to tell him for the hundredth time, "Stop leaning back in your chair or you'll break it," which had never happened in spite of her worries.

Like Andrew earlier, but without disdain, Miles took in the crowded walls of art posters and shelves of memorabilia his parents had collected. His eyes stopped on a photo of himself on a stage, curled up inside his father's drum, his mother trying to coax him out. He smiled at his three-year-old self and said, "You know, if your accountant thinks you would be comfortable in a cozy, modern apartment then he doesn't really know who you are.

And why does he care what you do with your money? I bet he has a heavy investment himself in that 'congenial dining room' he's trying to sell you on."

"Mom?" he called out, and when he finally got back her attention said, "You've got to stop doing that. Did you hear anything I said?"

Marisa who had bored of waiting for her son to fall back in his chair so she could say "I told you so," was imagining Jules in his own chair, something she'd been doing way too much, but was afraid if she stopped conjuring him up then he really would go away forever and that must never happen.

"Andrew thought I was too old to work at Macy's. What do you think?"

"Of course not. But you'll move in with me before you have to do that."

She laughed. "Where? On your floor?" Miles shared a small Brooklyn apartment with three other young men. He did okay as a graphic designer but living in New York was way beyond his budget, even in Brooklyn.

Miles's dark bushy brows arched up just like his father's when he was worried. "Then what are you going to do?"

She took a deep breath, pulled herself up straight and stated as much to him as to herself, "I've decided to rent out the two back bedrooms and move into your old room in the front." She hurried on before she changed her mind. "I haven't slept in our bedroom since"—she sucked in air and let it out. "I can rent out our old bedroom and the other back bedroom. I'll cash in your dad's IRA to pay off the debts and I'll call my publisher clients and get working again. You'll see. I'm not really desperate at all."

"Mom, I never said you were desperate."

"It's been nine months since your father's been gone, and I know I haven't been at my best, but I'm coming around. At sixty-five, I can't see any reason why I should move into an old people's home. I'm more than capable of taking care of myself."

"Hey wait a minute. Who are you talking to? I'm not your

accountant. I know you can take care of yourself. But taking in tenants? Is that really a good idea?"

"No, maybe not. But I don't see any other choice."

He swirled his glass and put it back down without tasting it. "Look, you're going to do what you want anyway. But be careful. I've read bad things about older women living alone in the City. And if you can't find the right tenants, maybe you really should consider one of those assisted living places where you'd be safe."

She leaned toward him. "Do you think your father would have wanted me in an old people's home after he was gone?"

Miles turned toward his father's chair and when he turned back to face her, he blinked back a tear that Marisa felt was her own. "No, but he'd want you to be safe. Maybe we can find something like that in Brooklyn. Near me."

She covered Miles's hand with her own. "Look," she said softly, "I know this hasn't been easy for you either. And I know you want what's best for me. But you've got to trust me on this one." They clinked their glasses and smiled, but her heart ached looking into his blue eyes and seeing Jules.

"Now let's eat and after dinner we'll look over your Dad's record collection."

"Okay, but please don't just take in the first stranger who comes to your door."

"Certainly not," she said, rolling her eyes up onto the lofty ceiling.

By Friday, Marisa was anxious. Her publishing house clients had no freelance editing work for her and no one had responded to the Craigslist ad. She'd pretended to be brave in front of Andrew and Miles but poverty scared her.

Ignoring Jules's ethereal suggestion that she be patient, Marisa sat down at her desk and was about to lower the rental fee from eight hundred to seven hundred when she received an e-mail from cb9p6-388846@rental.craigslist.org: Interested. Could I see? cb

She responded instantly: Dear cb. Yes. Come tomorrow at three. Address: 32 Murray Street. Take subway downtown to Chambers. Walk two blocks south. Look forward to meeting you. Sincerely, Marisa Bridges

It was only after she clicked send that she reread CB's cryptic message and realized what a rash, irresponsible act she'd taken out of desperation. What if she'd just opened her home to a serial killer?

2

While the cuckoo shrilled three times, Marisa gaped at a tall Goth creature with a viper crawling up her right arm. And Cassandra, who had planned to cover her tattoo under a jacket and her gel-spiked orange hair under a stocking cap before knocking on a door, was unprepared for the elevator to open onto an elderly woman's loft and a screeching clock.

Cassandra pushed the lobby button to escape, and the elevator door would have closed, whisking away Marisa's potential rental income, if Marisa hadn't thrown out her arm and stopped it.

Embarrassed by their reactions they both burst out laughing. Cassandra removed her black sunglasses, bent down to look straight into Marisa's eyes, and reached out her hand. "Hello. I think you were expecting me. I'm CB."

"Marisa Bridges." She smiled up at CB, hiding her distaste for the diamond nose piercing and silver rings that dangled from the girl's left ear lobe, as they shook hands.

Both women turned in the direction of the whistling teakettle. "Please come in," said Marisa. "I was just boiling some water for tea."

While Marisa poured water in the teapot and dropped in two tea bags, Cassandra took in the enormous loft space. The orange-tiled kitchen was a bit garish but showed a flair for color that she appreciated. The faux-painted orange walls could have come from the same bottle of dye she used on her hair. The bold colors lent an air of eccentricity to this little woman whom Cassandra already found appealing.

She turned back and found Marisa gawking at her. Marisa

apologized saying that Cassandra reminded her of her daughter, Camille, who also towered over her. "And when she was younger she had cropped hair like yours. Are you from New York?"

"No." Cassandra said. After a moment's hesitation she added, "The West Coast."

"Oh really? My daughter recently moved to San Francisco."

Silence. Then "That's cool. A lot hipper than L.A. where I'm from."

Marisa was finding this tenant interview quite awkward. And Cassandra's minimal responses didn't help. She tried again. "Should I call you 'CB'?"

The girl half smiled. "Cassandra."

"Cassandra?"

"Cassandra Blanche."

"Well, Cassandra, if you like I'll show you around while the tea brews."

Marisa led Cassandra down a long sunflower-yellow hallway explaining she chose bright colors to cheer up the bleak rooms in the back of her loft.

"Nice."

Entering what she referred to as the foyer, Marisa studied Cassandra's face in the overhead light. The heavy black liner artfully penciled around sad, tired eyes and the thick white face powder made it impossible to guess her age.

Cassandra glanced into a large deep-purple bedroom with a double bed, but then was drawn toward a pattern of mottled light on the wooden floor of the otherwise all-white bedroom next door. The sunlight was coming through its one window, which looked out on an airshaft and a wall of brick buildings.

This room was actually much larger than her studio in the East Village and far quieter since it didn't face the street. She might finally get some sleep. The bed was narrow, but she didn't plan to share it with anyone. She plopped herself down on it, tested its springs and puffed up the pillow. She wanted to lie down and take a long nap. "Nice bed."

Marisa glared at this young woman who'd sat down on her daughter's bed without asking. It had been years since Camille lived in this room, but it was still hers.

Cassandra felt Marisa's disapproval and stood to straighten the bedspread and replace the pillow. *I just lost ten points*, she thought, as she followed Marisa back out into the spacious foyer.

"This is a really nice space," said Cassandra standing next to a piano in the center surrounded by walls of blue sky and puffy clouds.

"This is where my husband worked."

"A pianist?"

"No … a drummer, but he composed music on this piano."

"Would I know any songs he wrote?"

"Probably not. You're from a different generation."

"Would I be sharing the foyer with him? Is that your bedroom?" She asked too quickly, pointing toward the purple room.

Marisa folded her arms and said crossly, "No. Both bedrooms are for rent and the rental includes sharing the foyer and the bathroom. Perhaps you're wanting more privacy?"

Cassandra swallowed hard. "No, I wouldn't mind sharing. I'll be out most of the time."

Marisa sat down on the piano bench, fingers hovering over the keys.

Cassandra expected her to play, but after a long moment, she tapped Marisa on the shoulder, "Mrs. Bridges?"

Marisa's misty eyes came into focus on Cassandra. "Sorry. Did you ask me something?"

"Are you going to play?"

"Goodness no. Do you play?"

Cassandra took in the full bookshelves of albums and CDs. "I used to be a singer."

"Why did you stop?"

"Let's just say life interrupted."

How interesting, thought Marisa. Did the girl know that "life interrupted" was Virginia Woolf's reference to life getting in the way of her work as a writer? She was curious to know how life "interrupted" Cassandra from singing. Instead she asked, "Have you read Virginia Woolf?"

"Yes, how could you tell?" She didn't wait for Marisa's answer. "She was one of my mother's favorite writers and then mine. I particularly like *A Room of One's Own*."

Marisa pressed a few notes and Cassandra flinched. "Ooh. That's way out of tune."

"It's been neglected for quite some time."

"Doesn't your husband play anymore?"

"Let's just say"—she shut the keyboard cover—"death interrupted." She looked up and smiled. "Shall we have our tea before it gets cold?"

Cassandra followed her down the yellow hallway thinking Marisa Bridges's moods were as eccentric as the technicolor-painted rooms.

Marisa arranged a tea tray laden with brightly colored Provençal pottery that matched the walls. Cassandra offered to carry it over to a table in the large open space facing the street.

During the long silence that followed Marisa searched her mind for the appropriate questions a landlord should ask a potential tenant, and then remembered she'd written them down in her Notes. She reached for her smartphone and ran through the list with Cassandra.

Though Marisa seemed to approve of her being an art student, Cassandra hesitated before telling her she paid for her classes by bartending. She relaxed when Marisa said her daughter had worked as a bartender when she was Cassandra's age and understood how important tips are for a struggling artist.

Marisa then told Cassandra that she was a widow and couldn't afford the loft on her own.

"I'm sorry. It must be difficult for you," said Cassandra with a down-turned mouth lined with black lipstick. "I lost my mother when I was quite young but my father didn't wait long to remarry. Said he couldn't bear the loneliness."

"It does take time getting used to." Marisa pointed across the room to another open door and said, "I sleep in there now. It helps."

In spite of the brightly painted walls, there was a pall of grief over the dim room they were sitting in that made Cassandra want to open the heavy wood blinds covering the enormous windows and let the light in. If she didn't know she was in a downtown Manhattan loft, she might have thought she was in a cave or, worse, a mortuary for the unliving.

Marisa responded as if she'd heard Cassandra's thoughts. "How silly of me. My son often has to remind me when I forget to open the blinds or turn on the lights."

"I'll open the blinds if you like?"

The sudden stream of sunlight melted any remaining chill Marisa had felt toward Cassandra. "Do you have time for a second cup of tea?" she asked, holding the teapot over the girl's cup. "Yes, please." They smiled at each other.

"Well, what do you think? Does the white bedroom suit your needs?"

Cassandra's face brightened. "You mean I can rent it?"

"Yes. As long as you understand that we'll have to take it month by month. I'm somewhat unsure of my future plans." *So am I*, Cassandra could have said, but didn't want Marisa thinking she might move out on short notice. She nodded in agreement.

"When could you move in?"

Cassandra would give her present landlord two-weeks notice and move in on the first of February.

"Shouldn't I sign something?" asked Cassandra as she stood to leave.

"No, that won't be necessary. I have a horror of contracts. I would rather shake on it, if that's all right with you?"

Marisa looked down at her yellow-skinned phone to make sure she'd covered everything and looked up. "Oh, how silly of me. I almost forgot to ask for two letters of reference."

Cassandra sank back into the chair and Marisa sensed—not for the first time—that the girl's world was not on solid ground.

"Mrs. Bridges I don't know if I can do that. I haven't been here very long and I don't know many people."

Marisa remained firm. "There must be someone who can vouch for you? Your boss or perhaps one of your art teachers or what about your current landlord?"

Cassandra recovered and stood up. "Yes—I suppose I could ask them. I'll get that taken care of right away."

"Good. You can e-mail them to me." She walked Cassandra over to the elevator and waited for the doors to open. "Seeing we're going to be roommates," Marisa said, "Mrs. Bridges sounds rather formal don't you think?" They both smiled.

"Okay then. See you on the first of February, Marisa." They waved good-bye as the elevator door closed.

Marisa ate the last cookie on the plate and washed the cups and saucers. Drying her hands, she wondered whether she'd done the right thing. Cassandra had told her very little about herself, pulling a curtain across her past, so Marisa was going mostly by instinct and curiosity. Why hide her lovely face behind that gothic makeup? And what was that ugly viper all about? But there was something else about this mysterious girl that had been the deciding factor. She had chosen the room where Camille had retreated during her troubled years living in New York City—a safe place to mend her broken spirit. Marisa felt Cassandra also needed a safe retreat and she felt good helping her.

The Craigslist responses picked up over the weekend and Marisa showed the other room to several potential tenants but none that she wanted to invite to tea.

A week had passed and Marisa was at Edward's, the neighborhood bar, reading over the short list of possible tenants that she'd interviewed. The deep bass voice of a young man drew her attention. He was telling the bartender that his roommate was getting married and wanted the apartment for his bride. He had to find something soon but had nearly given up in Manhattan. "It's just too expensive, and no one wants to rent to a jazz guitarist. I'm starting to look in Brooklyn's Sunset Park where studios are cheaper, but it's a long commute to my gigs in the Village."

Having been a drummer's wife, Marisa knew what it was like to be turned down by landlords and her heart went out to him. She tapped him on the shoulder and was not disappointed when he turned his soft caramel eyes onto hers. He smiled, "Yes, ma'am?"

"I couldn't help but overhear what you were saying and I have a room for rent a few blocks from here."

"That's very kind of you, but I'm looking for a studio where I can live on my own."

"Perfect." She smiled. "I have just the place for you."

"I don't think you understand, ma'am—"

"Just listen for a moment. I have two vacant rooms in the back of my loft. One tenant is moving in on the first of February. That leaves one still empty." She smiled. "And there's a piano."

"A piano? Hmm, now that makes it more interesting. But could I play it?"

"Why, of course, isn't that what a piano is for?"

"No." He laughed. "Often it's just décor. In my case, I use it to compose my music. But wouldn't you or your neighbors mind 'the noise'?" he framed in air-quotes.

"Not at all. I live at the other end of the loft and I won't hear you. And my neighbors are out all day at work."

"Tempting, but I doubt if I can afford it."

"How do you know without asking?"

"Okay. What's the rent?"

"Eight hundred a month," she said quickly, stopping herself from asking less. That wouldn't be fair to Cassandra.

He blew a quiet whistle. "More than my budget. But thanks." He started to turn away.

"But you can be in the Village in ten minutes."

He laughed. "Wow ... You *were* listening. Yeah, it would be much better here but I have gigs in Brooklyn too."

"All the subways to Brooklyn are nearby. You can take the F train right across the bridge. And I'm not asking for a deposit."

"Look, I appreciate your wanting to help me—"

"This is not charity. I need a tenant. At least think about it"—she stopped—"Oh dear, I've forgotten your name."

"No you haven't. I never told you. It's Martin. Martin Starks." He held out his hand. "And whom do I have the pleasure of meeting?"

Marisa was sure he was teasing her but she liked it. She reached over and shook his hand. "Marisa Bridges."

"Nice to meet you, Marisa Bridges." He tipped the brim of his cap then turned back to the bartender and ordered another beer.

A bit cocky, isn't he?

She smiled. Yes, but I like him. He reminds me a bit of you struggling to make it as a musician.

Then you better ask him again.

She finished her drink, got up to leave, and tapped Martin's shoulder, "Why not at least come by and see it?"

His charming smile gave her a glimmer of hope, and she wrote down her address on a bar napkin.

———

The following afternoon, when Martin stepped out of the elevator and she looked up into his warm, trusting eyes, Marisa knew she'd made the right choice.

She gave him the same tour she'd given Cassandra, but he barely glanced into the offered purple bedroom. His interest lay elsewhere. He returned to the foyer and sat down at the piano, playing a few chords. "This needs tuning."

She frowned.

"Not to worry. I can tune it for you." He crouched down to look through bookshelves of CDs and LPs. "Wow! This is a rare collection. You certainly know your jazz!"

"No, not really. They're my husband's. And so is the piano."

"Won't he mind me using it?"

A painful moment for Marisa, just like with Cassandra, when she had to face the truth head-on. A wave of sadness came over her, but she saw this one coming and dove under it, coming up on the other side still breathing. "He passed away last year."

"I'm sorry," said Martin.

She retreated from the light. "Shall we have a cup of tea? Or would you prefer coffee?"

"I really should get going." He saw her disappointment. "Oh all right, I could use a cup of java, but that doesn't mean I'm accepting your offer."

She smiled. "Of course not."

She'd just poured a second cup when Martin agreed to her terms. The deal was too sweet to refuse. Any other landlord would have insisted on the two months rent and a deposit that he didn't have. And then there was the piano to compose on. He could eke out enough income playing gigs and teaching his guitar students. He promised two letters of reference.

Waiting for the elevator, he said, "You're being more than fair and I really appreciate it."

3

Marisa's tenants were moving in this morning and, unsure of a landlady's responsibilities, she'd made the beds, hung two sets of towels (orange for Cassandra's hair, brown for Martin's eyes) in the bathroom, and kept walking to the back of her loft several times to see if there was anything else she could do to make their rooms more welcoming. She considered a quick trip to the florist.

My god, Marisa, they're tenants not houseguests, interjected Jules without being asked.

Marisa frowned at two stacks of cartons blocking the hallway. Too heavy to take to the basement on her own, she'd have to wait until Miles was free to do it and that could be a long wait. Unsealing a box, she sat cross-legged on the foyer floor, and put a bound manuscript on her lap, tracing her fingers over its front cover title embossed in gold ink: *SHA LA LA: LIVE FOR TODAY.*

In what she considered a reinvention of her life, Marisa had gone back to college as an older student to jump-start her second career as a writer. Accepted and enrolled in Columbia's MFA program, she wrote a memoir for her thesis, expecting to revise and publish it after she graduated. But that was before Jules was diagnosed with cancer and she became a full-time caregiver and part-time book editor. She opened the manuscript to the first page and read the dedication: *À mon cheri, Jules*. Her vision clouded with tears and she glanced sideways at the wastebasket.

No, Marisa. Your work has value, even shut away. Someday—

"Someday what, Jules?" she shouted into the vacant foyer. The door intercom buzzed, and she looked down at the sweats she'd been living in for months and sighed. There was no time to change, but she'd have to clean up her act now that she was no longer living alone, which was probably a good thing.

The elevator door opened on a disheveled, unshaven Martin in black jeans, and an unbuttoned red plaid lumber jacket. He carried a faded, worn-out duffel bag over his shoulder, and two battered guitar cases in his hands. "Hey, Marisa. Sorry about my appearance. I'm coming straight from a very late-night jam session, and after packing up my stuff, I must look pretty bad."

Marisa picked up one of the guitar cases and followed Martin down the hall where he tripped over a carton. "What the"—he caught himself against the wall.

"Oh, dear. That's my fault. I've been cleaning out your closet and was going to ask my son to store these cartons in the basement."

"I'll help you."

"You wouldn't mind?"

Martin lifted the two cardboard cartons and smiled. "Lead the way."

Inside the elevator, Marisa pressed B, but instead it went up to the third floor. She cursed under her breath. An impeccably dressed middle-aged man stepped in and the door slammed shut, locking the three of them in its tight cabin. She wished he would turn around and face the door instead of her as she felt like a fly caught in a spider's web. She said, "Good morning, Carl. What a surprise. I thought you were under the weather."

He hesitated, adjusting his tie. "No. I'm quite fine. Why would you think that?"

"Well … I've woken several times to you pacing back and forth over my head very late at night or even at dawn. I thought you might be having trouble sleeping?"

"Isn't your bedroom in the back?"

"It used to be. I've moved. I'm in the front bedroom now."

"That's unfortunate for you," he said without sympathy. "My office is right above you and I often take overseas calls."

"Do you think you could—"

"Where are you going with all these cartons, Marisa? Moving somewhere?"

Don't you wish, she thought. "No. Just storing some things in the basement."

"Need I remind you of the Board's rule regarding storage? Only thick plastic containers with tight fitting lids are permitted."

She grimaced but kept smiling. "It's only temporary."

"I do hope so. As you know, better than anyone, the rules are the rules." He turned to Martin leaning back against the wall taking a catnap. "And who are you?"

Martin opened his eyes but before he could speak, Marisa interjected, "He's my nephew. He came to visit his aunt and have a look around the city. Martin, this is Carl, my upstairs neighbor."

"I didn't know you had any nephews."

"Well, I don't, he's really Jules's nephew. Actually he had quite a few. Nieces too. Big family in the Midwest." Just then the elevator opened onto the lobby and Carl stepped out.

The front door slammed behind him and Marisa pushed the elevator's basement button.

"Wow. What a creep. Is he always that pleasant?"

"Look, Martin, I know I shouldn't have introduced you as my nephew, but . . ."

"Yeah, what's that all about?"

"I'm not actually allowed to have tenants."

"I thought it was your apartment?"

"It is—but not really."

"Huh?"

"New York co-ops are different. We all own shares in a corporation controlled by a Board of Directors. Carl's the Board president and he takes his position quite seriously. If I asked permission to rent rooms in my loft, the Board could vote me down and you'd have to leave."

"That's crazy."

"And even if they did approve, they have the right to ask me to pay the building a percentage of the rent I collect and I can't afford that. So it would be better if my neighbors think you're my husband's nephew."

They descended to the basement. Marisa unlocked the elevator's basement gate and bent down to pick up a box.

"That's too heavy for you. Let me take that one, Aunt Marisa." They both laughed. She pulled a string hanging from a naked bulb that illuminated an otherwise black space. Martin stacked a carton on a metal shelf against the far wall, and Marisa placed hers next to it, turning its label, *SHA LA LA: LIVE FOR TODAY,* toward the wall.

Not that Martin would have noticed. His eyes were riveted on several drum kits zipped up in black cases. "Whose drums are these?"

"My husband's," said Marisa, switching off the light. She stopped the elevator at the lobby, and as the door opened she pointed toward a gate, which led to the back staircase. "You can use this instead of the elevator."

"Does that mean you'd prefer it so I don't meet up again with your friendly neighbor Carl?"

She smiled. "Well, no—though I must confess that I use it for that very reason."

Back in the loft, Marisa handed Martin a ring of keys. She showed him how to use the keyed elevator, warned him not to leave the loft without the key, then showed him the cross-bar police lock on the hallway door, which led to the back staircase. She repeated there was no real reason to use the staircase unless he wanted the exercise or there was a blackout in the building.

"Jules used it to bring up those drum kits you saw in the basement."

Martin's face lit up. "Wait a minute. You said, Jules … and you're Mrs. Bridges … so then those drums down in the basement belong to Jules Bridges?"

"Have you heard of him?"

"Heard of him! What jazz musician hasn't?"

Blood rushed to Marisa's head.

"Wasn't he on stage the night he—"

Pretending she didn't hear him, Marisa plopped down in the nearest chair. "That excursion to the basement wore me out."

He didn't notice her discomfort and continued. "From all I've heard, he was not only an awesome drummer but a really cool dude."

She smiled up at him through watery eyes. "Yes, he was."

Just then the cuckoo jumped out startling both of them and giving Marisa a moment to blink back her tears and suck in air as they both turned toward the clock. "Oh my," she said, "is it that late? Cassandra will be here any minute."

"Cassandra?" Martin widened his eyes in mock excitement. "You mean the priestess?"

"No, not exactly. Your roommate."

"Oh," he said, with feigned disappointment and yawned. "Well, I better get some sleep. I've got a gig tonight." He tipped his cap like he had done at Edward's when he first charmed her. "See you later, Aunt Marisa."

"Sweet dreams, nephew."

Worried about Carl, Marisa sent e-mails to the building's Board members advising them of Jules's nephew's visit, adding that Jules's niece, Cassandra, was visiting too.

She poured herself another cup of coffee, and then sat down across from Jules's chair, bracing for what she knew was coming.

Why did you do that, Marisa? Why did you tell Carl your tenants were my relatives?

"I—I don't know. It's just what came up. If I told them the truth they might not allow it, and I couldn't risk that."

You mustn't worry so much. Haven't I told you everything's going to be all right.

"And I'm to believe you? The last time you said that to me you never came home. Yet you promised to be back in a few hours." Her voice faltered. "Well, I'm still waiting for you."

She considered telling her neighbors the truth—something she would have done before Carl became Board president. Lying back on the couch, her mind raked over the coals of resentment that never stopped burning.

After 9/11, the Tribeca neighborhood pulled itself out of the wreckage and debris and neighbors greeted each other graciously on the streets and in the stores, everyone so grateful to have survived the catastrophe and mourning those who hadn't.

And then Tribeca changed. As the towers were slowly rebuilt, luxury condos sprang up on every block. Those who could afford overpriced real estate moved in—the artists who couldn't moved to Brooklyn. Carl bought the loft above Marisa and was very pleasant—at first. He was so willing to take on his share of work maintaining the building that the Board asked him to be president after Rachel resigned. That turned out to be a big mistake.

Marisa remembered a Board meeting when, after being president for just six months, Carl proposed hiring a building manager.

"Why can't we continue to manage the building ourselves?" she'd asked when no one else spoke up. "We've done it for years."

"Because DIY types mis-manage buildings."

"I'm sorry but what's a DIY?"

"It means Do-It-Yourself. That may have worked in the past, but things have changed. We need to hire a professional building manager to take over the finances and everything else, like other co-ops are doing. None of us have the time to sweep the lobby or take out the trash."

That was when Marisa volunteered to do the chores herself. Why not? She was home taking care of Jules and, with him not working, they couldn't afford an increase in maintenance fees. Carl had brought up hiring a professional at every Board meeting since, but Marisa had managed to sway enough votes to her side.

The door buzzer interrupted her reverie. "Who is it?" she said into the intercom.

"Cassandra," came the broken-up response passing through the staticky intercom, barely audible over the sounds of trucks, buses, and cars honking and screeching in the street below.

Marisa's second new tenant carried far more elegant baggage into the loft than the first one had; a large Louis Vuitton suitcase and matching make-up case, a leather satchel, an oversized portfolio, and a wooden painter's box.

Marisa reached for the make-up case, but Cassandra jerked it away. "That's too heavy. Would you carry the portfolio instead?"

"I hope you don't mind the lack of light back here. It can be a bit dreary," said Marisa turning on Cassandra's bedroom light.

"Wow! You shouldn't have gone to so much trouble. But thanks. I love the down comforter."

The two women stood just inside the doorway and Marisa sensed Cassandra's hesitation. "It's okay. Sit down. This is your room now."

They sat together on the bed, and as Marisa was explaining the various house keys, Cassandra jumped. "What's that? It sounds like a quacking duck."

Marisa giggled—something she rarely did lately—and reached for the quacking yellow-skinned phone in her pocket. "You're waiting for me? Oh dear. With so much going on I completely forgot. No, don't go. I'm coming right now."

Marisa turned to Cassandra. "Sorry. I have to run. Make yourself at home and feel free to use the kitchen. I made a pasta sauce and there's a box of spaghetti and a fresh baguette on the counter. Help yourself."

Halfway down the hall, Marisa called out, "For Internet the password is SERENDIPITY and give it to Martin if you see him."

"Who's Martin?" asked Cassandra, but Marisa was already out the door and running down the backstairs to avoid her neighbors.

4

With her wooly plum scarf snug around her neck and a matching cloche pulled over her head, Marisa pushed hard against the bitter wind, making her way down the three long city blocks to Edward's. She cursed herself for forgetting her weekly artist-night-half-price drinks with Corina, which she always looked forward to. Far off, wedged between walls of the concrete and glass monoliths, the setting sun reflected on the Hudson River. Marisa squeezed through the slow pedestrians blocking her way.

After 9/11 the streets had been barren; Tribeca's population, afraid of either the next catastrophe or the grieving spirits floating in the atmosphere where the indestructible twin towers had once stood, had fled the neighborhood. But now it was as if nothing had ever happened. The population had tripled and new towers were being constructed to replace those lost.

Her stride was halted by a red traffic light. Marisa rested her eyes on the last slivers of sunlight, as she imagined standing in the golden fields near the French farm where she and Jules had spent so many idyllic summers.

Turning right onto West Broadway, she burst into Edward's warm taproom and approached Corina seated on a bar stool. "I'm so sorry. Will you forgive me?" she asked breathlessly.

"Don't I always?" Corina bent toward Marisa and kissed her icy, wind-burned cheek.

The bald and buff bartender, Stan, who knew Marisa well, smiled at her, while shaking her elixir in a cocktail shaker. She perched up on the bar stool and watched him pour the lime-infused Stoli gimlet into a frosted martini glass. "Thanks, Stan. You're the best."

In the bar mirror she admired her stylish friend in a tilted beret, her thick black hair spilling down off her broad shoulders. Corina's only sign of aging was a few strands of silver hair.

Marisa and Corina were older than most of the locals. In previous years they'd been noticed, flirted with, and bought drinks by men, in exchange for listening to their boring stories. No longer needing to ask those kind of guys to leave them alone so they could talk came as a relief. But there were times when Marisa would have liked waiters to pay a little more attention to her, like Stan did, when she wanted to order a drink or dinner.

Marisa turned to Corina. "I love being here with my dearest old friend." Corina's dark, intelligent eyes looked into Marisa's and they raised their martini glasses. "Cheers!"

In the past, they would meet for drinks at Edward's, their husbands joining them later for dinner. Seated at the bar, taking in the ethereal lights, Marisa could feel Jules behind her. *There you are,* he whispered. The warmth of his body pressing against her back, his soft lips caressing her neck then kissing her lips.

"The next round's on me," she said, breaking away from her habitual yearning for what could not be. "I owe you that for being late."

"I won't turn it down even though we both know I should." They laughed and clinked their glasses again.

Marisa had met Corina thirty years ago at a Lamaze class. Corina's daughter Ashley and her son Miles were born a day apart. Besides having their roles as wives and mothers in common, both women were aspiring writers who shared the disappointment of putting their manuscripts away to bring up children, care for their husbands, and make money as editors correcting other writers' books, when they'd rather be working on their own books.

The original reason for their weekly meetings at Edward's was to encourage each other to continue writing, to rekindle their creative sparks with conversations wrapped around plot twists, loose endings and character development. And to complain about how little writing they were actually doing and ask each other why they even tried.

To capture that deep joy that comes from doing something meaningful with your life. That's what Jules would tell her when she questioned the hours she spent struggling to finish a chapter or even a sentence. But that was before his illness divided her life into "before" and "after."

Corina was the first person she told when Jules was diagnosed five years ago. Then their conversations about writer's block were replaced with heartbreaking conversations about cancer. Marisa expanded her writer's vocabulary with words like metastasis, apoptosis, and cytotoxicity. Her weekly reports on Jules's health went from bad to worse. Clinical trials were pursued and finally, when they were desperate, crackpots who promised cures. After two stem cell transplants and chemo that had poisoned him so badly he couldn't get out of bed, she had to cancel her meetings with Corina.

And then the unexpected happened. After several years of illness, Jules, who never gave up, recovered. He beat the statistics. He became a cancer survivor against all odds and they thought they'd be together—

"Marisa! Marisa!"

"What?" She lifted her head and opened her eyes on Corina's concerned face.

"Are you all right? You didn't hear me calling."

"Sorry. I was thinking about Jules." She straightened her back and managed to smile before excusing herself. In the bathroom she took several deep breaths and splashed cold water on her face until the wave of sorrow rolled over her and receded out to sea.

She returned dry-eyed, jumped back up on the bar stool and, as if she hadn't left, asked, "How many pages did you write this week?"

"Do you really want to talk about that? We could talk about Jules."

Marisa shook her head. "No, I'd rather not."

"Well, if you must know, I haven't written since I last saw you. I've been too busy planning Ashley's wedding."

Marisa watched Stan rattle the martini shaker, while trying to decide whether or not to be brutally honest with her friend. She'd expect the same from Corina so she went ahead. "Sometimes I wonder if you even want to finish your manuscript."

Corina glared at Marisa who quickly apologized. "That wasn't fair, I know how hard you try to find time to write."

After Stan set their drinks down, Corina said, "No, you're right. My excuses are lame. The truth is, the further I get away from it, the blinder I become to the vision I started with. I forget why I'm writing the damn thing in the first place."

"It's good that you get angry about it. It means you still care about your work. I'm not sure I do." Marisa confessed that she almost threw out her manuscript.

"You do care," said Corina. "I remember how excited you were after a productive day writing. And now that you don't have to take care of"—Marisa's stricken face stopped her—"Oh Marisa, I didn't mean that. Really! Just sometimes I envy your solitude. Whenever I try to get some serious work done, Ben needs me to find something for him, or he wants his dinner or whatever, and another day passes without progress."

"I wish I had your problem. I'm finding it impossible to write because Jules isn't here. I just finished reading *A Widow's Story*, Joyce Carol Oates's book about her own grief after her husband's death. She thinks writing is a cure for grief, but I don't agree, at least, not yet."

"And how are you getting along in that big empty loft of yours?"

"Well, it's not empty anymore. I've taken in two tenants."

"Tenants? But why?"

Marisa looked down at her drink, "Because I can't pay my bills otherwise."

"You know if we can help—"

"Thanks, Corina. But I've got to find a way to provide for myself without help."

"Where did you find your tenants?"

Marisa laughed. "Well, one right here at this bar, which was serendipity at its best. The other on Craigslist."

"What does Miles think of your new tenants?"

"He hasn't met them. I'm going to tell him next week when we meet for dinner."

"How's he doing?"

"He's okay. His girlfriend breaking up with him just after he lost his father didn't help. But before we get wound up talking about our kids, let's get back to the writing. I read that chapter you gave me last week and it's really good. What a page-turner. You have to finish it or I'll never know how it ends."

"That's the problem." She banged her fist on the bar, almost spilling her martini. "I don't know how to end it."

Corina was telling Marisa how her unwieldy character just wouldn't give it up and die as she had planned, when Marisa's phone vibrated against her hip.

Strangers in your loft. Come home.

"Oh-oh! I've got to go."

Marisa rushed outside into the exterior world, a bit off-kilter after Stan's generous gimlets. Her feet almost slid out from under her on the icy sidewalk. *Slow down, Marisa,* Jules shouted. She'd prefer if he were there to take her arm, but she paid attention to his warning and tottered home slowly instead of taking her usual high-speed stride.

When she saw Miles waiting for her under the front door light, she waved and tried her best to walk a straight line toward him. "Mom, do you know who those people are in your loft?"

"People? Oh, you must mean Cassandra and Martin? But why are you standing out here?"

"What are they doing here?"

"They're my new tenants."

"Your tenants are eating your food, and drinking your wine?"

"Oh good, they took me up on the pasta. C'mon, let's join them. I'm starving." He followed her into the lobby.

"Mom, what if they steal everything?"

"Miles, aren't you overreacting? They're tenants not thieves. And I don't really have anything worth stealing anyway."

"Did you ask for references?"

She nodded yes but didn't tell him she hadn't gotten them yet.

Marisa didn't want her neighbors or her tenants to hear them arguing. Voices carried too easily up the elevator shaft. "Let's go upstairs. If you give them a chance, you'll find out they're quite nice."

He jammed his thumb on the elevator button. "I can't. I have a dinner date. I was just stopping by to move those boxes to the basement. I'll meet them some other time." The elevator door opened. "And, Mom, you better take it easy on those gimlets, don't you think?"

She searched her purse frantically for the key that would activate the button for her floor. She wanted to go straight up before Carl or anyone else called the elevator to their floor.

Now you've done it, she thought to herself. What is it about me that rubs my son the wrong way?

He shows his concern for you and you don't take him seriously.

"I don't know why you always have to take his side."

The elevator door opened on a scene from *The Lady and the Tramp*. Cassandra and Martin were seated across from each other eating out of bowls filled with spaghetti bolognese. They put their forks down and looked over at her while she hung her coat and hat in the closet. They were still looking at her when she approached the table. Martin said, "Some guy came in here, looked real shocked, and before we could explain anything, he left."

She poured herself a glass of wine and sat down.

"That was my son, Miles. I'm sorry if he was rude to you."

"He looked like he didn't really want us here. That's for sure," said Cassandra softly, lowering her eyes, reminding Marisa of

Lady's brown saucer-shaped eyes, thick eyelashes and heavy lids. But Lady was a spaniel and didn't have orange-spiked hair.

"This is all my fault," said Marisa. "I should have told him about you. He was just surprised to see you here."

Her look changed from one of concern to cheerfulness. "How's the pasta?"

"Delicious," said Martin twirling another large bite around his fork. "Thanks. It was really nice of you to do this for us."

"Let me get you a bowl," said Cassandra.

Marisa felt warm and fuzzy inside. Many a dinner had been shared with Jules and their friends at this table and seeing her new tenants enjoying her pasta brought back those good memories. She wished Miles were there to see that Cassandra and Martin really were nice people and he shouldn't worry.

"Cassandra, there is one thing I need to ask of you. I don't know if Martin told you that I have difficult neighbors. I know it sounds ridiculous, but if anyone asks who you are, please tell them you're my niece, here for a visit. I don't want the co-op Board to know I've taken in tenants."

"No problem."

They offered to help Marisa wash the dishes before they left but she told them not to bother—she'd just put them in the dishwasher.

They left together for the Village: Cassandra to bartend at the Bitter End and Martin to play at a club nearby. Martin thanked Marisa again for dinner, and Cassandra smiled in agreement before the elevator door closed.

The Bitter End was packed. Max, the other bartender, was relieved to see Cassandra arrive. He went outside to smoke and left her to take up the slack. Much later, when the bar thinned out, she sat on a corner stool exhausted. She listened to the band and sketched the musicians. They offered to pay something for her portraits, but it seemed only fair to give them away seeing she made more money in tips than they did playing music. Besides, she liked doing it.

While Cassandra sketched musicians at the Bitter End, Martin was finishing up his last set at the 55 Bar down the street. It was way after midnight and only a few local drunks were hanging out, talking loudly. It didn't bother Martin that they weren't listening. He'd had a good night. The first two sets had pulled in a good listening crowd. His agent had brought a few A&R guys from a record company who seemed to like the music though they didn't stay around for the second set. But most important he felt satisfied with his playing and the new compositions he'd tried out with his trio.

As the last song ended, he nodded to the drummer and bass player to lay out as he finished it off with a guitar cadenza before the final chord.

Packing up, he thought to stop by the Bitter End to see if Cassandra was still working, perhaps have a drink with her, but then he thought better of it. They'd shared dinner together happily enough, but on the subway ride she shut down. As he finished packing his guitar, a pretty fan came over to him and said, "Thanks for the music. You're really good." He smiled and invited her to join him for a drink.

Marisa checked her phone before turning out the light, hoping for a message from Miles. Tomorrow I'll call and apologize, she promised herself. Her nattering thoughts about her son and the building finally quieted down, and she fell asleep.

Her sleep was interrupted by Carl's pacing footsteps above her head. The digital numbers on her alarm clock were a blur without glasses but the cuckoo confirmed the time with six screeches. She stuffed rubber earplugs in her ears, but she couldn't fall back to sleep. She made coffee, brought it back to bed, and checked her phone for messages. There was a text message from Miles: Sorry about last night. Give me full names so I can run credit checks.

At her desk, Marisa began editing the Random House manuscript that was delivered the day before. If she didn't need the money, she'd have put it off a few more days because the graphic details of a pedophile's perversions were making her ill.

After correcting several chapters, she took a break and checked her e-mail. Since none of her neighbors had replied to her message about her niece and nephew, she was afraid Carl would bring it before the Board and try to get them thrown out. She wished she'd never lied but now she was stuck and she'd have to play it out.

She considered calling her neighbors and telling them the truth, hoping they would take her side.

Leave it alone, Marisa!

She quickly turned but Jules wasn't there. His absence brought on another wave of grief, but this time she was ready for it and gripped the desk until it passed.

She felt like taking a walk by the Hudson River, but there was no time to get distracted like that. A four hundred thirty-page manuscript sat on her desk and it was due back next week. "Why not work at the Yale Club library?" she asked herself and packed her briefcase. She wouldn't be distracted there.

She threw off her sweats, showered, put on an upmarket pantsuit and went down the elevator to face the world, or at least to pretend to face the world, like a well-adjusted, smooth functioning lady with places to go and things to do.

Fix your collar.

She looked in the lobby mirror and saw Jules was right. He had been her dresser, always making sure she wasn't askew. She adjusted her clothes in the mirror before pushing open the heavy door. She then braced herself against the gusty, winter wind and stepped out.

5

“Good morning, Mrs. Bridges,” said the beaming concierge when Marisa entered the hushed, old-world charm of the Yale Club lobby. “It’s good to have you back.” Jules and Marisa had been members for many years, possible because Jules had graduated from Yale. They considered it their silent oasis in the middle of the city. But it was Marisa who took the most advantage of its benefits: the gym, the lounge, and especially the library where she could work in silence surrounded by books.

“Thank you, Ali,” Marisa said, shaking his hand. She’d rather hug her old friend, but the club held to tradition, and physical contact between members and staff was frowned upon. She and Jules had often noted how ironic it was that they’d made friends with the staff and not other members in the club.

The Persian rug muffled her footsteps as she walked toward the elevator. She nodded to the receptionists at the front desk, all smiling, welcoming her back to what she considered her second home. She pushed the fifth floor button to the Gym-Pool, remembering when she pushed that button nine months ago, Jules was standing next to her, and he was fine. Or at least they thought so.

A smile composed on her face, she approached Ana and Adrian standing behind the sports club counter. Just where I last saw them—Marisa forced herself to finish her thought—before Jules died.

“Mrs. Bridges. What a wonderful surprise to see you. We’ve missed your smiling face.”

She reached over the counter and shook their hands. "I thought I'd work in the library today, then take a stride on the elliptical, and finish off with a Hilgardo margarita in the Lounge."

"Sounds like old times," said Adrian.

The television announcer was shouting into an otherwise empty woman's locker room. Marisa shut it off with the remote control and sank down on a bench near her locker.

It's going to be all right, she heard Jules say. *You made it this far; the rest will be easy.*

In the library, Marisa sat down at her favorite table by the window overlooking Grand Central and began editing the trashy novel she'd started at home. The genre was romance, which was really a bodice-ripper filled with unrequited desire, then heated sexual satisfaction, mixed in between chapters of violent crimes committed by pedophiles. Her editorial skills were limited to adding commas and dashes to phrases like "Oh, that feels so good" and "Oh, please do that again!" or "I'll do anything you want—just don't hurt me."

After several hours, she scratched out the fifth "I orgasmed" with her red pencil and politely recommended using instead "I had an orgasm." She marked that page with a yellow sticky note from where she'd start again tomorrow and packed her briefcase.

As planned, she worked on the elliptical for forty minutes, headphones sending funky beats to her speeding heart and rising endorphins, as she danced across an imagined dance floor to Jules's music. For the five-minute cooldown, she waltzed in Jules's arms to Gretchen Peters's "The Secret of Life."

Marisa had taken her shower and was dressed when Ana approached her in the locker room carrying a straw basket. "It didn't seem right to send these in the mail." She put down the basket and left quickly.

Ana had removed Jules's blue gym shorts and T-shirt from his locker, washed, and folded them. Marisa crushed his clothes against her bruised heart and cried out into the empty room, "Jules, I can't live without you. Come back, please." He said nothing.

Splashing her face with cold water at the sink, Marisa looked at her reflection and thought to go home, but heard Jules finally say something. *Fix yourself up and go see Hilgardo. I'm sure he's missed you.* Not what she wanted to hear but it was better than his silence.

She dimmed the fluorescent lights at the vanity table and rubbed tinted cream into her age spots, brushed mascara onto her thinning lashes, penciled in the arch of her eyebrows, and covered her dry lips with Sparkling Rose lip gloss.

With a parting smile to her aging reflection, she put Jules's clothes in a plastic Yale bag, stuffed it in her backpack, thanked Ana for her thoughtfulness and, holding on to her smile, pressed the elevator's Lounge button.

The Yale lounge was full of super-confident, self-important people who pretended to be seriously happy, confident and as satisfied as very large bank accounts could make them. She hesitated getting out of the elevator. It really wasn't her place and she knew it. Too much show and not enough real substance. These people were, in fact, probably the publishers of the bodice-rippers she had to suffer through as an underpaid copy editor.

Go home, she told herself, but she didn't. Instead, she grabbed *The New York Times* off a table and headed for the bar.

Hilgardo's face lit up when he saw her wedged between two businessmen. "The usual?" he asked. She smiled and nodded yes.

Marisa had been enjoying Hilgardo's strong margaritas ever since he started bartending at the Yale Club. She'd seen photos of his pregnant wife, and then his growing kids, and she had vouched for him when he had legal difficulties under the new immigration laws and had to apply for citizenship after living and working in the States for twenty years.

Leaning against the dark mahogany bar, she read the paper, sipped her drink, and nibbled on too many salty peanuts. Oh well, hadn't she just exercised? When the bar thinned out of businessmen downing that second Scotch before getting on the train to Scarsdale or Greenwich and going home to their country estates, perfect two kid families and trophy wives, Hilgardo came back to her.

"Can I get you another margarita? This one's on me."

"Thanks, but I better say no. Riding subways under the influence of two Hilgardo margaritas is not a good idea and Jules isn't here to . . ." Her voice faltered, and Hilgardo reached across the bar and gripped her hand, "I'm so sorry, Mrs. Bridges. I still can't believe it. The last time I saw Mr. Bridges he looked so healthy."

Marisa looked away and wiped her eyes with a cocktail napkin. "I better get home before I take you up on that drink."

She gathered up her gym bag, said her good-byes to Hilgardo, and took flight down the stairs and out into the brisk winter night.

The subway ride only made her feel worse. She looked at all the miserable people going home after working all day at meaningless jobs just to bring in a paycheck, and she wasn't any different. There had to be a way out. Jules would have wanted her to make some kind of meaningful statement with her life, something she could look back on and be proud of.

Disappointed to find her tenants out, Marisa busied herself scheduling a meeting for the next night and writing the House Rules, and then pasted a copy on the refrigerator door:

DON'T RINSE DISHES BEFORE PUTTING IN DISHWASHER.

TURN OFF LIGHTS WHEN YOU GO OUT.

CALL ME AUNT MARISA IN COMMON AREAS: LOBBY AND ELEVATOR.

OKAY TO USE MY WIFI CONNECTION. PASSWORD: SERENDIPITY.

PLAY MUSIC ANYTIME BUT USE HEADPHONES BETWEEN 11PM AND 9AM.

KITCHEN OPEN BETWEEN 8AM AND 10PM.

Martin showed up at the Bitter End after his last set. Cassandra concocted her house specialty for both of them and by the time the club closed at four she considered crashing on the club's storeroom cot. Martin insisted on walking her home.

They stumbled downtown to Murray Street in the freezing cold air, laughing and grabbing on to each other to stop from slipping on the icy sidewalk.

Back at the loft, Martin invited her to his room to listen to music.

"Anything in particular you'd like to hear?" he asked.

She shrugged. "Whatever."

"Do you like old R&B tunes? You know. Marvin Gaye. Otis—"

"Otis? I love that guy. Do you have 'Sittin' On the Dock of the Bay.'?"

"Sure you don't want to hear something more up-to-date?"

"You mean commercial stuff? Songs you probably never listen to?"

"Maybe not. But iTunes will carry it. Give me a title and I'll find it."

"No. I want to hear Otis."

Cassandra collapsed onto his bed, closed her eyes, and fell asleep listening to Otis whistling on the dock.

She woke up to Martin asleep beside her and slipped off the bed. She cursed herself for getting drunk with him and swore not to let it happen again. Her life was complicated enough.

On the other side of the loft, Marisa dozed in and out of sleep until she finally sat up around six and read her e-mail in the early morning light. She hesitated but couldn't resist clicking Miles's text message: Must talk. Meet at Edward's tonight at seven.

Oh dear, now what? Slightly moaning, she pushed her stiff, aching body out of bed, very conscious of the old woman she'd become, and slipped into her equally worn-out fuzzy slippers.

After her first sip of coffee, she felt revived enough to answer Miles: Can't do it. Meeting tenants at seven to go over house rules.

He texted back insisting she meet with him first.

Sundays don't mean anything to freelancers who get paid by the hour so Marisa returned to the Yale Club to put in another full day on *Broken Chastity*. It was much easier to concentrate in a hushed room surrounded by books than in a home surrounded by bittersweet memories.

At the end of the day, she put her briefcase back in her locker. There was no time for the elliptical or Hilgardo's margarita because she had to meet Miles at Edward's.

The subway car was overheated and overcrowded. Someone offered Marisa a seat. Usually she was too embarrassed that someone thought she was too old to stand up on her own, but this time she accepted the seat graciously. At the City Hall station, she rushed up the stairs and down Chambers Street toward Edward's, stopping to catch her breath before pulling open the heavy, glass door.

A woman sitting very close to Miles at the bar pulled away when she saw Marisa approaching.

Miles looked down at his watch before he said hello, kissed her cheek, and helped her off with her coat.

"Aren't you going to introduce me to your new friend?"

"Oh sorry," said Miles, turning red. How delightful, thought Marisa. She'd been hoping he'd meet someone who made him blush like his former girlfriend did before she dropped him.

"Sheri, this is my mother, Marisa." Sheri slid off the stool, and as they shook hands, Marisa looked up at this stunning woman—a face of perfect symmetry except for a charming one-sided dimple when she smiled. And was she even taller than Miles?

"What a nice surprise. Miles didn't tell me that he was bringing someone."

"He asked me to come along and after all he's told me about you, I wanted to meet you."

"Well then, let's have some libations." She called out to the bartender, "Stan, the usual please and give these kids whatever they want." Miles ordered a Coke and Sheri a glass of Merlot. "Let's move to a booth," said Marisa.

They sat across from each other in a red leather banquette. Miles waited impatiently for the waiter to bring the drinks, tapping his fingers on the table just like his father used to do, but Miles's tapping was a nervous habit whereas his father was usually practicing a drumbeat. As soon as the waiter walked away he said, "Mom, it's about—"

"Before I forget," she interrupted, remembering what she'd been carrying since yesterday in her backpack. "I brought you something." When he started loosening the tied string of the Yale Club bag, she stopped him with her hand. "Not now. Open it later. It's some of your dad's things."

He looked at it briefly and gave it to Sheri who put it beside her on the seat.

"We need to talk about Martin," said Miles.

"Martin?"

He leaned forward. "Yes, Martin. He has a record."

"A record? That's exciting. I had the feeling he was a good guitarist, but I didn't know he'd made any records."

"Very funny, Mom. I'm talking about a police record."

"Oh. I see. Well … I spent a few days in the clink myself, so it'd be rather hypocritical of me to hold that against him. It didn't make me a dangerous criminal."

"You don't need to bring that up now. I'm sure Sheri's not interested in hearing about your hippie days."

"Are you kidding?" Sheri smiled over at Marisa. "I'd love to hear."

Sheri got one of those censorial looks that Marisa thought Miles reserved only for her. It was harsh enough to make one pull back and be quiet, but Sheri seemed to have more going for her than a pretty face. Her eyes flashed back at him for putting words in her mouth.

"Can you both please stick to the reason we're here?" said Miles. Both women sat back and waited. "Your tenant got into a fight with one of his classmates. It was pretty ugly. Instruments got thrown around, some damaged. It cost him his Juilliard scholarship."

Marisa went wide-eyed. "Martin went to Juilliard? Why that's amazing. You're right, Miles, there is more to Martin than I realized."

"Mom, stop it. Can you be serious for just once. Martin might be dangerous."

"Oh no. That sweet young man? That's ridiculous. You really must meet him so you can see for yourself. You too, Sheri."

Miles nudged Sheri as if they'd rehearsed their parts earlier and she leaned forward. "Miles is only trying to make sure you're safe. He's very concerned about you."

"I know," said Marisa, sitting back in the booth and holding onto her chilled gimlet glass. "Tell me. How did you two meet?"

Miles looked at Sheri as if to say *see what I mean?* and returned to face his mother. "We're talking about your tenant, Martin."

"Yes, but unless you have more to tell me I'm far more interested in knowing how you two met?"

"Sheri has an office in my building, and after several hellos in the elevator, I asked her out. Over coffee I told her I was worried about your new tenants, and we searched Google."

"How romantic," mumbled Marisa.

Sheri laughed. "Well, maybe not romantic but it was pretty interesting when we finally found Martin on Facebook. He had a beard in his photo, but Miles recognized him right away. His page was inactive, so we made friends with his friends, checked out their walls and found out about the Juilliard incident."

Marisa looked toward the bar. "Sheri, would you mind ordering me another gimlet."

Sheri got up but Miles held her back and said, "Mom do you really think you should have another one?"

"Yes I do. Maybe Sheri would like another glass of wine."

"Thank you, Marisa, I'd like that," said Sheri.

Marisa didn't grimace this time when Sheri called her by her first name. She was beginning to admire the girl's spirit.

"Miles?"

"No. But I'll get yours."

"I don't mind," said Sheri. "I think your mom would like a little time with you alone." As she walked to the bar, Marisa noticed that she and Miles weren't the only ones who were admiring the wide swing of her supple hips.

Marisa hesitated, knowing her son wouldn't like what she was about to say, but she had to say it. "Miles, I would never judge a person by what was said on any social media site. I can't believe you would either."

"Mom—"

"No, let me finish. I'm meeting with Cassandra and Martin tonight to go over the house rules and settle them in, and that's that."

"What about your neighbors? What if they found out your tenant has a criminal record?"

"Knowing some of my neighbors, they'd probably try to throw him out the door. But they're not going to find out. I've told them my guests are Jules's nephew and niece."

"Tell me you didn't do that. Who are these people to you that you'd take such a risk?"

"These 'people' are two kids who need a break in this intolerant world we live in, and I'm going to help them. I thought you would understand."

"If Dad was here, he would never have allowed it." Miles looked down at his watch given to him by his father before he died. "Sheri and I are late for dinner with friends. We'll have to settle up and go."

After they left, Marisa nursed her gimlet or, truth be told, it nursed her. She stood up, put the forgotten Yale bag in her backpack, and told Stan she'd be back soon.

As she struggled into her coat, she felt someone helping her with the sleeves. She hid her disappointment when she turned around quickly and saw it was only Stan.

6

Marisa took in too much air hurrying home and arrived in the lobby with the hiccups. When she stepped into the loft, Martin was drinking a beer in the kitchen, looking rather glum.

"Where's Cassandra?"

"She's been in her room all day. I'm supposed to tell her when you arrive."

"By the way, how are you two getting along? I hoped you'd find some things in common as artists."

"I thought we were doing all right but now I'm not sure."

"Oh, sorry to hear that."

He dropped the empty beer can into the recycle bin. "I'll tell her you're here."

Martin was just thinking how unpredictable women were when he returned to the living room and found his landlady in the arms of her winter coat, dancing to "You've Really Got A Hold On Me" blaring on the big, old, garishly-lit Wurlitzer jukebox standing in the corner. In an impulsive moment, he held out his arms, she dropped her coat and let him spin her around the room. The tune ended as they stumbled into Cassandra, who had been watching them. They all laughed.

"Oh that was fun!" said Marisa breathlessly, her eyes glowing.

Martin collapsed into Jules's chair, and Marisa reminded herself that she had crossed off "Don't sit there" from the house rules.

Trying to be serious, she handed out copies of the house rules.

"Do you have any questions?"

"I don't. What about you, Cass?"

"Don't call me that," she said without looking up from scribbling in the house rules' margins.

"Sorry. But last night—"

She cut him off, addressing Marisa. "These rules are fine. Just one question."

"What's that?"

"Why do you have a rule against rinsing dishes before putting them in the dishwasher?"

"I learned how precious water is on a French farm when I had to scoop water from a well and carry it to my garden. And my landlady, Bridget, told me I was wasting water when she saw me rinsing dishes under the tap and then putting them in the dishwasher. I try to conserve water here in New York too."

Cassandra put away her pencil. "Okay. I can do that. If that's it, I have to get to work."

"Wait a minute," said Martin getting up at the same time. "We can go together."

When he returned with his guitar case, Cassandra was gone.

"Hey, why did she leave without me?"

"I don't know, Martin. I was going to ask you. Anything happen I should know about?"

He laughed. "Doesn't look like it, does it? I thought we had a great time last night but"— Marisa's mouth dropped open, and he quickly said—"Whatever you're thinking forget it. We just talked … or should I say I talked."

"I think she's been through some rough times and needs to work things out on her own for a while."

"Then you know more about her than I do."

"No, not really, but she reminds me of my daughter who went through some difficult times at her age. Don't worry about her. She'll come around in time."

Martin pushed the elevator button and went off to his gig.

Marisa was just settling in to watch *The Ghost and Mrs. Muir* when her iPhone buzzed with a reminder: Call Camille.

Camille didn't answer. Unlike her mother, she didn't always carry her cell phone and often forgot to even turn it on. Marisa left a message telling her she missed her and to call when she could talk. Then she snuggled down under her comforter to watch the young widow Mrs. Muir being charmed by Captain Gregg, a swash-buckling ghost.

An hour later, at the penultimate moment when Captain Gregg is looking down sadly at Mrs. Muir asleep in her bed, the phone's vibration startled her. She saw Camille and paused the film.

"Hi, Mom. Are you all right? Your voice message sounded like you'd been crying."

"No. I'm fine. I was just watching a sad movie."

"Why don't you ever watch a comedy? What is this tearjerker called?"

"*The Ghost and Mrs. Muir.*"

"Mom, you were watching that the last time I called. Doesn't that just make you miss Dad more? Why not watch something like *Ghostbusters* instead and get a good laugh."

"Very funny."

Knowing her mother's bittersweet pleasure in sad romances, Camille offered, "Do you want to call me back?"

"Heavens no. I hope all that rain you're having in California isn't depressing you?"

"Not at all. It encourages me to stay inside so I can finish the pieces for my gallery opening. But how did you know it's raining here?"

"I must admit I check in on your weather quite often. It makes me feel closer to you."

"Mom, if you want to feel closer to me just call or, better yet, visit. In fact, why not come to my gallery opening in San Francisco?"

Marisa looked up at Van Gogh's forlorn self-portrait on her Impressionist wall calendar for February. "What a great idea. When is it?"

"March seventeenth, my birthday."

"That's only a few weeks from now. Fortieth birthday, isn't it?"

"Don't remind me. Can you come?"

"I would certainly like to. Hold on. Let me look." She took down the calendar, flipped to March, and swiped over the blank, unfilled dates with her finger. "It just might work."

"What does that mean—*might work*? I thought you'd love to come."

"I do. But I need to feel comfortable with my new tenants first."

"Tenants? When did you take in tenants? And why?"

Marisa explained her financial situation briefly.

"Mom, why didn't you ask me to help? I just sold some pieces—"

"I know I can count on you but I want to be able to count on myself. And I rather like the idea of having some people living in my home again. It was getting quite boring around here."

"Anyone your age?"

Marisa laughed. "Not a chance. Both in their late twenties. Martin's a jazz guitarist and Cassandra's at Pratt studying art."

"Sounds like your kind of people. I'm sure you would never have taken them in if they weren't okay."

"Thanks for that vote of confidence. I wish your brother felt the same."

"Miles? Why, what does he say?"

"He was expecting a more serious screening process. I found Cassandra on Craigslist and I met Martin at Edward's."

"Good to hear you're starting to step out a bit. But isn't he a bit young for you?"

Marisa blushed. "Camille. It's not like that at all. I just couldn't resist a hard-working musician needing a helping hand? He's polite, soft-spoken, and quite charming. Calls me Aunt Marisa."

"Rather bold, don't you think?"

"I don't mind."

"And Cassandra? What's she like?"

"That's the surprising thing. If anyone was overexposed on social media sites, I thought it would be her. She's very afraid of something but doesn't talk about it. She recoils and I imagine the tattooed viper coming alive and hissing at me."

Camille laughed. "Has a tattoo does she? Well, if she needs help she's in the right place. If anyone can bring her out of a snake pit it'll be you. But be careful, Mom. Don't get too involved. You have your own problems to work through."

"Me? I don't have problems," said Marisa, looking at the empty calendar.

"Yeah, right. That's one of your problems right there—denial. Have you thought anymore about going to Bridget's farmhouse this summer?"

"I'd really like to. Perhaps if you and Alex came with me?" She flipped the art calendar pages to July, which was a painting of Van Gogh's field of sunflowers, and quickly closed it. Bad luck to look ahead.

"We can't. There's too much going on here for both of us. Maybe we could join you later in the summer."

Marisa was gazing at the dashing Captain, frozen in time, looking down at Mrs. Muir peacefully asleep in her bed. The poor woman didn't know that the gallant Captain was about to step out of her life forever and she would wake up tomorrow all alone, but it was only so that she could meet someone else, someone who wasn't a ghost.

"Mom, are you still there?"

"Uh-huh."

"You know you're always welcome here. You were never truly a New Yorker and now with Dad—"

"Oh, I don't know if I could ever leave Miles on his own."

"Mom, he's not a child anymore. I'm sure he'd visit you. And you can always communicate with him on Skype. Remember when he suggested we do that?"

"Yes, and the one time we tried all we did was laugh at each other and make faces into the camera. We felt ridiculous, and missed each other more than ever."

After they hung up, Marisa pressed play but now that Captain Gregg had walked off into the sunset, she couldn't bear to watch anymore and clicked it off. She drifted off to sleep a few moments later.

Cassandra wouldn't be getting to sleep for several hours. The Bitter End was packed. Not a moment to think about anything other than keeping her customers' glasses full. She wiped off one sticky table, set down a weighty pitcher of margaritas on another, and was back behind the bar taking another order when she froze.

At the end of the bar stood Ryan, the one person she never wanted to see again. His full soft lips blew her a kiss, and her heart betrayed her with an involuntary flip. But when he curled his finger and motioned for her to come to him, her mind cleared. "Fuck you," she whispered, before turning away to mix another pitcher of margaritas. She threw in too much tequila and forgot to add the triple sec but her rowdy customers didn't notice. The Bitter End's margaritas were about alcoholic content not taste.

His dark attentive eyes followed her every move. She turned to draw beer from the tap, the froth spilling over onto the counter.

Protected behind the bar, she approached him, "Are you going to order a drink? If not, why not go somewhere else?"

He smiled. "Couldn't you start by saying hello? I've come a long way to see you."

"Just to see me? I doubt it. I saw the ad for The Belles at Radio City."

"I wanted to tell you that I don't blame you for running away from me. I deserved it. I didn't treat you right."

"How did you find me?"

"It wasn't easy. You've covered yourself up really good." He touched the viper slithering up her arm. "Where did you get this?"

"I woke up with it and a hangover. Later I figured out it's there to protect me from myself." Cassandra crossed her arms, putting a hand over the viper's tongue.

"Is that when you cut off your long blond hair and became an orange-headed punk?"

She forced a smile. "No, I did that before I left L.A. How did you find me?"

"It wasn't hard. I would have come sooner, but I wanted you to have some time on your own to clear your pretty head. Things got a bit out of hand in L.A." He reached across the bar and touched her cheek. "CiCi, you don't belong in this shit-hole. Have you forgotten how good things were with us?"

She brushed his hand away. "I haven't forgotten anything. But you have. So let me set you straight. CiCi is history. My name is Cassandra now. Go find yourself another singer."

Ryan showed no anger. His deep-set eyes held onto hers and she couldn't look away. "You're still my CiCi. Nothing will change that. Come home with me."

Her body betrayed her and leaned toward him.

He whispered in her ear, "I've missed you, baby. I won't let you go again. You and me are meant to be together. You can't deny how you feel about me."

She pulled away. "I have work to do."

"Look, I know I hurt you. But it won't happen again, I promise. No more lies. I'll do right by you this time. Let me take care of you."

"No, Ryan. No! I'm doing fine on my own."

"Yeah, right." He stuck his phone out and showed her pictures he'd just taken at the bar. They were dark but the light captured the viper and the orange hair. "I thought I'd put these up on Facebook, so your fans could see what you've been doing since you left The Belles. I bet the girls would like to see them too."

She glared at him.

"What happened to your sense of humor? I'm just joking.

Watch. I'll trash them right now." She watched him do it. "Look CiCi, I know what you're thinking, but I promise this time we'll do it your way—slow and easy. And when you're ready, we'll stage your comeback. Just like we always planned."

Customers were yelling at Cassandra for their drink orders. Ryan opened his arms wide taking in the seedy bar and its drunken clientele. "Don't waste your time here, CiCi. You owe it to your loyal fans, if not me." She turned to go.

"Wait. Just hear me out. I've been in touch with one of the best Hollywood vocal coaches. He says he can help you to retrain your voice so it won't get damaged again. And I've added a studio to the beach house where you can work. A quiet space to write your own material."

"It's too late, Ryan." She whipped around and returned to her customers at the bar. When she looked up, he was gone.

After midnight, the more demanding customers had thinned out and Cassandra had time to think. Everything had gone from bad to worse. First Martin and Marisa befriending her when she just wanted to be left alone, and now Ryan showing up out of nowhere with his big plans. And in all that he had just promised, he never used the words "love" or "sorry."

The Souza bottle reflecting under the bar light tempted her just like Ryan had. Her hand reached for it, tightening around its neck. If she poured one drink, she'd pour another and then the fragile, protective wall she'd built would come tumbling down. She took the curled fifty-dollar tip he'd left on the bar out of her pocket. It had a slight dusting of cocaine on its edge. His hotel and room number were scribbled across it.

She slid off the bar stool, grabbed her coat, collected the rest of her tip money, shouted good night to Max and hurried out.

Walking down MacDougal Street and crossing over Sixth Avenue toward Seventh to take the downtown subway, she felt the wad of tips stuffed into the bottom of her purse. She'd make rent. And that would have satisfied her if Ryan hadn't shown up. She didn't know if she could say "no" to him the next time.

Down in the subway, she felt exposed under the glaring lights. She turned away from the rats scurrying through the trash on the track and climbed back upstairs. While taking some deep breaths of the brisk night air, she heard a haunting melody coming from the open door of a bar. A chalkboard hanging next to the door read MARTIN STARKS TRIO.

Last night when Martin told her about his love for jazz, she'd held back telling him the truth about herself; held back telling him that her voice had been her instrument; held back telling him that it was almost destroyed.

She entered the dimly lit cavern, slipped into a chair at a back table, and flipped her sketchpad to a blank page. A flickering flame in a red glass votive cast light on the page. After her hand stopped shaking, she put pencil to paper and sketched the band up front.

The bass player was soloing. Martin was nodding his head with pleasure when a bright streak of orange zigzagged across the back wall of the club and broke his concentration. The bass player finished his solo and motioned for Martin to come back in.

Martin's fingers pressed against the neck of his emerald green guitar. He plucked and pulled the strings, and bittersweet notes filled the room. Even the local drunks at the bar turned to listen.

After he finished, he looked for Cassandra in the back of the club, but she was gone. Or had she even been there, he wondered.

7

The intercom buzzing with shrill urgency interrupted Marisa's morning stretches. Irritated, she pushed TALK and shouted, "Who is it?" Static and a howling siren answered back. She called out again, "Who is it?" More static. She slipped on her robe, stepped into her slippers, and rode down to the lobby.

A deliveryman held out a long white box labeled Heaven's Door and wrapped in curly pink ribbons. She invited him in from the cold and signed for the delivery. These certainly can't be for me, thought Marisa. Jules had often brought home flowers to surprise her on an occasion or no occasion at all, but unless one believed in Heaven, and she certainly didn't, these were not from Jules.

The letter "C" was written on the card. It was too early to wake Cassandra. Marisa pulled off the ribbons, set the flowers in a vase, filled it with water, and stuck the sealed white envelope between the vivid yellow, orange, and purple Gerber blooms.

Then she put on her headphones and pumped her six-pound weights to Bob Dylan's "Maggie's Farm" shouting out: *I ain't gonna work on Maggie's farm no more / Well, I try my best To be just like I am / But everybody wants you / To be just like them.* Finishing off with a jig, she spun around, embarrassed to find Cassandra watching her with an amused expression on her face.

"Do you do this every morning?"

"I try to. It's a great way to start the day." She wished she'd closed her door and wondered how long Cassandra had been watching.

"I'm impressed. I never exercise. Wasn't that Dylan's song?"

"Oh my, you know "Maggie's Farm"? I thought your generation was clueless when it came to the good stuff."

Cassandra's smile broadened. "Yes, I suppose most of us are, but I grew up listening to my dad's records."

"Lucky you. A real musical education. I'd love to hear more about it. Would you like a coffee?"

"Sorry, I don't have time. But about those flowers in the kitchen."

"I hope you didn't mind me putting them in water."

"No, not at all. In fact they're yours."

"Mine? I assumed they were for you."

"You're right, they were for me, but I'd rather you have them. Consider it a housewarming gift."

After Cassandra left, Marisa boiled an egg and was engrossed in an article on Alzheimer's in *The New York Times* Science section when she heard eleven cuckoos and cursed herself for not having started her work day earlier.

She switched to her blog and read the many comments generated by her quote from Joan Didion's *A Year of Magical Thinking*: "I know why we try to keep the dead alive: we try to keep them alive in order to keep them with us."

No time now to comment, she told herself. I must get to the library before the entire day is lost.

While throwing out the coffee grinds, she saw the florist's card torn into tiny pieces in the trashcan.

You're not going to read someone else's mail are you?

Peeking over her shoulder she smiled and then picked out the shredded card.

Here's your second chance. Limo at your door at eight. Get in it, Cinderella, before it turns into a pumpkin. Your prince will be waiting for you. Left your name at Irving Plaza backstage door. R

All in all a very peculiar invitation. And who was *R*, she wondered.

At the Yale library, Marisa worked all afternoon editing the same bodice-ripper manuscript. She corrected the poor grammar and wondered if any bodice-ripper reader would ever notice or care. For relief, she turned to Serendipity and wrote a blog on *Magical Thinking*, confessing to her followers that she didn't want Jules to go away, ever.

Then she typed *Exuberance: The Passion for Life* on a new blog page. Dr. Kay Redfield Jamison wrote *Exuberance* while her husband was dying and without her husband's support and encouragement, she said she'd never have finished it. After his death, she wrote an autobiography entitled, *Nothing Was the Same.* Marisa recommended it as an intelligent book for widows and widowers who wanted to temper their grief and move on in their lives.

Her attention turned to an e-mail from the Center for BrainHealth. The Center was asking her participation in a new clinical trial that she had read about that very morning. The FDA was considering approval of a drug that when it was infused during a PET scan would light up, like neon, any plaque on a patient's brain. Plaque was a key diagnostic marker of Alzheimer's that up until now was only diagnosed at the patient's autopsy. But if plaque was found on a living patient's PET scan, the disease could be monitored and perhaps treated, like cancer. This test could also be given to children of Alzheimer's patients who were afraid they'd inherited mutant genes transmitted through their parents' DNA.

Marisa's mother, Helen, at age seventy, had shown signs of serious mental deterioration: forgetting that a red light meant to stop, not go; forgetting to eat; forgetting food left molding in the refrigerator; forgetting her friends' names … then her children's. Back in 1984, the test used to diagnose Alzheimer's was an oral exam:

Dr.: Do you know where you are?

Helen: A school.

Dr.: Who's the president of the United States?

Helen smiled: Why, don't you know?

Dr.: Who brought you here?

Helen: My friend.

Dr.: Why has she brought you here?

Helen: My mother's waiting for me. Must not be late. She worries.

Helen survived fourteen years as a *probable* Alzheimer's patient. When she died the autopsy report stated that her brain was covered in plaque.

During her mother's illness, Marisa had volunteered at the Center for BrainHealth. The clinicians were studying children of Alzheimer's patients for early symptoms and she'd participated in several clinical trials.

This new trial would be four days of tests: mental, neurological, and physical. Along with an MRI they wanted to take not one but three PET scans. Her brain would be explored and documented by a robotic camera eye looking for neon-lit plaque.

She hesitated in front of her monitor screen and then tapped a response to the clinician: I'll do it.

Shortly after Marisa got back from the library, Cassandra stepped out of the elevator. Marisa asked if she would join her for a glass of wine.

"Thanks," she said cheerfully, as she ran down the hall to her bedroom, "but I only have thirty minutes to shower and get dressed."

As Marisa numbed her loneliness with Camembert and crackers, well deserved after a strenuous workout earlier on the club's elliptical machine, she considered Cassandra's rather odd behavior. In the short time she'd known her, Cassandra was never this high-spirited and she never changed her clothes.

She wore the same black leather jacket and pants every day.

When Cassandra returned, her face was meticulously covered with merging silver and pink powders, in shocking contrast to the wings that arched up from the corners of her eyes; eyes that looked out at Marisa with intense energy. In contrast, her orange spikes had been matted down into a fringed pixie that gave her a more childlike, fragile appearance, and Marisa thought the thin silver lamé top with matching pants made her look even more fragile.

"My, aren't you dressed up. Are you going somewhere special?"

"No. I just felt like dressing up tonight," said Cassandra, nervously snapping off an orange Gerber. Her fumbling fingers couldn't get it to stay behind her ear, so Marisa helped her. "There, my dear. It's your amulet tonight. It'll protect you against all evil. Don't lose it."

"But I already have an amulet. Why would I want another one?" said Cassandra showing the viper on her arm. Marisa's eyes fell on the "R" tattooed in red ink on its black tongue.

"Oh, I see," said Marisa. "Well in this city two amulets are better than one. And Cinderellas should all come home before midnight."

The cuckoo poked his head out eight times and Cassandra rushed into the elevator.

I'd make a terrible sleuth, thought Marisa. Why did I mention Cinderella? Cassandra must know now that I read the torn-up note.

Cassandra looked out the lobby door's window at the black limousine parked at the curb. Part of her held back. *But why shouldn't I have one night of fun?* she argued. *Why not test my willpower over Ryan's?* Her reflection glared back at her, "Don't do it." Cassandra tossed back her head and walked out the door.

The limousine driver jumped out when he saw her, but then hesitated, until she said, "Yes, Mike, it's really me."

"Hello, Miss CiCi, it's been a while."

"Yes it has," she said and smiled. "Good to see you." Mike held open the backseat door and without hesitation CiCi gracefully slipped back into the diva role she'd run away from.

The locks snapped shut and the center driver's window rolled up. She sank back into the soft leather, turned the music on and joined Amy Winehouse on the chorus: *They tried to make me go to rehab, I said no—no—no.*

She opened the wood-laminated bar, considered a shot of whisky, but decided on a miniature bottle of champagne. She'd barely topped off her second glass when the door opened and Mike ushered her through the crowd to the Irving Plaza stage door. He made sure she was safely inside before he tipped his hat and left.

She said "Cassandra," to the door guard seated in front of a long list of names on a clipboard.

"Don't have that one. Only Cinderella. Is that you?" he asked gruffly, looking up at her for the first time.

"I guess so," she said.

"Yeah. Where's your coach, Cinderella?" His rotund belly shook at his own joke before he handed her a long blue ribbon with a plastic square hanging from it that read: BACKSTAGE PASS. ALL ACCESS.

"Don't lose it. The Valentinos are in the dressing room at the bottom of the stairs. Them and a bunch of other Cinderellas." Then to the waiting crowd, "Next in line."

The dressing room was crowded with band members and their entourage but no Ryan. She was noticing how young they all looked and how much older she suddenly felt, when cold hands covered her eyes and someone planted a wet kiss on her neck, then spun her around. It was Ryan. "Wow, don't you look good. Hate to leave you on your own, baby, but I've got to talk to the soundman. Don't move. I'll be right back."

Cassandra sat down on the couch and said "no" several times to a girl who kept passing a joint around the room. She couldn't have been older than sixteen. Having no one to talk to and bored watching everyone getting high, Cassandra decided to go watch the show. A security guard stopped her at the door, "You sure you want to go out there? I won't be able to let you back in."

"But I have a backstage pass," she said, pulling it out of her purse.

"Okay, but when this DJ finishes his opening set his fans will rush this door trying to get an autograph and you might not be able to get through. Why not watch from the wings?"

"I'll just go out for a minute and come back."

Cassandra squeezed her way across the dance floor to the bar and ordered a vodka martini, but was told they only served soft drinks. She was being bumped against the wall by gyrating bodies when Ryan pulled her toward him and hissed in her ear, "What are you doing out here. You might be recognized."

"I doubt it. Not in this crowd. Your band didn't even recognize me."

"Then maybe it's time for you to come back out into the limelight before you're completely forgotten. And you know I'm just the guy to make that happen."

This is not the limelight I'm looking for, she thought to say, but the music was deafening. Ryan ushered her back through the crowd and left her in the wings. "Now stay put this time. I don't want to lose you again."

She thought of making some quick sketches but as soon as the Valentinos started performing, their groupies started jumping up and down and screaming, blocking her view. When the set was over, the band ran off stage to wild applause and screams for more. Their girls wiped the sweat off their brows with towels before they ran back onstage for the encores.

Cassandra had had enough. This was not the evening she'd imagined. She was being treated more like a scullery maid than a princess considering the amount of attention she was getting from Ryan. While he took his band back down to the basement, she headed for the back door, throwing the pass down on a table.

She was about to walk out when Ryan called after her, "Hey, where are you going?"

"Home."

"What's the hurry? Is someone expecting you?

She ignored him and walked on. "Please CiCi," he said softly, catching up to her. "I've missed you, baby." He wrapped his coat around her shoulders. "Come back to the hotel and we can talk things out. Mike will take you home whenever you want."

Marisa told herself that she wasn't worried, but every time she heard the mechanical hum of the elevator coming up from the ground floor, she sat up in her bed. She was reminded of all the times she'd anxiously stayed up waiting for Camille to come home, knowing her daughter was hanging out with an older crowd who used drugs to lure her to their parties.

By the time Cassandra took off her shoes and tiptoed to the back of the loft, Marisa was asleep.

She didn't cry until she was under the shower.

It was my damn fault. I never should have gone back to the hotel with him. And why did I tell him I'd go back to L.A.? Am I crazy? I must never see him again. Never.

She swore to herself that when he came back to New York in three weeks to get her, she'd tell him no and this time mean it. *Why is that so hard to do?* she asked herself, who answered back sharply, "Because you're still in love with him."

She was trying to scrub off the viper tattoo with a washcloth when she heard Martin at the door, "Hey, are you all right?"

She didn't answer.

"You've been in there a long time. Can I take a pee?"

Wrapped in a towel, she ran to her bedroom.

Martin picked up her silk blouse off the bathroom floor and hung it on her doorknob. He went back to his room and started playing his guitar.

After a while, there was a tap at his door. Cassandra stood there wrapped in a comforter and asked, "Was that the tune you were playing the other night at the club?"

So he hadn't imagined her at the club. He nodded and kept playing as he hummed the melody to "Peggy Blue."

She curled up against the far wall, her eyes barely visible. When her head dropped to the side, he slipped a pillow under it, tucked the comforter around her, and turned out the light.

8

Marisa had finished editing the tenth "orgasmic" scene in Random House's soon-to-be published *Broken Chastity* and was so un-aroused she couldn't keep her eyes open. The actor Richard Burton came to mind. He had unfulfilled literary ambitions and suffered, he said, from the "indignity and the boredom of having to memorize the writings of another man." Poor Richard, she thought. Poor Marisa.

Desperate to do something creative, she turned to her blog and branched out from her bereavement themes by tapping out a line from Katherine Mansfield's journal: "To live as a writer is to draw upon one's real familiar life—to find the treasure."

When she'd read that to Jules, he told her she spent too much time taking care of him instead of seeking the treasure of her own life. She'd have time later, she told him. And now it was *later* and she was still not anywhere close to her own treasure.

Stop wasting time, Marisa, she heard Jules say.

Ignoring his intrusion, she clicked on MarketWatch only to see a correction in the stock market. Her father had put an early fear of poverty in her heart. After his career unraveled, she witnessed his depression under a very reduced lifestyle.

The library emptied out of students studying for exams in law and accounting. She wondered if they had considered becoming artists before the truth hit them that they needed real income. The vacant black chairs were like a long row of widows waiting. Waiting for what? she asked herself. Destitution? No. No. I'm not going to any poorhouse.

Deciding not to take the elevator, she pulled herself up the thirty steps to the gym while complaining out loud, "The library's too warm; the stairwell's too cold."

Jules interrupted her. *You're worse than the girls in the locker room and soon your complaints are going to fall on deaf ears because you've got to let me go.*

Marisa stopped. "What do you mean 'let you go'? Don't you pull a Captain Gregg on me. Let's make a deal. I'll stop complaining if you don't make any more threats about leaving me." Before he could answer, the phone vibrated in her jacket pocket: Lillian.

"No you're not interrupting. I was just talking to Jules … No of course I know it isn't really him … What? I can't hear you … Why? I don't know why … Yes of course, sounds great. I'll be there … No, a snowstorm won't keep me away from those madeleines baking in your oven … Yes, I'll be careful."

Marisa turned up Pink on her iPod and strode off on the elliptical until she reached the needed endorphin high and decided she could manage just fine without Jules. But, later, in the shower, she cried when remembering the conversation she'd had that morning with the Center for BrainHealth. Enrico, her clinician, had asked her to bring her husband to the first appointment so he could identify her. "I can't do that. He's unavailable." It was over nine months since she'd buried him so why couldn't she just say, "No, he's dead." Enrico then told her to bring a friend. Someone who knew her well.

While she massaged lotion into her dry, wrinkled skin, she ran through her list of friends: Lillian was occupied with her husband's care; Corina was occupied with her daughter's wedding; Rachel was occupied with her legal clients. Who else was there? She and Jules had spent so much time as a couple that they'd never made many friends. She splashed her face with cold water, put on lipstick, gave her reflection a happy smile, and headed downstairs.

The lounge was as hushed as the snow falling outside the lofty windows. Marisa chose a wingback chair near the warm, blazing fireplace. She frowned at misbehavin' Bill Clinton's portrait on the wall and picked up *The NY Times Art* section. Not finding anything of particular interest, she rested her head on the back of the chair and gazed up at the wedding-cake ceiling and sparkling chandeliers.

"Do you mind if I sit here?"

Marisa looked up into the eyes of a distinguished looking, older man with silver-flecked black hair, and then over at the many empty chairs. "It's a bit chilly tonight to sit by a window," he explained.

"Do as you like," she said, hiding her irritation with a forced smile.

Gilbert came over and asked, "What can I get you?"

Marisa ordered a Stoli flavored with fresh lime juice, a drop of seltzer and just a bit of ice. The stranger who had just sat down said, "You certainly know what you like." He ordered a Manhattan and asked Gilbert to put the nice lady's drink on his bill. Marisa insisted on paying for her own drink.

"I hope you're okay with me sitting here. I couldn't resist cutting in on you and Bill up there. And this really is the warmest spot in the lounge."

Was it too absurd to think he was flirting, thought Marisa, hiding her blush by returning to the play review she'd been reading? She had no intention of flirting back, regardless of how attractive he was.

"Do you like the theatre?"

She peered over the paper. "Yes. But I never find time to go."

"When I was young, I worked in the theatre."

"Oh, were you an actor?" she asked, looking away from his deep-set, green eyes and disarming wide smile that would have impressed any casting agent looking for a mature man.

"No, afraid not. Stagehand. Professionally though, I've had the opportunity to treat some of the best."

"Oh, I see," she said, though she didn't see at all and looked puzzled.

"I'm a psychologist."

Her phone chimed just as the drinks arrived. "That's my alarm. I have to leave soon."

"That's disappointing for me. What could draw you out into a snowstorm?"

She leaned forward as if taking him in her confidence. "If you must know, Marcel Proust is waiting for me and he insists on punctuality."

"Proust?" he asked. "Marcel Proust?"

"Why, do you know him?" she said, appearing quite serious. Now it was his turn to look puzzled. She laughed. "My friend and I are reading *Swann's Way* in French. We get together to read it out loud."

"That must be a challenge. I got bogged down reading it in English. Never got past the miserable love affair Swann was snared into by that seductress. What's her name?"

"Odette. You're not alone. Most readers stop there."

"Those excruciating long sentences."

"What do you read?"

"Usually anything I can grab at the airport."

Marisa slipped behind the newspaper to hide her disappointment.

He didn't get the hint. "Do you speak French fluently?"

She gave up reading and put down the paper. "I wish. But I like to practice. Keeps my brain alive. And I love the French culture."

"Formidable! Je suis un Francophil aussi," he said, with an impressive French accent. Raising his glass, he looked directly into her eyes and said, "Santé."

Embarrassed, she crossed her legs and held the chilled glass against her forehead, her eyes on the kindling wood, wishing he'd just disappear.

"Haven't I seen you here before?" he asked, as if he hadn't noticed her discomfort.

What's wrong with you? she asked herself. He's only being nice. Answer him. "I work in the library."

"Really? Are you the librarian?"

"I wish. I make a living editing those books you buy at the airport for cheap entertainment."

He laughed. "Are they that bad?"

"Let's just say they're formulaic. Don't tell me you haven't bought one rushing to catch a flight and just as you settled down in your seat for a good read, found out you'd already read it."

Marisa's phone alarm went off again. He got up with her and said, "Perhaps when we meet again you can suggest some books I might read that aren't so dimwitted."

"All right . . ."

"Serge," he said putting out his hand.

"I'm Marisa." Embarrassed again by his gaze, she withdrew her hand from his and picked up her purse.

"À bientôt," she called back trying to be casual as she fled down the staircase, but almost tripped when she realized she'd left her phone on the table and had to come back. At the top of the stairs, Serge, with a wide grin on his face, handed it to her and told her to watch her step going downstairs.

On the uptown Madison Avenue bus, Marisa's copy of Proust lay open in her lap, but she couldn't concentrate. Her mind and body revisited her encounter with the very alive and flirtatious Serge. Maybe he was a gigolo and had his sights on a recent widow. Why else would he have flirted with me?

Because you're a lovely woman and he found you interesting, said Jules from behind her.

"So you were there. Why didn't you say something? Weren't you jealous?"

Of course, but I can't expect you to stay with me forever. Not like this.

While Marisa was stepping off the bus at Seventy-second Street and walking toward Lillian's elegant apartment off Central Park, Cassandra was passing by below on a downtown Lexington Avenue subway, heading to Brooklyn for her drawing class at Pratt. She had been uptown to see the only person in the city who she could call an old, trustworthy friend.

She'd needed Margaret's calming reassurance that she could make it on her own without Ryan. She didn't tell her all that happened last night but enough that Margaret, who knew all about Cassandra's volatile relationship with Ryan, felt she had to warn her to stay away from him. "It took a lot of courage to get this far, CiCi, don't go back."

Margaret was the wardrobe mistress for The Belles and after many tours had become good friends with Cassandra. She was the only one who had visited her at rehab. And Margaret was the one who helped her get out of L.A. and away from Ryan.

Cassandra told Margaret about the promo photo of the new Belles with her replacement that she'd seen in Ryan's hotel room, where he'd strategically placed it so she couldn't miss it.

"Did you really think you were irreplaceable?" Margaret asked her.

"Oh, Margaret, why did I give all that up? And for what? To be a low-life bartender with some delusion of becoming a painter someday? How absurd is that when I was already a successful singer?"

Margaret shrugged. This wasn't the first time Cassandra had complained about the choices she'd made. Margaret had given up reminding her of how unhappy she'd been in the group. The best she could do for her was just listen.

Cassandra continued, "I made a huge mistake leaving The Belles and Ryan knows it. Why else did he have a limo pick me up? If not to remind me of what I've given up. Then having no one recognize me at the club. No one. Not even Ryan's band. Of course it was a really young crowd but it was still humiliating."

"But isn't that what you wanted—after you escaped Los Angeles—to become anonymous?"

"Yes, but not forever. I blew it, Margaret. And I don't know what to do about it."

On the train, Cassandra flipped her sketchbook to the drawing she did of Martin at the 55 Bar. He'd been so nice to her and he had no idea who she really was. Would he distance himself from her if she told him the truth? Or would he use her like Ryan had, to further his own career? She couldn't get the new Belle photo out of her mind and saw it now as the train roared through the tunnel taking her deeper underground.

The screeching brakes made her jump. She grabbed her sketchpad off the floor and escaped out the door just before it snapped shut.

After reading ten pages of *Remembrances* describing Swann's passion for Odette in fine Proustian detail, Lillian and Marisa settled back with their wineglasses on the purple velvet couch and ate fresh-baked madeleines.

"Proust is certainly a better read than what I'm editing. *Broken Chastity* is just pornography disguised as romance. A more appropriate title would be *A Book of Orgasms.*"

"Should I read it?"

Marisa laughed. "Heavens no. You'd hate it." She took another sip from her wineglass while thinking about the unexpected physical stirring that she'd felt sitting across from Serge. "This wine is so delicious. You're one lucky woman to have a man who loves you enough to bottle his new blend of favorite grapes in your name."

"So were you, Marisa. Your luck just ended a bit sooner. I'll be following in your footsteps soon enough." Her seventy-six-year-old husband, Eduardo, had just come out of the hospital after a stroke. "And don't I recall you telling me that Jules's wrote a song called 'Marisa'?"

"That's true," said Marisa. Her mind slipped away to the day he came home and played it for her.

"Marisa, Marisa, where are you?"

She looked up at Lillian. "Oh sorry. Did I drift off?"

"Yes you did. Perhaps you should stay here tonight? It's still snowing."

"No. I'm all right. The wine makes me sleepy."

Marisa told Lillian about her new tenants, the new blog post on writing she started today, and more about the dissatisfaction that came with editing other authors' books.

"Then why aren't *you* writing?" asked Lillian. "A long time ago you gave me a draft of the first few chapters of your memoir. I never forgot those scenes you recalled from your childhood. Why not finish it, now that you have the time?"

"Funny, you're the second person who mentioned my memoir this week. Maybe it's because I opened Pandora's box and looked at my unfinished manuscript?" Marisa reached for her glass. "But you live quite happily without needing a project. Why encourage me otherwise?"

Lillian hesitated. "But I do have a project—Eduardo. When I married him fifty-five years ago, just out of high school, I made him my project and, except for publishing that one art book, I've done just that. You . . ."

"I know. Widows can't have husband-projects. And you're right. There's no reason why between editing jobs I couldn't work on my manuscript."

"And when do I get to read it?"

"Oh, Lillian, you're ruthless. Just to placate you I'll write it down in my To Do list." Before she could write anything, Lillian said, "I don't imagine you've met anyone . . ."

Marisa's face turned crimson.

Lillian leaned forward. "You have?"

"Well, I did meet someone at the club tonight. He was a bit forward I thought but kind of cute."

"And?"

Marisa shrugged. "It was nothing. Just two strangers passing in the night. I'll probably never see him again." She reached for the last madeleine. "These are so good."

"Did you at least get his name?"

"Serge."

"Serge what?"

"I don't think he told me." Marisa picked up her iPhone. "The Notes app is perfect for those of us whose minds have become sieves. I don't know about you but I can't retain anything longer than a few seconds. For instance if I hadn't looked at my Notes just now, I would have forgotten to ask you when our next Proust night is? In two weeks, I hope."

"Oh dear, how thoughtless of me. I meant to tell you that Eduardo and I are leaving soon for Argentina and we won't be back for a few months."

"That long?" Marisa felt a lump forming in her throat. She walked over to a large Provençal landscape oil, wishing she could lie down on its golden field and sleep forever.

One of her few friends was leaving her. And she'd really miss their Proust nights: Eduardo pretending he was their butler and serving them tea and scones on a silver tray, Chopin playing in the background. Lillian and Eduardo lived in the insulated world of the wealthy. Inside their home, surrounded by original oil paintings, antiques, and soft amber lamps, Marisa felt protected. And when they read Proust together, she forgot her loneliness and grief.

Lillian put her arm around Marisa's waist and apologized for not telling her sooner. She promised to stay in touch by e-mail.

"Yes, do that," said Marisa, forcing a smile while brushing away a stray tear.

Eduardo came out of the study to say good-bye and help

Marisa on with her coat. Bundled up against the elements, she stepped out of their palace onto the deep snow covering the sidewalk. She turned back to wave at Lillian standing in the doorway with Eduardo's arm over her diminutive shoulder; their silhouettes backlit by the lights inside their home. Marisa felt her heart crack. She faltered and then stepped into the black night for the long, frigid walk to the subway.

A group of young students got off at Hunter College. They took the robust energy they'd created in the subway car with them and left some tired and forlorn people behind. All strangers. Some read books, some slept, some played games on their smartphones, some wore earbuds, and some, like Marisa, just stared blankly into the void.

Marisa got off at City Hall and walked slowly across the park. Why hurry? There was no one waiting for her.

No one was waiting for Cassandra either so she sketched a nude model in her studio class all evening at Pratt. But her mind wasn't on the model. Martin had brought someone home last night and later slipped that someone out the back door. Through the thin walls separating their bedrooms she could hear heavy breathing and pleasurable moans. Later, he played his guitar to that someone, which was against the house rules at that hour, but Cassandra wasn't about to complain to Marisa. Martin might think she was jealous and she certainly wasn't. He wasn't her type. But who is, she asked herself? Ryan?

She didn't realize how hard she was pressing on her pencil until her drawing instructor, Don, touched her shoulder and said, "Cassandra, are you all right?"

She looked up and saw the other students staring at her. On the floor were scattered shreds of paper. Don helped her pack up and would have taken her home, but she said she'd be all right on her own. She knew she'd disappointed him, though he pretended it was okay, saying that she must be coming down with the flu, or something.

Don was responsible for getting her into Pratt after he saw her portfolio of work, and had stood by her when the other teachers questioned her academics. She had quit the other art classes, but kept coming to his class because he believed in her work.

Outside, Cassandra took a deep breath and chided herself for losing control in front of her classmates who already found her strange enough. She shivered. Her leather jacket didn't keep out the cold. She remembered a café down the street that was usually empty at this hour.

She slipped into a corner booth. The waiter served her tea and a cup of broccoli soup. She brought out her drawing pad and sketched the bamboo chairs; the cracked vinyl booths; the tables, each a different height and color; and the bar stools that spun around, laughing at her until she captured them on paper. Then she sketched the portrait of a frightened girl, failing to recognize herself.

Marisa had been wrong about no one at home. Martin arrived at the same time. She asked him to come down with her to the basement to bring up a box. "What's in this heavy box?" he asked, leaning it against the wall as they rode back up the elevator.

"My past and perhaps my future lie inside that box."

"Hmm. Sounds ominous. But what about living in the present? Isn't that what we're supposed to do?"

She smiled. "Oh, that's in there too."

"Where shall I put it?" asked Martin. She pointed to the desk.

Martin scanned the tall, wide bookshelves. "Wow, have you read all these books?"

"Most of them."

"You're fortunate to have a room like this to work in. I have to rent space by the hour to practice the piano or rehearse with my band."

"Didn't I tell you that you could use the piano? Jules practiced on it all the time. No one will mind. Everyone in the building is out at their jobs during the day. And if I'm here, not to worry, I'm used to musicians practicing. I won't even hear you."

"I don't think Cassandra would like it. I'm getting the impression she's not into musicians. She hardly speaks to me."

"I'm sure she wouldn't mind you practicing. Shall I—"

"No. It's swell of you to offer but I'll ask her."

Marisa smiled. She hadn't heard anyone use the word "swell" in a long time. "Martin, are you originally from the Midwest?"

"Man, you caught me. Born and raised on a farm outside Indianapolis. I've pretty much lost my accent but occasionally my roots show through. I try to hide them because musicians from here think players from the Midwest don't know how to play jazz. They're pretty uppity about it. Ironically, the white musicians are the worse."

"Do you know where Cassandra is from?"

"No. But I keep thinking I know her from somewhere."

9

Marisa threw off the bed comforter, but she couldn't throw off the rerun of mindless, endless chatter rattling inside her head. Tense and miserable, she blamed the morning's angst on Carl, who had turned up the thermostat so high that the steam heat pumped through a banging pipe by her bed all night. And now his heavy footsteps above her head sounded like someone hammering nails into a coffin—hers. She felt pressed in on all sides and lay prostrate, helpless.

Open the window, Marisa, and move on.

She glared up at the ceiling. "Easy for you to say, my dear." An image of Jules floating out the window like Casper the ghost crossed her vision and she had to laugh.

After forcing herself to get out of bed, she pressed her hands against the wall to stretch out her stiff, aching back. She knelt down with a moan and picked up the pages that had fallen during last night's late reading of her manuscript, after Martin brought it upstairs. It had gone better than expected: She'd actually liked what she read—certainly far more exciting than getting worked up over Carl. And she had more control over the manuscript than she had over Carl or the steam heat.

She drew comfort from the large space on her desktop that had opened up after Random House's messenger picked up the edited *Broken Chastity* and she'd proudly set her own manuscript down in its place.

With a sharpened red pencil in hand, she stared at the ream of paper. Where to start? And then what? Maybe put a few chapters up on *Serendipity*?

The phone rang, breaking into Marisa's thoughts. It was Enrico calling to remind her of tomorrow morning's appointment. "Do I absolutely have to bring someone with me to the first appointment?" she asked again. "Couldn't you talk to someone on the phone who knows me? I could have my daughter call you."

"No, I'm sorry, Mrs. Bridges, but clinical trial rules are very specific and must be followed or we'd lose our financing. Why not ask your husband again?"

"Because"—she stopped. "I'll see what I can do."

Later that afternoon, the elevator door opened, and Cassandra stepped out looking like Truman Capote's Holly Golightly marooned in a storm.

"Cassandra, I need to ask you a favor," Marisa said abruptly before the girl could slip away to her room. "I need someone to identify me at my appointment at NYU Hospital—in case I should ever forget who I am."

"That's a pretty weird request," said Cassandra, who hesitated before adding, "Why would you ever forget you are Marisa Bridges?"

Marisa explained how her own mother had first forgotten her daughter's name and then even her own name. She explained how her mother's dignity had been ravaged by Alzheimer's, leaving her with no sense of self. And she explained that after her mother's illness she had volunteered as a patient to help find a cure.

Cassandra nodded her head sadly and Marisa asked, "Might you know someone with Alzheimer's?"

"No, but it sounds like a fate worse than death."

A shadow crossed over Marisa's face. "Yes, I suppose someone could see it that way."

"I'm sorry. That was a stupid thing to say to you after what you've been through. Actually I think it's really cool what you're doing. Of course I'll come with you."

"Thank you. We'll leave at nine o'clock tomorrow morning.

Or eight-thirty if you'd like to join me for a cup of coffee before we go?"

"Okay."

At the Center for BrainHealth, Cassandra quickly identified Marisa as her landlady. But when Enrico asked for her phone number, she hesitated.

"It's just a formality. Mrs. Bridges's husband's number is on file but it would be good to add yours in case he's unreachable."

Cassandra was about to mention how *unreachable* Mr. Bridges actually was, but if Marisa didn't want to tell them he was dead why should she.

"Actually, I don't have a phone," Cassandra said, surprising both of them. "I'll give you the number when I get one." She smiled. "Remember, I just live down the hall." She leaned down to kiss Marisa's cheek. "I'll see you at home, Aunt Marisa."

Marisa was taken by surprise again. Cassandra had never kissed her cheek before, perhaps she was just performing for the clinician.

Marisa found the mental tests more grueling than last year, but when she mentioned it to Enrico, he told her that everyone's brain shrinks with age. "And perhaps you're just tired today," he said casually. "You'll do better next time."

Easy for you to say, my youthful Enrico, she muttered to herself, when she got lost in the labyrinth of hospital hallways. It's not your brain that is shrinking.

By Sunday, she'd read through several *Sha La La* chapters at home and at the Yale Club. It was strange to look that far back over the years. Had she really been raised in Beverly Hills in the fifties and then morphed into a Hollywood hippie in the sixties?

After the initial excitement of revisiting her memoir, Marisa saw the uphill climb—all the work that was left to do. Was she up to it? There were so many other pressing things to attend to.

Like what, Marisa? said Jules, over her shoulder.

Not bothering to answer him, she put on her custodian overalls and went downstairs to pick up the trash left behind by the garbage truck. Then she decided to change the burned-out fluorescent tubes above the front door entrance and brought outside a 15-step ladder.

Concentrating on finding the most level spot to place the unwieldy ladder, she was surprised by someone behind her shouting, "Do you need help?" She swung around to see what idiot would ask such an absurd question when it was so obvious that she did. And there was Ed, her ground-floor neighbor, hopping up and down in his track clothes. He took out the earbuds that plugged him into the music that would spur him down the block to the Hudson River for his daily run.

"Hey, let me do that." Ed examined the fluorescent tube, and then looked at her again. "You're lookin' much better, Marisa." He returned to the tube in his hand as if composing his words. Marisa waited. "Look, I should have said this a while back, but Denise and I were real sorry about what happened to Jules. We wanted to come to his funeral but you know how it goes with work and the kids. How long has it been now?"

"Nine months."

"Wow, that long."

Fortunately for both of them, Josh from the fifth floor stepped outside, letting Ed off the hook. Josh looked haggard and older than his fifty-five years. But who wouldn't age fast, married to the extremely competitive and ambitious super-lawyer Suzanne. When younger peers threatened to take over her position in the law firm, she countered by having another Botox injection.

Suzanne didn't like people in general and Marisa in particular, but never knowing when she might need Marisa's vote at a Board meeting, she was polite during their brief encounters in the lobby and between floors in the elevator.

Ed handed Josh the bulb and sprinted off. After screwing in the bulb, Josh said, "While we have the ladder, don't you think we should replace the emergency lights in the lobby too?" He moved the ladder inside. "I'll pull one out and take it to the hardware store later to match it." The fluorescent tube slipped in his hand and crashed on the tiled floor.

"Oh dear," said Marisa. She came back with a whiskbroom and dustpan. "I hope this doesn't bring us bad luck."

"I doubt it. You've already had enough bad luck for both of us." He came down the ladder and stood in front of her, the broom between them. "Look, I know it's a bit late to be saying this now but I've been wanting to tell you how sorry I was about the way things worked out for you—and Jules. I don't think any of us realized how ill he really was or maybe we wouldn't have behaved the way we did."

"Thanks, Josh, for telling me that. It helps to know that everyone in the building isn't against me."

"Oh no. Everyone feels really bad about what happened. Things got way out of hand and Suzanne—well, I won't apologize for her, but I'm certainly sorry for the way we all ganged up against you. It all started with those e-mails." Tears welled in Marisa's eyes. Josh bent down awkwardly from his towering height and hugged her and the broom.

Depressed by the too-late sentiments of her neighbors, Marisa sat across from Jules's chair and sipped her Stoli gimlet, wishing he could join her. "Jules, did you really mean it when you said I should move on?"

Yes, I meant it. There's nothing to keep you here.

She sighed. "But where would I go? And how can I possibly go there without you?"

Do what we planned before I got sick.

Marisa's eyes flashed with anger. "No. That was *our* plan."

The loft had been on the market for only four weeks when they received an acceptable offer from a young married couple. After the buyers got an approved mortgage there was only one last hurdle, the co-op Board's approval. "That should be a shoe-in with our neighbors," Jules had said. "We're all old friends."

Marisa and Jules were the sellers so it would have been a conflict of interest to attend the buyers' interview with the Board. Rachel and Charlie came up the back stairs after the meeting to give them the news.

Rachel said that after the buyers supplied all the necessary references and tax records, it looked like the Board was ready to approve them. But then Suzanne asked the wife, who was pregnant with her first child, if she planned to go back to work after the birth. No, she was going to be a stay-at-home mom.

Suzanne thanked them for coming and said they'd let them know their decision right away. After they left, she convinced the Board that they were a nice couple, but they couldn't afford the mortgage and maintenance fees with only one income. Rachel had disagreed saying the husband made several hundred thousand dollars plus yearly bonuses, but Suzanne said the bonuses were not a sure thing.

Jules wrote to the Board members asking them to reconsider. When they didn't respond, he tried reaching them by phone but only got their answering machines. Carl officially wrote back to say the Board's decision was final.

Only a week later, an ambulance rushed Jules to the hospital with acute pneumonia. Not knowing how long Jules would be ill or if he would pull through, Marisa took the loft off the market. Then Jules survived. And after several months recuperating at home he felt up to booking a short tour. The first club date was in New York City. He was playing a drum solo when he collapsed. By the time Marisa reached the hospital his heart had stopped.

10

Martin hadn't planned on coming back to the loft so soon, but his student had cancelled. He was hoping Cassandra would be out so he could put in a few hours of practice.

He took the stairs to avoid Carl. Every time they ran into each other in the elevator, the man kept probing him with questions: "What was it like being the nephew of a famous drummer?" "Why weren't you here for the funeral?" "How long will you be staying?" Martin lied and gritted his teeth into a smile when he'd rather have slammed the dude against the elevator wall and tell him it was none of his goddamn business.

Martin caught his breath when he entered the loft through the back hallway. Cassandra was seated at the piano playing his new song "Peggy Blue." She was reading from his sheet music, one hand on the keys, the other scribbling in a notebook. He slid down against the wall and kept motionless, as she sang the lyrics she'd just written.

She sensed someone watching her and shut her notebook.

"Don't stop. *That* was amazing."

"I shouldn't have but—your music was on the piano and I—"

"Don't apologize. Man, that was so cool. No one has ever put lyrics to my music." He fumbled for his phone. "Will you sing it again so I can record it?"

"No!" she snapped. "You can't do that."

"Wow, you're jumpy. What's wrong with recording it?"

"It was kind of out of tune."

"What are you talking about? Your pitch is perfect. Hey, I know a singer when I hear one and you're really good. And those lyrics were right on. I'd just like to hear them again. It was like you knew Peggy Blue's story better than I do."

"It's just what came to mind listening to the melody."

He walked over to the piano but she'd put away her notebook. "Would you really mind me recording it? It's just for my own pleasure."

She stood up. "I've got to go. I have a class."

"Wait a minute. I just got a great idea. I'm playing at 55 Bar this Friday. Why don't you come and sit in?"

"Sit in?"

"You know, sing with my trio. We could do 'Peggy Blue.'"

"No!"

He held up both his hands. "Okay. Okay. Lighten up."

She softened her voice. "Maybe some other time."

"Hey, gigs in the city aren't that easy to come by. You don't have to sing 'Peggy Blue' but maybe some standards. Blues? Jazz? Your choice." He smiled. She frowned. "It's not a big deal. I'd just like to hear you sing again."

Even while he was saying it, he was surprising the hell out of himself. Usually he didn't want to have anything to do with singers, but Cassandra's sultry contralto voice and her lyrics were too good to pass up.

"I told you I'm not a singer."

"Yeah, right, and I'm not a musician." She started toward her bedroom. "Wait. Will you at least give me the lyrics?" She tore out the sheet from her notebook and handed it to him. "Thanks."

When she returned to the foyer wearing her black leather jacket and carrying her art briefcase, he was seated at the piano reading the lyrics and playing the melody. He looked up. "Do you know if Marisa's home?"

"She told me she was going to her club to work in the library. Why?"

"If she was home, I might spend some time with her. She's kind of lonely, don't you think? Sometimes I see her just sitting on the couch staring off into space, and when I call her name she doesn't hear me. I've even seen her talking to that beat-up chair. Do you think she's all right?"

Cassandra shrugged. "Probably just missing her husband. But—"

"What?"

"I don't know whether she'd want me to tell you but Marisa volunteers at a research clinic that's looking to cure Alzheimer's. Her mother had it so she might get it too. I think it worries her a lot but she'd deny it."

"That's a drag. How do you know about this?"

Martin made room for her on the piano bench. "She needed someone to go with her to the Center for BrainHealth—the name alone is creepy—I went with her yesterday. We walked down hallways lined with freezers filled with autopsied brains. She said one of them was her mom's."

"That was nice of you to go with her."

She stood up. "There was no one else and she seemed kind of desperate."

"I don't think anything like Alzheimer's is going to happen anytime soon. Most of the time our landlady is quite sharp."

"Tell me about it. I can feel her pulling my thoughts right out of my head."

"Yeah, I know. I think she's just curious about us. Now what about sitting in on my gig on Friday?"

She half smiled. "You don't give up easily do you?" She left without giving him an answer.

Alone in the elevator, she beat her fist against the wall. "Stupid. Stupid." *How stupid can you be, girl? Why not just give him an autographed CD and be done with it. Now he's going to figure out who you are for sure.*

As Cassandra had said, Marisa was at the Yale Club. After forty minutes on the elliptical, she showered and slipped into a little black dress she'd brought from home to wear to a literary event at the club library on the fourth floor. She'd read the author's book, *The Mesmerizing Svengali,* and liked its insightful description of the personalities of charismatic manipulators and the overwhelming difficulty their victims have in breaking away from them.

All the library tables had been moved to the side except for one center table, which was spread with cheese and fruit plates rather than laptops and heavy textbooks.

If Jules had been there, the two of them would have mingled with the members, but now on her own, Marisa sat down in a chair in the back row, a good seat for slipping out if the author wasn't as fascinating as his book.

She was stunned when Serge, the man she'd met in the lounge three weeks ago, approached the podium. What was he doing there? A woman next to her had a copy of *The Mesmerizing Svengali* on her lap and there he was on the back cover. But why had he said his name was Serge?

Even from far away, she could feel his eyes on her. His smile sent a shiver up her spine that was undeniably pleasant. She brushed the fallen peanuts off her lap and reached for her notebook.

Serge described a case history of one Svengali-like character's powerful seduction of his female victim. When everyone clapped enthusiastically at the end of his lecture and held up hands to ask questions, she was surprised. She wouldn't have expected a Yale Club audience to be interested in Svengali-type men. But why not? Those kinds of men did not exclusively target the poor.

She looked down at the notes she'd taken, wondering how she could fit a review of Serge's lecture onto her blog as an appropriate topic. Marisa thought to ask Serge some questions, but too many Yale Club members had surrounded him.

She was waiting at the elevator when a hand touched her elbow, "Wait. Why are you leaving before we talk?"

"Oh, hello—I wasn't expecting to see you here. Why didn't you tell me your real name when we met? Why *Serge*?"

"Serge is what my friends call me. And if you hadn't had to rush off to your date with Proust, I would have told you."

Marisa looked over at the line of buyers waiting for Serge's autograph at the display table. "Don't you think you should talk to your fans?"

He hesitated. "Will you wait for me?"

Marisa couldn't remember the last time a man, other than Jules, asked her to wait for him. She heard herself saying yes before she could shake her head no. She watched Serge give each fan a few moments to ask their questions, before autographing his book.

"Hi, Marisa." She had no idea how long Louise had been standing there. "How good to see you at one of our events. I saw you earlier in the library but I didn't want to disturb you." Louise lowered her voice. "I was so sorry to hear about Mr. Bridges. He was one of my favorite members, always going out of his way to be so thoughtful and kind."

"Thank you," said Marisa.

Louise asked if she was still working on her book.

"Yes, I am," said Marisa, amazed that Louise remembered she'd been writing a memoir before Jules got sick. "I plan to spend more time in the library now."

"Please do. And come to our events more often."

"I will if they are as good as tonight. Are you responsible for booking Steven Anthony?"

She smiled and nodded her head. "It was a real coup. My committee didn't think there would be that much interest in his book, too controversial, for our conservative members." She looked around the room. "They were certainly mistaken seeing the response we got tonight."

"There you are," said Serge suddenly appearing without warning and with such a welcoming smile that Marisa blushed. He turned to Louise and said, "I hope you don't mind, but I've invited Marisa to join us at the library committee's dinner."

Marisa started to interrupt when Louise said, "Mind? Not at all. But I didn't know you two knew each other, though it makes perfect sense that you would."

Votive candles on white tablecloths reflected on the wine and water glasses at the Yale Club's rooftop restaurant. Marisa paused by a ceiling-high window to look out on the towering skyscrapers and the open sky above them, a sky she never saw from the street. And there was a full moon to hold her attention even longer.

"Do you often wish upon a star?"

"How do you know I'm wishing?"

He smiled. "I'll tell you my wish if you tell me yours."

"You should never do that. It breaks the spell."

Louise had saved a chair for the honored guest and put Marisa on his other side. After conversing with the other guests at the table, which included his publisher, his agent, and a few members of the library committee, he turned his attention to Marisa. He listened attentively while she told him about her literary blog and how she'd like to review his book, if she could decipher all the notes she'd scribbled down. He said he'd answer any questions she might have and handed her his business card.

Relaxing back in her chair after eating a delicious crème brulée, Marisa felt Serge's arm around the back of her chair. The tips of his fingers lightly touched her shoulder. She shivered. When she said it was the draft from the air conditioning, Serge took off his jacket and put it over her shoulders.

After the customary thank-yous and good-byes, she floated through Grand Central station and down the stairs into the subway. She felt radiant after her evening out in the bright world she had once inhabited before grief had confined her to her home.

The following morning Marisa literally jumped out of bed and opened her arms to the early morning light.

After breakfast, she responded to her e-mails. One was from a reader commenting on her recent book review of Annie Dillard's *The Writing Life*. He asked her not to stop her "Grief Literature" reviews. As a widower, he found them quite consoling. She wrote back that she would continue to review books on grief, but she wanted to branch out into other subjects too.

She turned to Dillard's book to get into a writing mood for her memoir and read, "Find a place to enter, to continue . . ."

She tried that, but by the end of the day, she was disappointed with her work. No enthralling phrases or heart-throbbing scenes had made it onto the page. Not even after a bar of chocolate, three cups of coffee, and a glass of wine.

At least she could be proud of the lamb roasting in the oven. She'd invited Martin and Cassandra to dinner. In a whimsical moment, she'd thought to invite Serge then remembered he mentioned leaving on a promotional book tour and that his home was in L.A., but she thought he might be in New York again on business. On his card there was only his e-mail address, nothing more. She stopped herself from going on Internet to learn more about him. How could she do that after admonishing her son for the very same thing?

"What did you do today, Marisa?" asked Martin coming into the kitchen.

Marisa half shook her head in defeat. "Too little for all the time spent doing it. Remember that box you brought up from the basement? You asked what was in it. Well it contains a memoir that I've worked on for several years but never finished."

"A memoir? About you and Jules? I'd love to read it."

She laughed. "Sorry to disappoint you but it's about my life before Jules. I've been struggling with it all day. Tell me Martin, what do you do when you're working on a song and it's not going anywhere?"

"I stop and go away from it," he smiled, "or I bang my head

against the wall. Or I get someone whose opinion I respect to listen to what I've written."

"Jules was my editor. I guess now I'll have to revert to banging my head against the wall."

Marisa looked in the drawer for the silverware and wondered why there wasn't enough. In the dishwasher? Then she saw the table was already set. "Did you do that, Martin?"

"No." He laughed. "You must have."

She turned away, embarrassed.

"It's no big deal, Marisa. I've caught myself putting headphones in the refrigerator and I'm only twenty-nine. It just means you have more important things on your mind."

At that moment, Cassandra stepped out of the elevator carrying one budding orange rose, a bottle of wine, and a wide smile that surprised them both.

"Why, that's very thoughtful of you, Cassandra. Is that for me?"

Cassandra nodded, handing her the rose.

"Yeah," said Martin, "Why didn't I think of that?"

Marisa and Cassandra rolled their eyes.

"Cocktail hour," said Marisa, bringing out the refrigerated Stoli. "May I shake you a gimlet?"

"Absolutely," said Martin. Cassandra said she'd prefer a glass of wine and opened her bottle.

Cassandra lit the candles, Martin carved the roast, and they sat down to eat.

For the first few minutes of eating, they hardly spoke other than to ask for salt and pepper. But underneath their silence they were all feeling the same thing: How pleasant it was to be sitting here together having dinner.

Marisa told them about her evening at the Yale Club and how she was surprised to find Serge behind the podium. She told them she'd met him a few weeks before but he hadn't mentioned he was a writer. When she told them about the concept behind his book, Cassandra's interest sparked. As Marisa expected, Martin showed no interest. Male domination wasn't a subject men were usually comfortable with. The audience at Serge's lecture had been mostly women.

Marisa was offering to loan her book to Cassandra when Martin interrupted with, "Hey, guess what? A record company heard my demo and two guys came to hear me play at the 55 Bar. After my set they said they'd be in touch." Marisa thought it was great news and wished him good luck.

Cassandra said nothing. She seemed far away. Finally, she raised her glass, "Congratulations, Martin. But be careful. Don't sign anything without a lawyer representing you." Marisa nodded in agreement.

"Thanks. It's a little early to be thinking about lawyers and contracts but it's good to know I've got two pros to turn to if something does happen."

"Oh," said Marisa, raising her eyebrows. "Are you in the business, Cassandra?"

"Of course not. I don't know where Martin got that idea. I've just heard stories about what can happen if you get bad advice."

Martin started to say something but changed his mind and instead got up for a second helping. "Anyone else?" Marisa said no. "Cassandra?" She shook her head.

After dinner, Cassandra brought out her notebook and sketched Marisa and Martin.

"These are really good," said Marisa, looking over her shoulder. "Have you been studying for a long time?"

"No. Just something I like to do."

"Well, I'm impressed. I hope you plan to continue at Pratt."

Cassandra got up, apologized for not helping to clean up, but she had to leave for work.

"You're going there now at ten o'clock?"

"I promised Max, the other bartender, I'd take the late-night shift. He has an audition tomorrow."

"That's too bad. I was going to invite the two of you to watch a movie. Martin, what about you?"

"Sorry, Marisa, I'd love to but I've got a sideman gig at Small's."

Marisa's face fell. "Hey, I've got a great idea. Why don't you come with me? Maybe Cassandra could join us later."

"Now?"

"Why not? You were going to stay up and watch a movie. My gig's close by in the Village. Come home when you get tired."

Marisa was tired now, but the thought of an empty house got her out of her chair. "Okay, but let me pay for a cab. I don't want to ride the subway."

"It's a deal. We'll drop Cassandra off first."

Settling back in a booth, Marisa watched the musicians come up on stage to set up their instruments and amps. She knew the routine well; she'd spent more than half her life managing bands. The drummer was always the first to setup, because he had the most hardware. The horn player was the last musician to arrive. It felt odd sitting in a booth on the sidelines with nothing to do other than listen. She had a sudden craving to go outside and bum a cigarette from someone like she used to do when she wasn't needed backstage, but what a foolish idea that was, no one smoked anymore.

She and Jules had met in a bar like this—dark, crowded, and, back then, smoke-filled. She held her crooked middle finger up to the light and her mind drifted back to their first date at Riverside Park. He'd called and invited her to join him and his friends for a friendly baseball game.

Jules sent her to the outfield and told her to catch any ball that came her way, but that didn't happen until the last inning when a big hunk of a guy, Jules's bass player, threw a ball right at her. She wanted to make a great impression and reached up to catch it, but the force of the ball snapped her middle finger back and she dropped the ball.

When Jules saw the red, swollen finger he went to get the sticks from the ice cream bars they'd just eaten and used his Swiss

Army knife to cut his handkerchief into strips. He used the sticks as a splint and tenderly wrapped the strips around her finger. As she watched him care for her, she fell in love.

She covered her face in her hands.

Don't cry, Marisa. You came to hear Martin play. Just listen. It will do you good.

She looked up just as Martin took a solo. His playing drew her in and she heard enough to know he was a talented musician. She drifted in and out of the rest of the set and only listened closely when Martin was featured. The other players were excellent technicians but she couldn't feel them in her heart. Martin was special. He was someone who would have sparked her interest back in the day when she managed bands.

You're right, said Jules, *he's good, but give the other players a chance. They just haven't hit their stride yet.*

Jules was always kinder than Marisa when it came to judging musicians. She drifted off again until Martin slid into the booth and nudged her.

"Hey, Marisa. Are you all right?"

"I'm fine. I was just resting my eyes. Is it over?"

He laughed. "Yeah, ten minutes ago. Sorry it wasn't a better set. The trumpet player's solos were way too long and he doesn't have that many ideas. He got a record deal right after he graduated from Berklee so he thinks he's hot stuff. I fell asleep during that last one myself."

"I'm glad I came. It was great hearing you play. You sounded really good. Did you go to Berklee too?"

"No." She hoped he would tell her about what happened at Juilliard but when he didn't she let it go. She wouldn't have known he even went there if Miles hadn't told her. And she still wasn't sure the story about Martin was even true.

"Thanks for coming, Marisa. Next time I'll invite you to hear my own band. Did you hang out at Jules's gigs?"

"Always. I was his manager."

"His manager? Wow, you're full of surprises. Did you go on the road with him too?"

"All over the world. But that was a long time ago. I'll tell you about it sometime, but for now let's get this old woman home."

"Marisa, you're far from old!"

She was about to deny it when she heard Jules whisper in her ear, *It's true.*

11

Marisa was squirming in her chair at her monthly widow's support group meeting at Gilda's club in the Village, when she felt her iPhone vibrating in her pocket. "Oh no, I forgot," she said out loud. She was meeting Miles and Sheri at the club and now she was late. She got up and said some hasty good-byes and headed for the subway.

When she rushed into the Yale Club lounge, Miles was just popping a large martini-soaked olive into his mouth. "Nice of you to stop by, Mom."

"Please don't give me a hard time, Miles. The meeting went late at Gilda's."

He dropped the olive pit into his empty glass. "Sheri and I have been waiting an hour and you know this isn't my favorite place to hang out." He took off his sport jacket in defiance of the club's dress code and his mother's respect of propriety.

Marisa dropped her eyes down on the inebriated olive at the bottom of Sheri's empty martini glass and looked up at Sheri's glowing face. "Will *you* forgive me?"

"Are you kidding? Forgive you? This place is awesome. It's so quiet and removed from that insanity going on outside. I wish I'd graduated from Yale just so I could hang out here."

"It was my father who went to Yale," said Miles. "My mother had a different kind of education. After Yale he turned left and got into music. This wasn't his favorite place to hang out in either. He only came here to please Mom."

Marisa waved her hand to bring over the waiter. "Would you

please have Hilgardo make me one of his special margaritas? And two more martinis. Make them special too." She looked at the empty bowl of peanuts. "And another bowl of peanuts for my hungry guests."

Miles said he didn't want another drink, but Marisa told him it was her peace offering for being late.

"It's good to see you again, Sheri. We didn't have much time to talk the first time we met. Miles told me how you met in his office building but he didn't tell me what you do? Are you a graphic designer too?"

"Mom, please don't interview her."

"I don't mind. My mother would do the same thing." Sheri turned to Marisa. "I'm a marketing manager for *Cosmopolitan*."

Watch what you say, said Jules from behind Marisa. He knew well when she was in a spicy mood. She didn't heed his warning. "Cosmopolitan? Why, isn't that a drink?"

The young woman sat back in her chair.

"Sorry, Sheri. I should have warned you about my mom's warped sense of humor. She meant that to be funny. Of course she knows the magazine. Let her hear a sample of your work."

"I don't know if she wants to hear ad copy," said Sheri.

"To the contrary. I'd love to," said Marisa.

Sheri leaned forward to sip Hilgardo's special martini, and Marisa's eyes couldn't resist wandering over the full breasts barely concealed under a low-cut silk blouse.

"Okay. Here's one of my most recent ads. '*Cosmo* is the life stylist for millions of fun, fearless females who want to be the very best they can be in every area of their lives.'"

"That's great stuff. Maybe I should subscribe. I'd like to learn how to be one of those *fun, fearless females* myself."

"I'll send you a free subscription if you really want one but you're probably already one of those fearless females."

"That she is," said Miles, grinning widely at his mother. "I have an idea. Why not ask Sheri to give you some writing tips for your memoir."

Sheri giggled. "Oh, Miles, I'm not a real writer. I studied literature in college, but then I interned at *Cosmo* and well," she shrugged, "here I am. Marisa, have you ever written anything for a magazine like *Cosmo*?"

"No, my dear, I don't think my work is really *Cosmo* material."

"I don't know about that," said Miles. "I think coming out of a cake to celebrate your thirtieth birthday would be a titillating story for *Cosmo* readers. Why just this month there was a feature called 'Feel Great Naked'!"

Miles put a little too much emphasis on this last phrase and his voice ricocheted through the somber room. Several coat-and-tie members peered out from behind their newspapers and turned their heads toward their table. Maybe Hilgardo's drinks were a bit too special tonight, thought Marisa, nodding pleasantly to the onlookers who returned to their papers.

Sheri was giggling into her napkin. "Really? You came out of a cake? That's sensational. I'd love to read your memoir." She plucked out the martini olive that was more than pleased to be held between her full rosy lips.

"Hey, why don't you ask Sheri to find you an agent," said Miles. "She has a handle on everyone in publishing."

Marisa had no doubt this was true after watching the unguarded stares from several of the men who walked by. Sheri, on the other hand, seemed oblivious to her assets. What a charming girl, decided Marisa, just what Miles needs in his dreary life.

"I do know a few people in publishing I could contact."

"Thank you, Sheri, that's very kind of you. Perhaps once I've finished—"

"Finished? You've been saying that for years," said Miles.

Marisa threw him a censorial look. "It's time for dinner." She pushed herself out of the chair, a mistake realized too late when the Yale Club lounge tilted and went into a spin.

Miles leaped up and put his arm around her. "Are you okay?"

"I'm fine. I just got up too quickly. I'll feel better after I've had something to eat."

Sheri took Marisa's other arm, and as they walked past the club members, Marisa imagined them smirking behind their papers. Begrudgingly Miles had put back on the required sport jacket, but it hardly covered his wrinkled shirt and stained painter's black jeans.

The Grill Room was busy but Jake, the maître d', smiled when he saw Marisa. He gave a warm hello and ushered them to the quiet corner table where she and Jules used to sit. As if he knew what she was feeling, Miles gripped her arm until the wave of grief receded and she could sit down.

Between courses they got on the subject of memory. "Just the other day I found my keys in the freezer and had no idea how they got there," said Marisa. "And balancing my checkbook has become a real chore. And those stressful tests at the Brain Center"—she slapped her hand across her mouth.

Miles turned to Sheri. "My grandmother had Alzheimer's, and Mom thinks she has to help find a cure, so she volunteers for one clinical trial after another. Those researchers are taking advantage of her."

"Clinical trials kept your father alive years longer than anyone thought possible. And brought the researchers closer to a cure for his cancer. Why shouldn't I want to do the same for Alzheimer's?"

Sheri frowned. "She's right, Miles. What your mother is doing sounds really worthwhile. Why are you so against it?"

"Because I don't see the point. What if they did discover she had Alzheimer's? Nothing can be done about it."

"If I knew for sure, I could at least prepare for it," said Marisa. "And do things I really want to do before I become helpless."

"Like what?" asked Sheri.

"Well, I'd find a nook somewhere where I can read and write and look out at towering green trees rather than towering gray buildings made of glass and cement. Maybe travel. And

I'd like to spend more time with my daughter in California."

"That sounds like fun. I've never been to California," said Sheri, beaming.

"What about your mother, Sheri?" she asked, not realizing until it was too late that her son was kicking her leg under the table not because he didn't want her to interview his new girlfriend but to warn her not to mention Sheri's mother. "Do you see her often? Is she as cheerful as you are?"

Sheri paled and bit her bottom lip. "My mother died last year. I wish we'd spent more time together, but I didn't even know how ill she was until she called me from the hospital in Chicago—the same hospital where she'd given me life. And now all I have left of her are a few photos." Her eyes moistened. "You're fortunate, Miles, I wish my mother had written a memoir. I know very little about her life before I was born."

Marisa reached across the table and squeezed Sheri's hand. "I'm so sorry. You're quite young to have lost your mother."

"She'd just turned fifty. Breast cancer." Sheri turned to Miles. "That's why I find your mother's volunteering so admirable. I sign up for the Cure for Cancer walk every year but it's not enough."

Sheri excused herself and when she returned from the bathroom, Miles and Marisa were discussing Occupation Wall Street's anniversary. Miles had gone with his mother to the protest in Zuccotti Park the year before. They were both surprised when Sheri spoke up and said she'd been there too and had written an article.

"For *Cosmopolitan*?" asked Marisa.

"No," she laughed, tossing back her long blond tresses with a sweep of her hand. "*Cosmo* readers are more interested in reading about 'Steamy Sex Positions for Every Mood' or 'Hot as Hell Heels that Get You Noticed.' I wrote that article for the *Village Voice*."

Both Miles and his mother stared at her in amazement.

"My mother was a political science professor and an activist too. She encouraged me to study journalism. As you can imagine, she wasn't too happy about my writing copy for *Cosmo*, but she always read everything I wrote for the *Voice*."

Over a shared hot fudge sundae, they made plans to have dinner again at the club in two weeks, and Marisa, after Sheri's dogged insistence, promised to bring her the first three chapters of *Sha La La*.

12

While Marisa was having dinner with Sheri and Miles, Cassandra was back at the loft sitting at the dining room table with Marisa's laptop open in front of her. Her own computer had been stolen a while ago and Marisa had told her to go ahead and use hers. She'd left two cookies and a note on the table. "Have Fun!" Cassandra smiled at the good wishes, and the cookies, but doubted what she was about to do would be fun.

She opened up the Facebook account she'd been avoiding for several months. She'd stopped writing on her Timeline after she'd left L.A. Her fans didn't know she'd been in rehab or that she'd moved to New York.

It pleased her to see they hadn't given up on her and were still sending "Get Well Soon" messages. And there were messages from DiDi and MiMi, her former singing partners, saying they were worried about her, which she didn't believe seeing they'd made no effort to contact her when she was still in L.A. So why now? And she wondered why Ryan hadn't told them he'd found her bartending at the Bitter End, because he must have seen The Belles later that night after their performance at Music City Hall, as he was still their manager.

She was considering what to write on her Timeline as her current status so her fans wouldn't worry about her, when a new post flashed across her homepage: CiCi working on solo album. Stay tuned. Ryan Peters—CiCi's manager.

She'd forgotten Ryan administrated the CiCi Belle account and had full access to it. "Damn you, Ryan, leave me alone!" She yelled at his handsome photo attached to the post.

A huge thunderclap brought her to her feet and she ran to close the windows before the rain soaked the floor. She was lost in thought watching the rain stream down the windowpanes when she felt someone behind her and jumped.

"Sorry," said Martin, "I didn't mean to frighten you but you didn't answer when I called your name, so I walked over."

She turned back to the window, her heart still thudding.

"Quite a storm isn't it?" he said. "I just made it inside before getting completely soaked. I think it'll blow over soon. New York thunderstorms usually do."

"I hope so. I want to go out for something to eat." She didn't tell him that someone might show up at the loft that she didn't want to see. Three weeks had passed since her date with Ryan at Irving Plaza when she'd told him she'd go back with him to L.A. and he might take her up on that at anytime, even tonight.

"Me too. I'm starving. When it lets up we can run around the corner. Jerry's has amazing pizza."

Cassandra turned and hesitated but the friendly smile on his face was so charming and guileless. And right now she needed a real friend much more than she needed hundreds of virtual friends reaching out to her on Facebook. She logged out and shut down Marisa's computer.

Between bites of pizza, they talked about living at Marisa's. Martin said how cool it was having a rehearsal space with piano, and Cassandra said how happy she was to have somewhere to go at the end of the night where she felt safe.

On his third slice, Martin told her again how much he liked her lyrics to "Peggy Blue." How awesome it was that she'd captured what he was feeling when he wrote it after reading E.E. Schmitt's novel, *Oscar and the Lady in Pink*.

"Do you know the book?"

She shook her head, no. "What's it about?"

"This ten-year-old kid, Oscar, lives in a children's hospital. Dame Rose, an older volunteer nurse, befriends him. She tells him what the doctors and his parents are too afraid to say—his leukemia is incurable. Dame Rose helps him find happiness before he dies.

"While Oscar's in the hospital, he falls in love with another child who has been nicknamed Peggy Blue because blood has a hard time reaching her lungs, and her skin has turned blue."

Cassandra withdrew into the booth's shadowy corner. "Those poor kids."

"Yeah. When I finished reading Oscar's story, I was feeling so bad for him that I wrote down a melody and called it "Peggy Blue." When I heard your lyrics about a girl heartbroken by a guy who took his life, it brought up the same sadness I felt when I wrote the melody. And your lyrics about how she could see his face everywhere, how she hates him and loves him but mostly misses him were right on. Man, I can't get your lyrics out of my head."

"I had no idea what your song was about. I was just responding to the bittersweet melody."

Martin considered his words before he looked at her again. "Listen, Cassandra, I need to ask you something. And please don't shake your head no until I finish. Okay?"

"Okay," she said, averting her eyes by picking up a blue crayon and circling around the wrinkled water rings that were on the paper tablecloth.

"I was in the studio last night with my band working on songs for the new album." She reached for another crayon and he stopped her with his hand. "Hey, do you like my day-old beard?" She took her hand away, continued drawing circles, and then without looking up, mumbled, "Is that really your question?"

He laughed. "No. Just trying to get you to look at me." She put down the crayon and looked up. "Everything's sounding really good except for one track, 'Peggy Blue.' It is missing your vocal. So my question is, Will you sing your lyrics on top of my melody?"

She shook her head, no, and called out to the waiter for the check.

"Why not?"

She shrugged.

He said, "Pleeeease."

She said she'd think about it.

Dawn was creeping into Marisa's window while Carl paced above her head. Would he understand the hint if she gave him a pair of furry slippers? Probably not. Was he upstairs plotting to evict Cassandra and Martin? Probably.

She welcomed the morning light, which meant that lying awake in the dark talking to herself was over. While waiting for the coffee to brew, she sat on the bar stool and read *The New York Times* headlines on her iPad. She shook her head at the constant bickering in Congress and, for that matter, all over the world. How little things have changed, she thought, and recalling the popular Kingston Trio song from the sixties, she sang its lyrics, *They're rioting in Africa, there's strife in Iran. / There's hurricanes in Florida, and Texas needs rain. / The whole world is festering with unhappy souls. / What nature doesn't do to us, will be done by our fellow man.*

After a sip of fresh-brewed coffee, she sat across from Jules's chair and told him all about dinner at the Yale Club with the kids after he left her on her own.

"Why did you leave so early?" she asked, remembering how she'd ignored his early warning to be careful about what she said to Sheri.

You didn't need me.

She shivered, wrapped herself in his blanket, and shut her eyes, so she couldn't see his chair. "Don't ever say that again, Jules. I'll always need you."

In the back of the loft, Cassandra woke up thinking that her evening with Martin had been nicer than she wanted it to be. After returning from Jerry's, they'd made popcorn and watched *The Ghost and Mrs. Muir*, which was still on Marisa's laptop. She smiled, remembering what an enjoyable, corny evening it had been.

Sitting up, she took out her sketchpad planning to draw the scene taking place across the airshaft; people working at their computer screens. Instead, she decided to scribble down some more lyrics for "Peggy Blue." After leaving L.A., she'd stayed away from songwriting, concentrating on drawing. It felt good to fall into it again as it satisfied her in a way drawing never could.

Martin woke to Cassandra singing the lyrics to "Peggy Blue" at the piano. He lay back and listened. What was it about her phrasing that sounded so familiar? He was sure he'd heard her before … but where? He hesitated then turned on his phone's recorder.

By mid-morning Marisa was settled at her desk reading a request from a blog follower, *whatnext*, whose husband had died last month. The widow was looking for a book that would tell her what to expect in the months to come and how to manage it.

The poet, Robert Seymour Bridges's verse: *I will not let thee go. /I hold thee by too many bands/Thou sayest farewell, and lo! /I have thee by the hands, and will not let go*, came to Marisa's mind but it was too sad for someone wanting to know what was next.

Instead, she suggested *Nothing Was the Same*. Kay Redfield Jamison claimed that grief wears itself out, that time spent alone in grief can be restorative, and that a drink or other anesthetic can blot out the ache of what remains. Marisa had felt less guilty after reading that when she drank one too many gimlets. She gave *whatnext* some other reading suggestions—Joan Didion's *The Year of Magical Thinking*, Joyce Carol Oates's *A Widow's Story* and Gail Godwin's *Evening at Five*. All those writers found that through their work they could blot out their husbands' absences and still feel close to them.

Snowflakes silently fell onto the city street below like someone above was shaking the feathers out of a pillow. A thin white line settled across the fire escape railing. It was an early March dusting that didn't stick on the oil-stained street below. Trucks and cars were restrained below her window by the red light at the end of the block. When the light turned green, they lurched forward, and the pedestrians cursed them for spraying their clothes with the dirty rainwater from last night's storm.

The few trees on her block were now naked sticks. Her own building had invested in two tree planters back when everyone cared about such things, back when 9/11 was still a reminder of life's vulnerability and seeing a tree survive the seasons on a congested, polluted street in Manhattan gave one joy and hope.

Her eyes traveled across the street into an exposed apartment window. During the time she and Jules had lived on Murray Street, the brick-and-mortar nineteenth century building across the street had been demolished and replaced with this glass and steel cube. Through its glass sheets she'd watched a woman go through pregnancy, and then saw the twin infants grow into five-year-olds under an au pair's care.

A Portuguese bank had bought the adjacent six-floor building for twenty-five million and after moving out the tenants kept it vacant. The ground floor had been an outlet store and every morning, Monday through Saturday at 8 A.M., like clockwork, Marisa used to hear the scraping sound of rusty metal shutters. Even in snowstorms when there were no customers and the commute from New Jersey was dangerous, the shop owner was there at 8 A.M. raising the shutters. When Marisa asked her why she came on such bad days, the woman replied that she was a widow and preferred being alone in the store rather than alone at home. In the store someone might come in and say hello.

Marisa's eyes dropped down on the black, graffiti-covered nightclub called 20/20. Now that she'd moved to the front of her loft, the late-night noise of party animals and the screams from bar brawls in the street below woke her. Even earplugs couldn't keep out the grating sound of metal-wheeled carts being pushed down the street. Before dawn, around the same time Carl started pacing upstairs, a large metallic-blue vegetable truck always parked in front of the 20/20 Club to make its daily vegetable and fruit deliveries to street vendors. The vendors showed up with their noisy carts, loaded them up and pushed them to street corners where office workers stood in line to buy their produce. The truck driver was not shy about bantering at high volume with lots of four-letter words, and, without fail, he would give the departing vendors some parting shots, *get two dollahs a pound for banana, a dollah apple*, his voice ricocheting through the chambers of her brain. There was something to be said for having a quiet bedroom in the back where her tenants now lived.

Her eyes returned to her neighbor's window across the street where the twins were playing. Children who would grow into adolescents while she grew into an older woman. She dreaded the day that these same neighbors would look down from their glass towers and see her carried away in a silver-blue body bag. That's the only way that I'll ever get out of here, she thought, anxiously.

My dear, that's just not going to happen. Don't let anyone stop you from moving on, not even yourself.

Marisa grabbed the phone.

"You're coming!" exclaimed Camille. "That's fantastic news. Alex has been looking so forward to meeting you. And I really want you to be at the gallery opening!"

"Are you sure I won't be in your way while you put up your exhibit?"

"Mom, you'd never be in the way. If anything it'd be a great help to me just having you here. You know how nervous I get before an opening and this is a very *very* important gallery."

Marisa went online to Kayak and checked flight availability.

She found a reasonable fare to San Francisco and bought her ticket. Quite pleased with herself, she e-mailed Camille her arrival time and then started a packing list.

It wasn't until evening that she finally paid attention to *Sha La La.* It had been glaring at her from across the desk where she'd stacked it days ago. She sharpened a red pencil, and set to work on revisions: *"When I was twelve my father announced that we were leaving Beverly Hills and moving to Palm Springs where the night sky is undisturbed by glaring streetlights."* She smiled, and wondered what her father would have to say about the narrow space viewed outside her window. If she stretched her neck out she could see New York City's night sky but it was very disturbed by a multitude of electric lights.

Cassandra had other things on her mind besides starry nights. She was at the Bitter End counting off each of the five hours until the end of her shift at midnight. Finally, with three minutes to go, she was wiping down the beer-stained bar for the last time when she heard, "Hey, bartender, bring me two double shots of Don Julio." Her hand froze. She knew that voice, she also knew that none of her regulars would order $50 shots of tequila. She turned to the other bartender, "Hey, Max, could you take care of that guy's order? I'm out of here."

She dropped the dirty, stinky rag in the bucket and slipped into the bathroom. What was she going to do? Martin was expecting her at the 55 Bar. She looked up at the window. It was too small to get through and someone was knocking on the door. There was only one way out. She strode out of the bathroom, determined to get by Ryan.

He blocked her at the exit door. "Hey. Where are you going? I just ordered your favorite tequila." He took her arm and brought her over to the bar.

"Sorry. But I'm meeting someone and I'm late."

He didn't let go of her arm. "You're not going anywhere until you tell me why you ran out on me the other night without saying good-bye. I would have come sooner but I had to go to Europe with the Valentinos on a short tour. I'd have called you but you don't have a phone. And now you're running away again. Why?"

"I never should have said I'd go back to L.A. with you."

Max put down the tequila shots Ryan had ordered along with a plate of sliced limes and salt. Ryan paid no attention to him. Max shrugged and walked away.

"Baby, you've got to quit flipping out on me like this. It makes me uptight."

"Well, speaking of feeling uptight, why did you go on my Facebook page and say I was in the studio recording an album?"

He smiled. "I thought that was very cool. Your fans were thrilled. And it went viral immediately. That's why we've got to get you back to L.A."

She controlled her voice. "Ryan, you're not listening. I'm not going back to L.A. I'm not going into the studio. I'm not leaving New York."

"Come here." He pulled her close and kissed her softly on the lips. He could tease her with his kisses until she'd do anything he asked and he knew it. That's why he pulled away now; his kisses were rewards for good behavior and she'd have to earn them.

"After you said you'd come back to L.A., I lined up a band and everyone else we need to make this happen. I've got writers working on material and record companies are already showing interest. Everyone loves the idea of you going solo. I know I can get a deal." He leaned toward her as if he was going to kiss her again, but instead traced her lips with his finger.

He picked up a shot glass and slid the other one over to her. "Cheers," he said.

Cassandra licked her hand, shook out the salt, tossed back the tequila, and bit down on the bitter lime. He threw back his shot and coughed. "Damn what is this crap?"

She laughed. "It's the best we have. You should have chased it with a lime."

"Baby, let's go back to my hotel where we can drink the good stuff. Don Julio misses you almost as much as I do."

The tequila gave her courage. "I'm late. I've got to go."

He threw back his head and laughed. "What's wrong with you, girl? I'm offering you everything you ever wanted and you talk about being late." He stroked her cheek. "Who are you meeting that could be more important than that?" He drew her closer, whispering in her ear, "It's okay, baby. I'm going to take care of you." He wrapped his arms around her. "Nobody cares about you like I do."

Cassandra woke up in Ryan's hotel suite and looked across the room at the half-empty Don Julio bottle and her clothes piled on a chair. She didn't remember putting them there.

Ryan came out of the bathroom whistling. He was cleanly shaved and dressed in pressed jeans, a silk shirt under a tailored jacket. He told her he was meeting with several record companies today to offer them her comeback record. He'd sign her up to the highest bidder. Then he was leaving that afternoon on a one-week tour with the Valentinos. When he got back he wanted to take her to a bed and breakfast he knew in upstate New York. Before she could answer, he said, "Mike and I will pick you up at your apartment next Saturday morning at ten sharp."

As if waking from a stupor, she pulled herself up and shook her head. "No."

"What do you mean, no," he said severely, coming toward her. "You're not going to flip on me again are you, baby? Not after last night."

"It's just I have an early art class on Saturday mornings. It would be better if I met you here at ten."

He smiled. "Okay, but you better make it your last class. I've got big plans for you." He tossed the room service menu on the bed. "Have whatever you want. It's on me."

At the door, he turned back. "Oh, I almost forgot. I got you a present. You'll find it in your purse. Don't throw this one away. We need to stay in touch."

13

At the San Francisco rendezvous point Marisa and Camille fell into each other's arms. Camille took her baggage and led her to the parking garage. Minutes later she was leaning back in Camille's convertible, staring up at the big blue California sky. There was an early March chill in the air. Camille handed Marisa a blanket and turned on the heater full blast. Back in New York, it would take a blizzard to get Camille to put the top up.

Speeding down U.S. 101 South, Marisa looked over at her daughter and noted she'd put on a few pounds. She knew Camille gained weight when she was depressed, but Marisa didn't think that was the reason now. She looked too happy. As the wind whipped her lush, wavy hair, Marisa admired the reddish-blond strands burnishing under the California sun.

When they stopped for gas, Camille, having read her mother's mind turned and said, "No, I'm not depressed. And yes I could lose a little weight!" They both laughed. "Let's put on some country music for the ride."

Marisa closed her eyes, and for the hour drive to Los Gatos, drowned her worries under Gretchen Peters's soulful lyrics and the sunshine. They pulled off the highway onto a country road then onto Bear Mountain Road where they wound around several breathtaking hairpin turns before Camille drove up a steep driveway lined by oaks and eucalyptus trees and said, "We're home."

Marisa was surprised to see a mid-sized house with several independent cottages built along the property's ridge. It was more like a compound. "All this for just the two of you? It's large enough to raise a family."

"Yes, it is," said Camille, pulling out Marisa's suitcase from the trunk. "And that was Alex's plan before Sarah's car accident. His only child, Lucy, visits us on her breaks from Stanford and stays in the bedroom that's been hers since childhood."

Marisa followed her along a stone path. "That's Alex's office over there." Camille pointed down another path to a white, shingled cottage with green shutters. "My studio is on the other side of the orchard." She stopped in front of a white cottage with red shutters. "And here's where you'll be staying. I hope you like it."

"Like it? Why I certainly do," said Marisa as she entered a small living room with a stone fireplace and stepped through French doors onto a small terrace. "Look at this view! Why I can see"—she counted on her fingers—"eight mountain ridges and beyond. And look at that vineyard! You better be careful, my dear, or you'll never get rid of me."

Camille hugged her. "Would that be such a bad thing, Mom? I'd love you to move out here. Come look at the bathroom. It's got your name on it."

"Camille, tell me, how on earth do you afford all this?" she asked, admiring the sunken marble Jacuzzi.

"This all belongs to Alex, not me. When he was a young man, he sold an upstart company to Apple and invested in this property."

"This is quite a change for you, isn't it? Last time I visited you in San Francisco, it was a small, dark studio and I slept on the floor."

"I'm still getting used to it." Camille looked at her watch. "Do you want to nap before you meet Alex?"

Marisa stood up straight. "Why? Do I look tired?"

"No but—"

"Then no. And considering the time difference, it's way past cocktail hour."

Camille laughed. "Oh Mom, you never change. It was always difficult keeping up with you. I'll check with Alex, but why not come up in thirty minutes if you don't hear otherwise."

"Just after five," mumbled Marisa, as she adjusted her watch to West Coast time before strolling across a garden path toward the main house.

Inside, she heard peals of laughter and looked down a hallway to a half-opened door at the far end. Resisting the urge to eavesdrop, she entered the living room and scanned the bookshelves for a clue to Alex's character. The alphabetized *New York Times* bestsellers, first edition classics, and enormous coffee-table art books told her that Alex had expensive taste and preferred tidiness to chaos. She wondered where Camille's banged-up art and poetry books were. Probably in her studio.

Another peal of laughter from Camille. "Jules, can you hear that?" she said, raising her eyes to the skylight in the vaulted ceiling. There had been no laughter from Camille when she visited Jules in the hospital and saw his pallid face and emaciated body. At his bedside, Jules told her not to worry about him. He encouraged her to take some leaps of faith, just like he had to do. It would please him so to see that she was doing that with her new home, her new boyfriend, and a new studio.

Back when she was earning a living waiting tables, Camille had considered giving up on her artistic dreams. But now, with Alex's help, she could be that full-time artist.

Marisa looked down at the polished oak floors. "This is a floor meant for dancing on, isn't it, Jules?" she said softly. "If you were here, you'd take me in your arms and twirl me around."

But I am here, whispered Jules. With her eyes closed, she felt his arms wrap around her and they spun across the room.

Woozy, she landed in the big arms of an overstuffed chair. "Oops," she said looking up at Camille. They both giggled.

"You always did make a memorable first impression with my boyfriends." She then turned to a thin man of medium height, and an older face than Marisa had expected.

She guessed from the lines extending out from the corners of his somber gray eyes and furrowed forehead that he was approaching sixty and wondered why Camille hadn't told her. Or was he younger than he looked and just worn down from paying for all this?

"Sorry about that. But your floor was meant for dancing."

"Alex, this is my Mom."

Alex reached for Marisa's hand and pulled her out of the chair saying how happy he was to finally meet her.

———

When Marisa saw the fresh limes from their orchard in a fruit bowl, she offered to make gimlets.

Alex placed the drinks on a tray and said, "Let's have these outside. I want to show you the view before the sun sets." They walked out onto an expansive deck with a view of Monterey Bay in the distance and several pastoral fields below.

"Is this all yours?" she asked.

He smiled. "No. Just the view." He draped his arm around Camille. "And your lovely daughter when she's feeling generous."

Marisa hadn't seen a clear one-hundred-eighty-degree view like this since she'd left France and her heart leaped. She turned to tell them what a stunning view it was but quickly turned away when she saw Alex kissing Camille.

What does his age matter as long as he treats my little girl right? thought Marisa. She and Jules had been through all the bad choices Camille had made. The manipulative guys who'd wanted a beautiful mannequin, an object to admire and later discard, blind to the real beauty and gentle, loving heart behind those soft amber eyes.

"Mom?"

Alex and Camille were staring at her.

"Sorry. Did you ask me something?"

Camille giggled. "Mom, you've been gazing off into space."

"I think I'm in shock. It's just so beautiful here in contrast to the city I left this morning."

"I've often asked myself how you and Dad lived there all these years."

"We just got so busy keeping it all going that we forgot what it was like to be in nature. But we did have our summers in France. This reminds me of Beaulieu."

"And what do you do when you're in New York?" asked Alex.

"Let's see. What do I do? Well, I spend a lot of time on my blog. I recommend books on grief and bereavement to my readers and I have to read the books first ... I edit other authors' books and, when I have time, I do some writing myself. By the way do you have a Wi-Fi connection?"

"Of course, Alex couldn't survive without one," Camille said, looking over at him. "Though sometimes I wish we didn't."

"Camille's referring to the fact that I'm online a lot of the time."

"Why?" asked Marisa. "Don't tell me you're playing video games."

Alex smiled. "That's what Camille thinks I'm doing." There was a stony exchange between the two of them that made Marisa wonder if all was as nice as it seemed up on this gorgeous mountaintop. She asked, "So what do you really do online?"

"I design applications for smartphones, iPads and other devices. Like the ones you use all the time."

"How did you know I use apps all the time?"

"Camille. She says we could compete for who spends the most time online. I hope you're not as addicted as she thinks I am."

"Alex, I never said you were addicted," said Camille, defensively. "After all, it's your work. I just wish you spent more of your time with me." She turned to Marisa. "Alex is very disciplined, like Dad. He doesn't tolerate distractions. That's why my studio is so far away from his office. It's where he used to house his in-laws."

Marisa felt she needed to say something to break the sudden chill between Camille and Alex. "I'd love to see your studio. Can we go now?"

"Sure. Let's"—Marisa saw Alex shaking his head at Camille—"On second thought, it's getting dark. Tomorrow I'll give you a full tour in daylight."

Marisa was disappointed. "Okay. But was that a chimney I saw?"

"Good eye. My Alex has thought of everything to keep me happy, including a kiln." Camille put her hand through his arm and reached up to kiss his cheek.

"Shall we go in, Marisa?" said Alex. "You must be hungry after that long flight."

Camille insisted that her mother do nothing while she and Alex prepared dinner. Marisa was surprised at Alex's command of the kitchen, even telling Camille what silverware to use. Having only moved in six months ago, perhaps she was still getting used to living with him. Or was it the other way around?

The candlelight dinner began with Alex's freshly made mushroom soup followed by veal piccata, from-the-garden asparagus, and Asiago potatoes. Every bite was delicious and Marisa was sure she'd gone to heaven. They told her to sit and enjoy being waited on and she did just that. And the wine, well the wine was out of this world too. So, when Camille, who was fairly quiet during dinner, asked her mother to extend her stay after the gallery opening, so they could have more time together, Marisa didn't hesitate to say yes.

The air was warm enough to sit out on the deck before going to bed. In the moonlight, Camille saw a whimsical smile cross her mother's face and asked her what she was thinking about.

"Oh, nothing. These stars just reminded me of a recent evening at the Yale Club when I was up on the rooftop dining room."

"What were you doing there?"

"Oh ... someone had invited me to dinner."

"Really? Who?"

After Marisa told them briefly about meeting Serge, Camille asked, "Are you going to see him again?"

"I don't think so."

"Well, I think you should. Don't you, Alex?"

"That's up to Marisa. Maybe she's not ready yet—"

"I'm not suggesting she marry the guy, but it would be nice to have a companion sometimes. You certainly didn't waste anytime"—Camille stopped.

"I think it's time for me to turn in," said Marisa, standing up.

"Good idea," said Alex. "We're all tired. The path to your room is a bit treacherous at night. Let me get the flashlight and I'll walk you down."

As they walked, Alex told her how sorry he was to hear of her husband's passing. He too had lost his spouse and understood how lonely it could be. He had tried to replace his wife with someone else soon after her accidental death but it hadn't worked out. It was only, years later, after meeting Camille that he thought he could try again.

Before he left her, he said, "Your visit has made Camille very happy. As beautiful as it is here, she gets lonely sometimes, even depressed, and you've cheered her up. Thank you."

Marisa watched him walk back to the house, with his shoulders bent over he seemed even older. At some point, when they were alone, mother and daughter needed to have a heart-to-heart talk about Alex.

Before getting into bed, she e-mailed Miles and Martin to let them know of her plans to extend her visit. She would have sent a note to Cassandra but there was no way to reach her. Her last e-mail went to Carl requesting a postponement of the scheduled Board meeting until her return. His response was swift, even though back East it was two in the morning. Did that man ever sleep?

She really didn't want to read his reply until morning but her curiosity got the better of her. After, she wished she hadn't:

> Please be advised that this meeting cannot wait another week and it is in your best interest to be here. We would rather have done this in person but you force me to tell you now of a very urgent situation in our building. It has come to our attention that your boarder Martin Starks is not your nephew but a paying tenant. As you know the co-op rules do not allow tenants without Board approval. One can only assume that your effort to hide the truth of your true relationship with Martin was premeditated and manipulative. I have been unable to question Cassandra as she keeps very strange hours, but I'm quite sure she is not your niece. The Board did consider changing the front door lock but in good faith we will not take any such action until after we meet with you. Know that we did not come to this decision lightly. You have been in the building many years and that compounded with your recent loss has kept us from taking any legal action against you.
>
> You should also know that the other night Martin and several of his rowdy beer-drinking friends were riding the elevator up and down. Shouting and laughing. One was smoking a cigarette. They continued to party in your loft and someone was banging on the piano. I bore the brunt of their shenanigans and could not sleep at all.

At breakfast Marisa told Alex and Camille about Carl's e-mail. She said she could go to the gallery opening but would have to keep to her original schedule and fly home right after.

14

The cabbie dropped Marisa off on Broadway, a half block from her loft and a cheaper fare. She was weighed down by her suitcase, exhausted after her delayed red-eye flight into JFK, overwhelmed at reentering the City, and she was freezing. She tripped on a loose pipe and nearly fell on her face.

A construction worker called out gruffly, "Hey lady, watch where ya goin'!"

Marisa tried to shout above the digging machine, "What do you mean 'watch where you're goin' it's your damn pipe I tripped over!"

When she didn't get the slightest rise from him it enraged her even more. "If my husband were here"—she sputtered. She shouldered her bag and then felt Jules at her side.

Go with the flow. It's not that important.

Cancer had taught him his priorities. Marisa was still trying to figure hers out.

Five anguished minutes later, she unlocked her building's front door, put down her suitcase and let out a deep sigh. The newly installed fluorescent tubes sizzled. She'd have to remove one of them or she'd never be able to face herself in the lobby mirror again.

Utter silence greeted her homecoming and she turned on the radio to NPR just to hear a voice. There was a note on the kitchen counter from Martin. He said he needed to talk to her and would be home around six. She sat at her desk and checked her e-mails, Facebook notifications, and blog comments. She was disappointed that very few of her blog followers had visited her site while she was away.

"Is that you, Martin?" she called out hearing the back door open and wondering why he hadn't taken the elevator.

"Hi, Aunt Marisa," he said. "Welcome home."

It's hard to resist that charming smile, but I have to be firm, she thought, coming toward him in the kitchen. "Don't Aunt Marisa me, young man. You promised to be the perfect tenant—invisible. Instead, Carl e-mails me about you and your friends riding up and down in the elevator like it was a Disney thrill ride and waking everyone up with your shouting. And how did he figure out you weren't my nephew?"

Martin put his hand down on the kitchen counter with a little too much force. Marisa flinched.

"Sorry but that's *his* story. I had some friends over but we never rode up and down the elevator and we didn't shout. You know, he really is a bad dude. I'm sure in a past life he was some sort of a Spanish inquisitor and probably nailed me to a cross. I take the stairs now to avoid him cornering me with questions. Like 'What side of Jules's family do I come from?' Or, 'When was the last time I saw Jules?' Man, he had me so turned around that I must have somehow slipped up." He stopped for air. "Look, I'm really sorry. Believe me, I tried."

He looked sincerely sorry and Marisa couldn't stay angry. She sat down on a counter bar stool. "This isn't your fault. If I'd told the truth in the first place Carl wouldn't have such a hold over me. I'll do my best, but if I can't stop him, I'm afraid both you and Cassandra will have to leave."

Marisa explained that she came home earlier than she had planned to attend a special Board meeting tomorrow tonight.

"This really sucks. Sorry but there's no better word for it. He shouldn't be allowed to do this."

Marisa sighed. "I know, but I don't have any leverage. I'm afraid he can do whatever he wants."

"Leverage? You say you don't have any leverage? Well, I think you do."

"What are you talking about?"

Martin started to tell his side of the elevator story, but Marisa interrupted, "Wait. Let's talk this out over gimlets."

"Good idea. I could use a drink."

"I hope you're hungry. I ordered a large pizza."

"Ah, Marisa, the quality of my life really picks up when you're around. Pizza and gimlets. I don't remember the last time I was treated so well."

After Marisa made their drinks, they sat at the kitchen counter. "Now tell me why you think I have leverage?"

"I had unexpected visitors from out of town. They didn't have anywhere to stay so I thought it would be okay if they stayed here, in my room, of course. Cassandra said she was going out of town for the weekend so it didn't matter to her. I realize now I should have asked you even if it was only for one night."

Marisa nodded while thinking how curious it was that Cassandra had gone out of town seeing she hadn't mentioned any family or friends living nearby. She had assumed Cassandra was quite alone in the world.

You're wandering Marisa. Stay tuned to what Martin has to say. It might be helpful, she heard Jules say.

"The guys were high school friends from Indianapolis. It was really great to see them. We went down to Jerry's to hang out and get something to eat. Yeah, we drank beer but we weren't drunk, just having a good time. We closed Jerry's around two. We got in the elevator but before I could get my keys out to unlock the damn key for your floor it started going up. Then the door opened onto Carl's floor." Martin burst out laughing.

"What's so funny?" asked Marisa.

"Well, just Carl. All he had on were some red plaid boxer shorts and he was wrestling with a woman wearing a flimsy nightgown. It was like we were watching a bad movie. She pushed him away and shouted, 'Let go of me, you fool,' and rushed into the elevator with us!"

Marisa immediately recognized Martin's impersonation of a woman's raspy voice. "Suzanne!"

"You got that right. So, while we were gawking at her, she got in the elevator acting all cool like, and we rode up with her to the sixth floor where she got out without saying a word. The elevator seemed to have a mind of its own because it brought us back again to Carl's floor. Maybe he pressed the button hoping she'd come back down, but there he was again right where we'd left him.

"We tried to stop laughing, really we did, but he looked so ridiculous standing there in his boxer shorts and white socks. While I was fumbling to put my key in the lock for your floor, one of the guys yelled, 'Look out,' and there was red-faced Carl coming toward me waving a broom over his head. The elevator door slammed shut before he lowered it on my head."

Marisa was too shocked at first to laugh. Who would have ever matched those two icebergs? But when she imagined them in such a ridiculous compromising position, she had to burst out laughing herself.

"So as I was saying, you have leverage. I'm sure Carl wouldn't want me to say anything about what I saw."

"You're right, of course, but that's the wrong kind of leverage. I don't want to blackmail Carl to win my appeal. I wouldn't feel right about it."

"Why not?" Martin asked.

Yeah, why not? Jules added.

The buzzer shrilled and Martin went downstairs to meet the pizza deliveryman. When he came back up, Marisa told him she would only consider blackmail if Carl or Suzanne ganged up on her at the Board meeting, and she might lose her appeal.

As she cut into the pizza, she said, "What I need for tomorrow night is a badge of courage like the Wizard of Oz gave the Cowardly Lion after he fought the wicked witch. Do you know the story?"

"Sure do. If I remember correctly the wizard awarded the badge to the lion because the lion didn't realize how brave he was without it. That's like you, Marisa. You don't realize how brave you are. So here's your badge of courage." Martin ceremoniously put an imaginary necklace over Marisa's head.

She felt tears stinging her eyes. "Thanks Martin. I'll be sure and wear this tomorrow night. Now enough of this talking. The pizza is getting cold."

Martin lit up the jukebox and pushed a few buttons. Marisa lit two candles and they ate pizza while listening to Jules's jazz trio.

Later Martin asked, "Do you think you could tell me about Jules now?"

Marisa woke to the sun streaming through her window as Louis Pasteur's words of wisdom passed through her lips, "Happy is he who bears a god within, and obeys it." A heavy weight, like a block of cement, lifted off her body and dispersed amongst the rays of dust motes above her. She was sure the trigger for this sudden lightness came from talking to Martin last night about her memorable life with Jules, a life she had locked away inside, afraid that if she brought it out in the air it would turn to ashes. But that wasn't at all true. By telling stories about Jules, he rose from the ashes like the phoenix and came to life again. And not just for her but for Martin. She could tell it in his eyes that he too would never forget how special Jules was.

But by the end of the day, when the cuckoo chirped seven times, and Marisa rode down the elevator to the Board meeting, flanked by Rachel and Charlie, the weight had returned and her spirit had faltered.

Be strong, Marisa. Be strong. I'm right here with you, whispered Jules.

A dozen shareholders were seated around the boardroom table when they entered the ground floor corporate office of Denise and Ed's. They had divided a large storefront in half. The front section was their architectural office and the back section, now hidden behind a screen façade, was their living space. A far cry from the days when the Board members sat back on Rachel and

Charlie's couches, sipped wine and nibbled on appetizers while amiably discussing the building's problems. In this corporate office environment, no wine was offered. Not even water.

She relaxed a bit when Josh asked if she'd enjoyed her California trip. But Suzanne, Carl, and Denise ignored her and spoke in hushed tones as they reviewed their notes. Not to be intimidated by them, Marisa called out, "Hi, guys. How is everybody?" But they didn't even look up.

All right, thought Marisa, we'll do it your way. She turned to Josh and said, "Have you been away?"

"Yes. I was working in Washington. Why?"

"Oh, nothing. I was just thinking the other night how lonely it must be for Suzanne being left on her own all the time, because of all the traveling you have to do." She turned sympathetic eyes on Suzanne. "Perhaps next time Josh is out of town you can ride the elevator down to my floor. I'll order pizza." Suzanne still didn't look up. Marisa continued, "No need to dress, we can pretend it's a sleep-over and eat in our nightgowns." Suzanne and Carl now glared at her.

"Why that's a wonderful idea," said Josh. "Suzanne could certainly use the company." Marisa took the last empty seat, sipped from her water bottle, and tried to act like she didn't have a care in the world.

Carl called the meeting to order. "We're here to discuss Marisa's illegal tenants, and also to vote on deleting the subtenant rule from our co-op by-laws. Our lawyer has advised me that if we ever want to refinance the building's mortgage, financial institutions would reject us if there were any subtenants."

Marisa was taken aback. Carl had just attacked her with a double whammy. If the subtenant rule were deleted she wouldn't even be able to plead her case, because any tenants in the building would be considered illegal. She sat back and considered her options before she rose to speak.

"It's my understanding that the subtenant law protects our

rights as homeowners. If any of us should come upon hard times or a serious illness this law allows us to sublease until we get back on our feet."

"A moot point. Most of us at this table will never put ourselves in a position of such dire circumstances," said Carl, smirking at the other Board members.

She continued. "Also, our real estate agent told Jules and me that our building's lenient subtenant clause increased our loft's market value. People won't invest in a building if the shareholders don't have the same rights as homeowners." A few members nodded in agreement.

"I motion that we take a vote," said Suzanne. Carl seconded it. "Those in favor of eliminating the sublease by-law raise their hands." Hands went up quickly but not enough for the required two-thirds majority. Marisa tried not to gloat but it wasn't often that Carl didn't get his way.

"Let's get on with the second item on the agenda," said Carl. "I recommend that we take an immediate vote on evicting the illegal tenants."

Charlie jumped up. "Now just hold on a moment, Carl. For one who follows the rules so strictly, you know that's unacceptable. Marisa gets a chance to speak."

"Thanks, Charlie," said Marisa. "I'll be quick." She looked down at her notes and took a deep breath and then, as difficult as it was to do, she looked at each of her neighbors before saying, "I want to apologize to all of you for lying. The truth is, I was desperate. As you know, the building's maintenance has increased thirty percent. Without Jules's . . ." she took a sip of water and swallowed back her pain.

"I've come here tonight to ask you to approve my tenants so I can afford to keep my loft." No one said anything but all eyes were on her. Marisa was surprised her knees didn't give out. "Thank you for hearing me out. I'll wait upstairs for your decision."

She didn't have long to wait. Fifteen minutes later Charlie and

Rachel were knocking on her back door. It wasn't a good sign that they'd avoided the elevator.

"I'm sorry," said Charlie. "Carl convinced most everyone that you could afford to live here without taking in tenants."

"But that's not true. Incredible. He'll say anything to get his way," said Marisa, shaking her head. "Why is he doing this?"

"I don't know. But I do have some good news."

"Yes?" she asked hopefully.

"The majority of shareholders said it was too punitive after what you've been through to throw out your tenants immediately. Surprisingly, this time not only Josh but Suzanne voted against Carl."

Marisa smiled. So she did have a bit of leverage after all.

"Your tenants can stay through May."

"Well, two months is certainly better than tomorrow, said Marisa trying to make light of the Board's decision.

It's time to move on anyway. You just have to take the first step, whispered Jules.

Marisa stood up and heard herself say, "Tomorrow I'm going to call my agent and put the loft back on the market. What with Carl so determined to get rid of me maybe this time the buyer will pass Board approval."

"But where will you go?" asked Rachel with concern.

"Not to worry," said Marisa. "There are many possibilities. Camille and her boyfriend Alex have invited me to live with them in California. Or I might consider returning to France—that is if I could work up the courage to live there without Jules. And then again, maybe once I've sold the loft other opportunities will show up."

After they left, she raised her wineglass to Jules's empty chair. "Thanks for sticking by me tonight. I couldn't have faced the Board without you."

Oh yes you could. You did a good job.

She blushed. "Oh, Jules, you always say the nicest things."

15

Martin got to the 55 Bar and saw people waiting outside to get in. Once inside he had to squeeze his way through the crowd to the bandstand and his mood lifted higher every step he took. Months of low paying gigs had finally paid off. The word was out. The Martin Starks Trio was a happening New York band.

Carlos, the bass player, and Stuart, the drummer, were already set up and ready to start, so he quickly hooked the wide leather guitar strap over his shoulder, plugged into his amp, and tuned his guitar. He nodded to Stuart who counted off 1-2-3-4 and they settled into a funky groove. It was one of Martin's favorite compositions and the groove held for the following forty minutes.

After two more songs the set ended with a loud applause and shouts for "more." Martin turned to Stuart and Carlos who were nodding their heads, smiling, and giving him the thumbs up.

As he was leaning his guitar against the wall, a short, chubby man came up and introduced himself. He said he loved the set, and asked if he could buy Martin a beer. At first, Martin thought he was a fan and begged off saying he needed to talk to the band, but then the man handed him a card that said he was the promoter for the Blue Note. He bought Martin a beer and offered him a one-night gig at the Young Lions Festival, a festival of young undiscovered players on the New York scene. Someone had cancelled, and he wanted to put Martin's band in the Friday night slot, on the last weekend in April.

Trying to be cool and not show how hungry he was for a gig at the Blue Note, Martin took his time, pulled out his phone, checked his calendar, took a swig of beer, and finally said yes, the band was available. Later, when he told Stuart and Carlos they didn't believe him until he flashed the promoter's card.

Down the street things hadn't gone as well for Cassandra. The bar crowd was keeping her busy but she couldn't shake off her dark mood knowing her stay at Marisa's would be short. She'd felt comfortable there. She even looked forward to coming home. She even liked having Martin as a roommate though she kept denying it. Just as she was thinking this Martin walked through the door. He had decided to stop by after his last set. He looked at her across the bar with those gorgeous wide-open eyes and in his gentle, persuasive voice asked her if she wanted to go out for coffee before she went home.

Without saying yes or no, Cassandra took away some empty beer bottles and wiped down the bar with a wet rag. Max was blinking the house lights so the last stragglers knew it was time to go home.

Martin said, "I played three sets and I'm beat. I'm only suggesting a cup of java. There's something I want to talk to you about."

"Isn't that what you said last time?"

"Exactly. And if you recall we both crashed when we hit my pillow. Come on. It's important. We need to talk about Marisa and the loft situation. Please?"

"Okay. We can go to Caffe Reggio around the corner."

"Whatever," said Martin, picking up his guitar case.

No harm in having a cup of coffee, is there? thought Cassandra, reaching for her purse and following him out. But she felt surprisingly excited when he opened Reggio's door for her and she passed under the bridge made by his arm. She walked over to her favorite table in the shadows.

"Do you come here often?" asked Martin.

"After work I stop by on my way home." What she didn't tell him was that she came here to observe the unsuspecting customers like Martin, who she would later draw from memory. The thick brows. The wide eyes. The bump on the bridge of his nose that would be difficult to capture on paper.

"I like it. It has that old feel," said Martin.

"It's the oldest coffee bar in Manhattan."

Martin held the menu up to the flickering candle, read "Since 1927" and looked at the selections. "So what's good?"

"I like the chocolate cake and a cappuccino with a splash of Amaretto."

"Cool. I'll have the same."

If Cassandra had known how cramped her favorite table was for two people she'd never have sat there. She needed space to temper the unwanted and unexpected warm feeling she felt every time her legs and knees touched Martin's, which was way too often.

"Tell me your thoughts and I'll tell you mine," said Martin.

She blushed. "I'd prefer not to."

"Why that's one of my favorite Melville lines. Bartleby, right?"

When Cassandra didn't reply, he added, "Bartleby would say that when someone asked him to do something he didn't want to do and then he'd turn and face a brick wall. Please don't you do that. I much prefer to look at your face even if it is hidden behind shadows." She moved into the light and returned his smile.

"That's better." Their eyes met for a second longer than either was comfortable with. They turned away and reached for their cappuccinos, but they were too hot to sip.

Martin put his mug down on the wobbly marble table. "God what a jerk that Carl is. Marisa has to humiliate herself by saying she can't afford the loft unless she takes in tenants and he still says no. And she's a widow for Christ's sake. Man, I'd like to take out that hypocrite and I'd do it if I thought it would do Marisa any good."

"Well, it won't. Marisa knew the risk she was taking when she lied to her neighbors. At least they've given us some time to find somewhere else to live."

He stretched out his legs under the table, brushing against hers. "Exactly what I wanted to talk to you about." He licked the foamy cappuccino cream off his lips with his tongue. "Hmm. Good call, Cassandra. So this is what Amaretto tastes like."

She moved her legs away from his. "What were you going to ask me?"

"What do you think about us looking for another place to live?"

"What do you mean—*us*?"

"I thought we might continue being roomies somewhere else."

"Martin, I know you're just joking around but let's cut out this *together* stuff. It's been nice but don't make anything more of it than just that." She took a sip from the strong espresso, but that wasn't what was making her heart beat faster. It was his eyes undressing her. She withdrew into the shadows again.

"Okay we'll forget about that for now."

He told her about the Blue Note gig. "It's an awesome opportunity for me if I pull it off right." The waitress put down two plates of chocolate cake, which gave Martin a moment to consider what he'd say next. His plan had made a lot more sense before he was actually facing Cassandra who had moved as far away from him as was possible in this small, crowded café. All he could see were her round eyes staring at him like a deer caught in his headlights. He took a bite of the cake and put down his fork. "So I've been thinking about adding a singer. I've considered it before, but I never heard the right voice until I heard yours." It was too dark to see her reaction so he plunged ahead. "So how about us working on some tunes, rehearse with my band, and try it out?"

She leaned forward into the light and her reaction was not favorable. "Now you've really lost it. Why would you want to take a chance on me singing with you on such an important gig? And why do you keep thinking I'm a professional singer?"

"Because I heard you sing. Listen, you might think I'm a

Midwest hick but I know what I hear, and your voice didn't just come out of nowhere. Or are you going to tell me you owe it all to singing in a church choir."

That brought a half smile. "Actually I did sing in a choir when I was young."

"But after that. C'mon, tell me the truth. Why's it such a big deal?"

She held her gaze on the wooden floor wishing it would open up and swallow her.

Martin knew he was stressing her out, but he couldn't stop. He had to know. "Ever since I heard you sing 'Peggy Blue' your voice has haunted me. I'm sure I've heard it before, but I can't remember where."

Cassandra's knee hit the table and her coffee splattered just missing Martin's sleeve. He pulled back. "Wow, that was close!" She started to leave. "Please. Hear me out."

"No Martin, you hear me out. I might be capable of throwing some lyrics together but a vocal performance is something else. And what about your band? Jazz musicians aren't known for wanting to share the stage with a singer."

"You're right about that. The truth is when I told the guys I wanted you to sing a few songs they resisted until I played your recording of 'Peggy Blue' and—"

"What? You recorded my voice! How could you do that?"

"Hey, chill out. It's not like I'm going to release it on YouTube."

"You should have asked first."

"I did. Remember you said 'No.'" Martin's voice softened. "Look. You're right. It was wrong of me to record you like that, and I'm sorry. And I'll be even sorrier if it means you won't consider my offer."

Cassandra let out a deep sigh of resignation and bit her underlip.

"Look. Let's just leave this alone for now. No pressure. Maybe after you've had some time to think about it you'll reconsider."

"Martin," she said. "You're an impossible optimist." They both laughed.

He paid the bill, saying it was the least he could do. She could consider it payment for their recording session. She didn't find that funny and asked him to please destroy the recording.

"Who was that?" said Martin jumping out of the cab in front of Marisa's building. "You weren't expecting anyone were you?"

"At two in the morning? Of course not."

"Well, somebody just came out from the shadow of Marisa's doorway and ran off down the street. I don't see how you could have missed him."

"Well, I did. I was paying the driver," she said, defensively.

"Marisa?" he called out when they got upstairs. No answer. "Marisa!" he shouted. She came out of her bedroom squinting, groggy and rather discombobulated from being awakened. "Martin? Cassandra? What are you two doing up at this hour? Why are all the lights on?"

"Somebody jumped out from the doorway when we came home and took off down the street. I was worried about you."

"Oh, my dear Martin, that's so considerate. But I'm fine. At least I think I am." She looked down at her old flannel nightgown, mumbled to herself, and returned covered in a bathrobe, not aware it was inside out.

"How good it is to see you together—I mean—Oh dear, what do I mean? Let's try this again. It's good that you're both together right now so I can tell you what I've decided." She pulled herself up to her full height of five feet three and said in a righteous tone, "If you go, so do I. And Carl wouldn't throw a helpless widow out in the street"—she stopped to smile—"or would he?"

"What do you mean 'If you go, so do I?'" asked Cassandra, finding it difficult to follow Marisa's line of thinking.

"Exactly what I said. You can stay here until I go."

"Where are you going? And when?"

"I don't know yet but I notified my real estate agent to list the loft. My first open house will be next Sunday. I will have to ask you to keep your side of the house tidy for unexpected viewings by potential buyers. But until it sells, know that my casa is your casa."

"But the Board said we have to be out of here by June first. Are you seriously going to ignore that?"

"For the moment, yes. And he might not have a legitimate case against me, because from now on you are my friends, not my tenants, and there is no law against friends staying in my home." She shuffled in her fuzzy slippers over to the window and opened it wide. "It's hot in here, isn't it?"

Marisa turned back to find them still staring at her. To get the spotlight off herself, she walked over to a Netflix envelope sitting by the monitor screen and surprised herself by saying, "Listen, if you two are home tomorrow night, would you join me for what I'm told is a thrilling thriller. If you do, I'll make popcorn."

"Love to," they both said at once.

"Good. Now run along and let me get some sleep. I'm worn out from all this activity. Up until you arrived, it was so quiet around here."

Before getting back into bed, Marisa dumped her nightgown in the wastebasket. Now that she had tenants to mirror her reflection, as Jules had once done for her, she must go shopping for a fresh wardrobe, beginning with a new nightgown.

Naked she slipped between the sheets. Something she hadn't done since Jules's warm body had been there to heat hers. Seconds later she slipped back out of the icy bed and put on Jules pj's, the ones she hadn't been able to part with.

16

"Why not invite Serge to join you for dinner? With his background in psychology maybe he could help Miles understand. And"—Camille laughed—"it would be a good excuse for you to reach out to Serge again."

Marisa had called Camille to ask her advice on the best way to tell Miles she wouldn't move to Brooklyn when she sold the loft.

"Dear daughter, I have never reached out to Serge and I'm not about to reach out to him now."

"It's just an expression, Mom, you don't have to take it so literally."

"Well, if you're envisioning a romance between me and Serge, forget it. We had a lovely evening together but it just happened by chance. Besides, I haven't heard from him since."

"And have you tried to reach—contact him?"

Marisa hesitated. She'd googled Serge on Internet and he was scheduled to be in New York for a reading this week. She crossed her fingers and said, "Certainly not! Besides, I'm really not interested in dating anyone. My last date before Jules was over thirty-five years ago and I'll never forget his sweaty hands holding mine through *Rosemary's Baby*. I was more repulsed by him than by John Cassavetes manipulating poor Mia Farrow into being raped by the Devil. I'd rather be lonely than have an experience as unpleasant as that was."

"You needn't get huffy about it, Mom. I was only suggesting dinner. I'm sure Serge doesn't have sweaty hands."

Marisa blushed, knowing Camille was right. He had squeezed

her hand briefly under the table at the Yale Club dinner party and it had been firm, dry, and warm.

After they hung up, Marisa felt tempted to follow through on Camille's suggestion. But would it really be *fun* or just embarrassingly awkward. Undecided she went to bed with her iPad and tried to work on her translation of "Swann in Love," but found it impossible with her mind in an uproar. Why shouldn't she, a single woman, invite Serge to dinner? Why feel so damn guilty about it? You cannot betray a man who is not alive. But on the other hand wasn't she betraying his memory. No, that's ridiculous. Hadn't Jules told her that he wanted her to be happy after he was gone, even if it meant being with someone else?

She crossed the loft and stood over his empty chair. "Well, Jules, say something. Tell me what I should do." Silence, an unbearable deep silence.

She clicked onto her e-mail account and entered the address written on Serge's business card and then tapped into the subject line: A DINNER INVITATION TOMORROW—THURSDAY. In her message she didn't tell him Miles would be joining them. He might be uncomfortable at a family dinner. He might assume she wanted him to meet her son, for his approval. For god's sake Marisa, it's just a dinner invitation. Stop reading anything else into it.

She held her breath and hit send. Hearing the sound of the successful *whish,* she jumped onto an imaginary broomstick and zoomed through virtual clouds to Serge's hotel room, where she found him in bed reading his iPad. She tumbled back into her own bed and returned to Proust for literary company.

She labored over his endless descriptions about his unrequited, impassioned love for Odette. Her e-mail binged but she was immediately disappointed when she saw it was Miles confirming their dinner. She was embarrassed at feeling like a lovesick adolescent. Her phone binged again with another e-mail.

Hi Marisa. Thanks for the invite. You must be telepathic. How else could you know I'm in New York? I was going to call you but I just walked into my room an hour ago.

Yes. I would love to join you for dinner. Meet you in the Yale lounge at seven. Serge.

Okay now you've done it, she thought, and snapped her iPad shut. She couldn't sleep, anxious over whether to wear her black pantsuit or the more alluring wine-colored, low-cut silk dress that draped her body nicely. No, then she would be overdressed and it might raise flags with Miles who, standing in for his father, would think it his duty to protect his mother's virtue.

Marisa hoped Serge didn't use the Yale gym. She'd be embarrassed if he saw her in pink spandex shorts. She jumped onto an elliptical machine, inserted her earbuds, and pressed JB's Playlist, bringing up all her favorite R&B tunes that Jules had downloaded when he gave her the iPod.

Little Willie John bellowed out a gut-wrenching "You Give Me Spasms," and she quickly reached an enthused stride, her eyes squeezed shut against the stabbing fluorescent glare. In her mind she slipped into the past and imagined herself twirling around a room to Jules's drumming. Out of breath, she stopped to take a sip of water. Her eyes opened onto a grinning Serge standing in front of the elliptical. She paused the music and took out her earplugs, hoping he wouldn't notice her embarrassment.

"Hi there, Marisa. You're having quite a workout. What were you listening to that makes you take off like that and forget your surroundings? I was just about to give up on you ever coming back down to earth."

Breathlessly she said, "Just a few old R&B favorites."

"R&B? That's surprising. I'd imagined you to be more of a classical girl."

"It all depends on the company I keep. And it would be rather difficult to burn hundreds of calories listening to Debussy's 'Claire de Lune.'"

"I see what you mean. I tried to get your attention earlier when you walked by the squash court where I was playing. It cost me a point."

She sat upright and sucked in her stomach. "Did you win the point back?"

His smile broadened. "Not yet, but watching you has been an inspiration. I'll go back and give it my all in the next game. See you at seven in the lounge."

She felt like she'd just been promised a date at the prom, and took off again striding to the beat of her pounding heart. When he was out of view, she glanced in the wall mirror grateful she'd worn a Yale T-shirt that draped over her shiny pink Spandex pants, hiding any bulges. Not bad, she said to her reflection, and increased her speed to keep up with Hank Ballard's "Finger Poppin' Time." She left the slim young girls loping on their treadmills—in the dust.

Miles and Sheri were already in the lounge when Marisa arrived, breathless and red-faced. Miles jumped up alarmed. "Mom, what have you been doing?" He ushered her into the chair next to his.

"I'm fine," she said. "I hurried to be here on time and took the stairs because the elevators were full. You can let my hand go now. I assure you I have the beating heart of a young woman. In fact, I bet I could outstrip you on the elliptical."

"Probably true," said Sheri in a teasing voice. "I've been trying to get Miles to come with me to the gym, but he always finds excuses. I think he's worried about the competition I'd give him on the treadmill."

Miles ignored them and went to the bar to order drinks.

"There you are," said Serge, smiling down at Marisa. "And you look just as radiant now as you did in pink Spandex."

Amused, Marisa stood up and formally introduced him to Sheri. Miles returned with a tray of drinks. "Miles, this is my friend Serge. He's joining us for dinner tonight. Serge, this is my son."

Miles was obviously stunned and the drink tray began tilting in his hands. Serge grabbed it just in time.

"Mother didn't tell me we were having an *extra* dinner guest."

"Well," said Serge, turning to Marisa, with a question on his face, "I hope it's as pleasant a surprise for you as it is for me, because I didn't know I was going to meet you either."

"I thought we'd make a nice foursome," said Marisa, smiling up at both men.

"Absolutely," said Sheri, patting the seat next to her for Miles to come join her so Serge could sit next to Marisa. But he plopped down next to his mother and Serge sat next to Sheri.

"I guess Marisa didn't tell you that we met here several weeks ago."

"No," said Miles, looking at his mother. "I think she's been keeping you a secret."

Marisa looked at Serge and wondered if it was really the burning logs next to her that made her feel warm all over? She hadn't felt this exuberant since—

Since when Marisa? she heard Jules ask.

Since you were alive, she admitted.

Soon Serge and Sheri were laughing and chatting away like old friends. Sheri realized that Serge had written an article for *Cosmo.* It described warning signs that would help women avoid falling in love with dangerous, overpowering men, a subject *Cosmo* readers apparently found quite interesting—and useful.

Miles remained on his best behavior at dinner, and Marisa pleasantly noted that Serge was not one to brag; he hardly said anything about himself unless asked.

When Sheri went off to the powder room, Marisa turned to Miles. "You'll be happy to know that I've taken your advice and re-listed the loft with an agent. She thinks I have a good chance of selling it quickly because of its downtown location. We're having the first open house this coming Sunday."

"Well, that is good news," said Miles. "Now we can start looking at places for you in Brooklyn."

Okay, here goes, thought Marisa. "Miles, I don't like to disappoint you but I don't want to move to Brooklyn. When I sell the loft I'm leaving New York."

"I'm sorry to hear that," interjected Serge. "May I ask where you're going?"

She smiled. "I don't know yet."

Miles raised his hands in disbelief. "How can you sell your loft if you don't know where you're going? And why leave the City? You've lived here for years."

"Because I'm simply not as happy here as you think I am and haven't been for quite some time. At my age I want to be closer to nature. Shall we say embrace it before it embraces me."

Sheri returned, freshly made-up, and cheerful. "Did I miss something?" she asked, noticing an awkward silence.

"My mother just informed me that she's selling the loft because she wants to leave New York to embrace nature." He turned back to his mother. "What will happen if you get a buyer right away? Where will you go then?"

"There's lots of possibilities," said Marisa, echoing what Jules had said to her earlier. "Maybe I'll return to France. Or maybe move to Los Gatos, California." She turned to Serge. "My daughter, Camille, lives there."

Serge must have understood her silent appeal for help. "Wonderful possibilities," he said, encouragingly. "Los Gatos is a great location. Near San Francisco yet not far from the beach. And France isn't a bad choice either."

"You got that right," said Sheri. "I hope you'll invite me to visit you in either place."

"Me too," said Serge, smiling at Marisa.

"Mom, why not move temporarily to Brooklyn?"

"I'll only get stuck again living somewhere I don't want to live. I want to leave New York and sometimes, my dear, one has to make a giant leap of faith."

"It's those giant leaps that I'm afraid of," said Miles. "What if I'm not there to catch you when you fall?"

"I volunteer," said Serge, raising his hand. Marisa blushed. Sheri giggled in her napkin. Miles frowned. Serge asked for the bill.

17

While Marisa was having dinner at the club, Cassandra was behind the bar at the Bitter End struggling with her own plans. For the past week, she couldn't stop thinking about Martin's offer to perform with his band at the Blue Note. The thought of singing again in front of an audience thrilled her, but it also terrified her. In a dream last night, she was performing onstage but couldn't get one note to come out of her mouth. The audience's admiration turned to ridicule. They roared with laughter. She woke up in a cold sweat with her mouth open, screaming but voiceless.

Then she re-remembered her last year with The Belles; the pressure to deliver night after night to audience expectations, the grueling days on the road with brief moments on stage, where the thrill of performing rewarded her, but always afraid her voice would betray her after so much abuse. And no one to talk to except Ryan, who pumped her up with drugs and alcohol when she got so stressed she was afraid to go onstage.

She shuddered at the thought of him. Luckily he had to go back to L.A. on urgent business and had cancelled their weekend upstate. Instead, she spent it with Margaret. He'd left messages on the new phone he'd given her at the hotel, but she hadn't replied except once, when she told him she wasn't coming back to L.A.

"Hey, where are our drinks?" called out a customer.

When things slowed down again, her thoughts returned to Martin. She'd have to tell him the truth. But what if he changed his mind when he found out he'd be sharing the stage with a former diva?

On her break, she pulled out Ryan's phone and texted Martin that she would come to his last set at 55 Bar. She had something important to tell him.

Moments later he texted back: OK!!!

When she looked up, her smile disappeared. Here he was again, that arrogant, tall, bulky son-of-a-bitch, ordering a shot of tequila, and it looked like he had already had a few somewhere else. And her shift wasn't over for another hour.

"What do you want, Ryan?"

"You, baby. Are you flipping on me again?"

He reached over the bar and grabbed her arm. "CiCi you know how angry I get when you flip on me. You've been doing that a lot lately and I don't like it. Now get me a drink."

She slapped a full shot glass down on the counter and glared at him.

"Chill, girl. If we're going to call this thing off, at least have one last drink with me. You know, one for the road." He puckered his Mick Jagger lips and threw her a kiss.

"No, Ryan. It's over. Drink up and get the hell out of here."

"No! Goddammit. It's not over!" he shouted back.

The bar crowd looked over at them and Ryan's sneer melted into a charming smile. He threw back the shot of tequila and called out to Max for another. Max set down the glass and glanced at Cassandra. "It's okay," she said.

"Thanks for the drinks, man." Ryan reached up and stuffed a fifty-dollar bill in Max's shirt pocket. "Keep the change."

He turned to Cassandra. "I want to see your digs. See how you live."

She shook her head violently. "That's not possible. House rules. No guests after midnight."

He grabbed her arm and pulled her nearer, "You're messin' with me, CiCi. I don't like it when you do that. You know better than to lie to me."

"You're hurting me."

"You should show some gratitude to your former partner, girl.

Have you forgotten the hole you were in before I saved you? And now you're blowing it again. The minute you're out of my sight you dig yourself into another hole and I have to come rescue you. When will you get it, CiCi? You need me." He clicked his tongue and shook his head. "Or have you forgotten what I've done for you?"

"No, Ryan, I haven't forgotten."

She knew the signs when he was on the edge of a tantrum; his eyes ablaze, his bottom lip reddened by his gnawing teeth. He pressed his arched body toward her. She cringed. He wanted to hit her but he wouldn't. He never exposed his lunacy in public.

"Now I'm gonna tell you what you're going to do. You're going to tell your buddy Max that you're not feeling so good and you need to go home. Then we are going to flag down a taxi and get in it. And if you don't want me to get any angrier than I am right now, don't call out for help from any of these punks. They're no match for me and you know it."

In front of Marisa's building, Cassandra searched through her purse. "I can't find my keys."

"Buzz your nice old landlady, she'll let you in."

"I told you. Nobody's home. Let's go to your hotel."

"Good try, sweetheart, but I see a light up on your floor. Number two, right? That's where I sent the flowers." He pressed down on the #2 button.

"How did you find out where I lived?"

"Did you think I would let my biggest, future investment get away? I know where you've been these last three months right down to those funny art classes you're taking. This is a nicer address than that dump in the East Village."

Marisa's sleepy voice: "Who is it?"

"It's Cassandra. Could you let me in? I forgot my keys."

"No problem," said Marisa. She pressed the door button, and went back to bed.

Cassandra gestured to Ryan to do as she did and take off his shoes but he didn't. He followed her down the hall to the back bedrooms.

"Wait here. I want to see if my roommate's home."

"You mean, Martin?" So he knew about Martin too. "Just point me to the bathroom, baby. You wouldn't want me to wander into the wrong room." He laughed.

She cracked open Martin's door and was relieved he wasn't there. He was probably waiting for her at the club or he'd gone looking for her when she didn't show up.

She went in her bedroom and turned on the light. Ryan had found Martin's terry cloth robe and walked in to her room wearing it, untied.

"Don't look at me like that, baby. It's not like you've never seen me naked before." He stretched up his arms and opened his mouth in a wide yawn. "Man, am I tired."

In the dark, she listened to him settling into her bed. "Hey CiCi, I'm cold. Come keep me warm, baby."

He rolled over on top of her pinning her arms above her head. "You feel real good."

The back staircase door slammed shut. Ryan pressed his hand over her mouth, when Martin tapped on the door. "Cassandra, are you all right? Cassandra?" The doorknob rattled but Ryan had locked it.

Martin's footsteps faded. His bedroom door closed.

She lay there like a rag doll staring up at the ceiling while Ryan slowly pulled off her jeans and panties. When he spread her legs and entered her, she bit down on her lip and screamed. It was a scream only she could hear, like her dream earlier.

When the bed started banging against the thin wall, she heard Martin's radio blasting. The harder the bed shook and the louder Ryan moaned, the louder the music screamed back. The radio went silent after Ryan rolled off her. Moments later he was snoring. She slipped out of the bed and picked up her clothes off the floor.

When she came out of the bathroom, Martin's body was framed in his doorway, a silhouette lit behind by his bed light. She waited to see what he would do.

"Have you seen my bathrobe?" he asked, walking toward her.

"Baby, come back to bed," shouted Ryan.

Martin and Cassandra locked eyes briefly and then both walked to their separate rooms. After Ryan fell asleep again, she curled up on the floor in Martin's bathrobe and muffled her cries with her hands.

Cassandra woke up to Ryan whistling in the shower and the back door slamming shut.

After he dressed, he told her he was leaving that night for Tokyo with the Valentinos. He'd be away for two months. When he came back, they'd go together to L.A. She said nothing. "See you soon, baby." He kissed her forehead and left.

Cassandra pulled the sheets off the bed and washed them with Martin's bathrobe in the washing machine. When they were dry, she hung the bathrobe back on the bathroom door as if nothing had happened. But it had.

She didn't know where she would go but she couldn't face Martin. He was better off without her. And so was Marisa.

She was bringing down her suitcase when Martin knocked on her door and said, "Cassandra, can I talk to you?"

"Not now, Martin," she said, holding back her tears.

He opened the door and saw the suitcase. "Where are you going?"

"A friend in Brooklyn offered to share her apartment and since we won't be able to stay here much longer it seemed like a good idea to take her up on it."

"Her apartment? Don't you mean *his* apartment?"

Cassandra shrugged, strapped her backpack over her shoulders and tried to get past him but he blocked her.

"Look you're right, it's none of my business. As you've told me enough times, there's nothing happening between us. I was just pissed off at you saying you'd meet me at the club, then not showing up, and finding you here with that dude. If you're moving in with him then why not just tell me the truth?"

She put down her backpack and faced him. "It's not that I wanted to—"

"Oh, c'mon Cassandra, I heard what was going on in here last night. And for Christ's sake, if you didn't like it, you could have screamed out for help. I almost busted in here anyway just to stop him from grunting like a pig."

Cassandra walked over to the window and stared out. He came up behind her putting his hands gently on her shoulders. "I keep saying the wrong thing, don't I?"

"It's what I deserve."

"No it isn't. You just need to figure out what you really want."

She stiffened. "I'm so tired of people telling me what I need to do. Just leave me alone, please."

"Okay, but don't move out because of me."

She shouldered her backpack and, after she left, Martin put the suitcase back up on the closet shelf.

After a week of Cassandra's cold silence, Martin had given up on salvaging any kind of relationship with her. He wasn't even sure that he wanted to. Then one night just after he had turned off his bedroom light and gotten into bed, she slipped into his room and sat cross-legged on the floor, barely lit from the lights in the building across the way.

"Martin," she whispered, "I want to tell you something."

He sat on the edge of the bed and said, "You mean about The Belles?"

"So you know."

"Only that you once sang with them. Is there more to know?"

"Yes, there is." She leaned her back against the wall and stretched out her legs. "The three of us met in high school. Ryan heard us at a local singing contest and told us if we let him be our manager, he'd make us famous. We signed on. And he kept his promise. He got us a recording contract and put us out on the road. Our names were his idea. I thought he'd get with MiMi, all the guys went for her, but he chose me instead. Back then, I thought I was lucky. The group had a hit. Then another one. He gave me anything I wanted—a car, clothes. We traveled first class all the way. It was a fairy tale that I never wanted to end. I was really happy for the first time in my life."

Martin sat back on the bed and waited for her to continue. In the dim light, he saw her close her eyes.

"The more popular we became, the more Ryan took control. I started to see another side of him and it wasn't nice. We weren't allowed to choose our own songs or even our own musicians. Our performances turned into Broadway productions with sets, designer wardrobes, pyrotechnics, and bigger and bigger bands. We were always on the road. You'd think we'd be rich by then, but all the money was fed back into the expensive tour productions and we were only given small per diems. Our record company advanced us the money for recording, advertising, and tour expenses and then deducted it from our record royalties. Ryan would tell us that with the next album we'd start making some real money. Meanwhile, he kept us out on the road doing long one-nighter tours. That's when I started drinking.

"He hired a big time hit-making producer who had written songs for us for the new album, and when I told him I wanted to choose my own songs, he threw a tantrum. He told me I was ungrateful, even threatened to have me replaced. I moved out of his house in Malibu and got my own apartment.

"I was exhausted. We were recording our next record and we were rehearsing for a world tour at the same time. Rehearsals, dance classes, vocal lessons. We never had any time off. The producer had written what everyone thought would be our highest charting single yet, and I was the featured vocalist.

"One night at a recording session, I was in the vocal booth and saw Ryan through the glass window laughing with the engineer and the producer, coking up, while I stood singing into the mic until my voice was raw. And he didn't care. He kept telling me to do another take. Take One. Take Ten. Take Twenty. Finally, I pushed the mic over onto the floor and walked out.

"It was raining hard. Ryan came after me. I told him I couldn't keep it up any longer. I wanted to quit. He told me I just needed a break. He told me not to worry, he'd arrange everything."

Cassandra stopped to take a deep breath. Martin wanted to go to her but he held back. "And what did he arrange?" he asked softly.

"He took me to a rehab center. He told my fans that I'd been to see a voice specialist who said I needed to rest my voice or I might injure it permanently. The Belles and our wardrobe mistress, Margaret, were the only ones who knew where I really was.

"When I came out two months later, band rehearsals started up again and so did all the bad feelings. I just couldn't take the pressure anymore. I told Ryan I wanted out. This time he gave in. Told me if that's what I wanted he'd manage my solo career.

"The Belles left on tour with my replacement and Ryan brought me out to his house in Malibu. He started me on a rigorous schedule of rehearsals and vocal rehab training. We were in the recording studio working all the time. The pressure was worse than when I was with The Belles. When I told him my voice was strained and I needed a break, he stopped being kind. By then I was drinking pretty heavily and he threatened to send me back to rehab if I didn't get my act together."

Silence. "And did he?" he asked.

"No. One night when he was out, I packed my bags. A couple of kids picked me up on the highway and drove me to my friend Margaret's. I hid out there for a few days and then flew to New York."

When Martin saw her open her eyes, he slipped off the bed and sat next to her.

"How long have you known I was CiCi?" she asked.

"My piano player thought it was you when I played the tape ... I should have figured it out when I first heard you sing 'Peggy Blue.'"

"I was coming to tell you that I wanted to sing with your band when Ryan showed up again. There's no way I can do that now."

"Yes you can, but we need to talk to Marisa first."

"Marisa? Why Marisa?"

"Because she's had lots of experience in the music business. She was a manager for many years and she really knows what this stuff is all about. If you really want to sing with my band, we could make the Blue Note gig your comeback and she could help us set it up."

She turned to Martin. "Are you sure you want to do this?"

In the dark, he squeezed her hand. "Yes, I am. It's all going to work out the way we want it to."

"Okay, I'll talk to Marisa, but I don't want her to know about Ryan."

"If we're asking her to help us, you'll have to tell her." Still holding her hand, he lay down on his back and stared up at the ceiling. "Where's Ryan now?"

"On his way to Tokyo, touring with one of his band's. He'll be gone two months." She hesitated. "He plans to pick me up on his way back to Los Angeles."

"Do you want to go?"

"No."

"Well, this isn't Pakistan, you know. Women have rights."

"Not with Ryan."

"You've got to stand up to him, Cassandra. You can do it and I'll be there to help you."

He pulled her down next to him and she fell asleep secure in his arms.

18

Marisa hadn't seen Cassandra since the night she buzzed her in and heard a stranger's footsteps in the back hall. Martin had stayed away too, slipping out quietly or using the stairs.

Then after a week of worry, while she was preparing her morning coffee, Martin walked into the kitchen with Cassandra right behind him. "Marisa, we have something we want to talk to you about."

"Sure. As long as you don't mind seeing me in my new bathrobe."

"Nice. I like you in red."

"Why thank you, Martin." Marisa was so flattered she plunged down the coffee press so quickly it almost gushed over.

Martin took a sip. "Just what I needed. Thanks."

"Now let me make some toast and then you can tell me what this is all about."

Cassandra perched on the bar stool. Martin sat at the table and Marisa got out apricot jam and started cutting the bread.

"I'm not who you think I am," burst out Cassandra.

"Oh?" said Marisa, stopping the bread knife in mid-air and turning to Cassandra.

"And I'm not really an art student, I'm a singer. I'm CiCi Belle." She looked at Marisa as if she expected her to know who CiCi Belle was.

But she didn't. At least, not at first. "CiCi Belle?" She rubbed her forehead. "Yes, that's it. Awhile back I saw an ad in the paper announcing The Belles performing at Radio City Music Hall. It looked like quite a big production. Are you one of those Belles?"

"I was, but not anymore."

"Well then, CiCi Belle, how on earth did you end up in my kitchen?"

Cassandra sighed and sat down across from Martin and Marisa. "Nearly a year ago I had a bit of a breakdown and I had to recuperate for several months. Later, when the rehearsals started up again, I became severely depressed."

Cassandra didn't explain why she'd become depressed and Marisa didn't think she had the right to ask. She poured her another cup of coffee and Cassandra smiled gratefully.

She told Marisa the same story she'd told Martin, but left out Ryan's name and didn't mention that they were once lovers or that he planned to pick her up on his way back to Los Angeles. She avoided looking at Martin when he got up and stood at the window looking out.

After she finished, Cassandra stretched her arms out and let out a big sigh. "I came to New York, chopped off my hair, dyed it orange, and bought a large pair of very large sunglasses. It helped that I'd lost a lot of weight.

"But why?"

"I wanted to be anonymous until I had time to figure things out."

"I see," said Marisa putting a piece of toast on Cassandra's plate. "And have you figured things out?"

"I know I want to sing again, but I don't know how to start." Her plaintive eyes touched Marisa, deeply, and she stopped spreading jam to listen. "I abandoned my fans when I left The Belles. That's another thing I didn't do right. What will they think when they find out I'm bartending at the Bitter End?"

"They'll love it," said Marisa. "You're being way too hard on yourself. You're certainly not the first singer to fall on hard times and many have overcome worse circumstances than yours. I'm sure your fans will support you when you tell them the truth."

Cassandra shook her head in disbelief.

Marisa considered another way to convince her. "What about your manager? What does he think you should do?"

"He's no longer my manager," snapped Cassandra, tossing back her head. A gesture Marisa had often noted and now realized that it must be an old habit from when Cassandra had a full head of luscious hair to toss. When Cassandra looked at her again, her eyes were soft, "I'm sorry that I've been using your home as a refuge."

"I don't mind. I find it all rather exciting." Marisa turned toward the window where Martin was still standing with his back to them. "Don't you think so, Martin?" He returned to the table and shrugged before reaching for another piece of toast.

"If you're asking my advice," said Marisa, and I'm not sure you are, then I encourage you to tell your fans and former partners that you're all right. And if you want to sing again then do it."

"Exactly," said Martin. "That's why I've offered her a gig at the Blue Note when I play there next month with my band."

"You're playing the Blue Note! That's wonderful news." Marisa poured herself another cup of coffee. "But I'm still not sure how I fit in to all this. Why did you come to see me this morning?"

"Isn't that obvious? You're a music pro. You managed Jules and his bands and you've worked with singers. You would know how to promote my Blue Note gig and CiCi's comeback."

"Kids, I've been out of the music business for years. I think you need to find someone a bit more hip, someone who knows what's happening today."

"That doesn't matter," Martin argued. "We need someone we can trust and that's you, Marisa, please say yes."

She was touched by his offer and sat with it for a moment before answering. "Let me see if I have this right. You want me to plan out a press campaign for Cassandra's comeback performance. One that the media will pickup on as positive, exciting news. A campaign that will obscure your—shall we say—past mistakes and celebrate your return to the stage. Have I got that right?"

Martin and Cassandra nodded in agreement. And whatever

was bothering Martin earlier when he left the table he seemed to have gotten over, thought Marisa.

"Well, how about—*Singer conquers depression and returns to the stage.* Your fans will love that."

Neither looked impressed and even Jules said, *Marisa, I know you can come up with something better than that.*

"Okay, we'll get back to that. But isn't there a more serious problem here? The Belles are pop singers, right? Martin's music is rooted in jazz … shall we say, outside the commercial pocket. A female jazz vocalist is a far stretch from harmonizing with a pop group."

Cassandra uncrossed her arms and legs and leaned toward Marisa. "But that's the point. That was why I wanted to leave The Belles. I wanted to go solo as a jazz singer. And if I have enough time to rehearse with Martin's band maybe I can pull it off."

Marisa frowned. "My dear girl, what do you mean, *maybe* pull it off? You'll have to do better than that. This gig is far more important in launching Martin's career than your wanting to sing jazz. He'll need to know you can do your part." She hadn't meant to sound so harsh but she felt a natural impulse to protect Martin even though she wasn't sure what she was protecting him from.

Cassandra was offended by Marisa's sharp and unexpected criticism and an awkward silence followed until Martin said, "I'm sure she can pull it off."

Marisa smiled at both of them. "Okay, then so can I."

"You mean you'll do it?" said Martin.

"How much time do we have? When's the Blue Note gig?"

"Friday, April 26."

Marisa walked over to the wall calendar to avoid expressing her shock. That date was the anniversary of Jules's death and even more awful, he was performing at the Blue Note the night he died. Marisa managed to shove this coincidence into the back of her mind and pull herself back into the present before she returned to the table and said, "That doesn't give us much time, does it?"

Martin shrugged. Cassandra looked unsteady.

"Right away we must shoot out a press release with a photo and bios of Martin and his band members. That will be a lead-in to inviting music journalists to come hear the Martin Starks Trio. We can invite the jazz labels too. But we'll hold off until a day before the gig to announce your special guest—CiCi Belle." Marisa was thinking fast. She didn't want CiCi's comeback in anyway to take away from Martin's performance. And this way there would be no time to schedule any interviews before the event when journalists might ask embarrassing questions that Cassandra would rather not answer.

"And Cassandra, let's see ... how about you are returning from a *self-imposed exile*. Yes, that's good. Simply confess it all. But wait until a day before the gig to post it on Facebook. Then tell them you were very depressed because you were not fulfilled as a pop singer. You went into retreat to find a new musical direction, a more challenging, unique vocal style. And you found it in Manhattan, working with Martin Starks, a very creative musical director."

She smiled over at Martin and returned her focus on Cassandra. "Maybe tone down the bright orange shag a bit." Cassandra looked ready to object. "Okay. You decide on the image you want to project, but you'll need a new photo when you post online. Once the word is out, I'm sure your New York fans will come to hear you at the Blue Note."

"Wow, Marisa," said Martin. "You sure know how to fire things up."

Cassandra paced up and down the room several times before she sat back down and said, "Look, this is an important gig for Martin and I don't want to spoil his night." She cast her eyes down onto her folded hands and her bottom lip quivered. "There's a good reason I got into self-medicating with booze. I'm embarrassed to admit this but it got to the point where I couldn't get on stage unless I had a few too many drinks. I'm not sure I can be trusted to get through this sober."

Marisa came around the table and massaged Cassandra's tight shoulders. "I've never known a singer who hasn't been paralyzed by doubt at some point in their career. And I've known several who needed something before going on stage to fend off the demons. It's the manager's job to keep those demons under control. Perhaps your manager didn't use the right technique." Marisa felt Cassandra's muscles cramp and she massaged deeper into the knots.

Martin got up from the table and said he'd be right back.

Marisa was certain now that something was being held back from her. She had the frame of the puzzle but there were lots of missing pieces, and she was sure it had something to do with that flower delivery on Valentine's Day and that bizarre invitation from "R." She'd never mentioned it to Cassandra but she had looked out the window and seen her get in the limousine before it drove away. And then more recently, those footsteps following Cassandra to her room.

Marisa's kneading was working magic. Cassandra's shoulders had come down several inches. In a hushed voice she told the older woman that her manager had actually done a good job keeping her demons under control and was always there to calm her when she panicked. She didn't know if she could perform without him, which was something Martin would never understand.

"Then why not talk to your manager? Tell him what you want to do and see if he wants to help."

Cassandra shook her head violently and Marisa removed her hands. She sat down in front of the girl and said what she could to encourage her to take a chance.

As Martin came back into the room he heard Marisa saying, "You'll never forgive yourself if you don't take Martin up on his offer."

Cassandra walked over to him. "What do you think? It's your band. Are you sure you want me to sing at your gig?"

"Hey, I'd be lying if I said I'm not a little uptight about turning my gig at the Blue Note into some kind of a media event but, what the hell, I'm willing to go for it." He shrugged. "After all, it's just a gig."

Later, Martin asked Cassandra if, when he left the room, she'd told Marisa about Ryan. She said telling Marisa that she had a drinking problem was hard enough. And why mention Ryan when he wouldn't be back for two months? Martin told her that it was a matter of trust. Cassandra promised to tell Marisa after the Blue Note performance.

19

Marisa had dropped out of the music business many years ago. She was at the top of her game when she suddenly realized that her success was based on her artists' success. Her identity was tied up in their identity. She was only as good as the last performer she put on stage. By then she'd toured the world with many successful and not so successful artists and had begun to realize that they were having more fun than she was. They had something to call their own, something they'd created. She was just the enabler. She was helping others, but she wasn't helping herself, and she was bored. After her epiphany she decided to become a writer and join in on the fun.

But she'd forgotten how much fun it could be to produce an event until she sat down to work on Martin and Cassandra's press releases. It had been years since she'd done anything like it, but like riding a bicycle, once you've learned it, you don't forget it.

She started by looking up CiCi Belle on Google and was astonished to find many pages of information plus photos showing CiCi at various stages of her career, both the good parts and the not-so-good parts.

She befriended CiCi and on her Facebook newsfeed found a river of theories on why she had disappeared and where she was now. All these speculations would end when her performance at the Blue Note was announced.

Marisa saw a reference to her manager, Ryan Peters. Was this the "R" who sent the flowers and picked her up in a limousine? Then she remembered Cassandra telling her that she couldn't imagine performing onstage without her manager. How very interesting.

At this point, she felt overwhelmed trying to understand the inner workings of Facebook and shut it off. She was relieved that Martin's drummer, Stuart, was handling the band's social media for the gig. She was clueless as to how Facebook worked, but seeing that CiCi had accumulated 3,200 friends, she could understand that it had a lot of potential and had made it part of their marketing campaign.

As planned, twenty-four hours before the gig, Stuart would announce on his Facebook account that CiCi was going to be a guest with the trio at the Blue Note and there'd be a picture of her with the band. At the same time, CiCi would write to her fans about her self-imposed exile and her surprise coming-out gig the following night at the Blue Note. Everyone hoped the news would go viral.

When Marisa started in the business, "viral" was the cause of colds. Back then she'd spent painstaking days designing "flyers" to promote gigs and then taking them to the printer. Then came Photoshop and all that went out the window. Now one could put out a press release in seconds as long as you had the content prepared. No more stuffing envelopes or trips to the post office. Marisa had fond memories of the days when she first met Jules, and he invited her to come out after midnight and help him paste flyers on telephone poles illegally to promote his band. She shook her head at how crazy that had been and how much fun.

She could hear Jules laughing and looked over at his empty chair.

Fun? Why you hated pasting up those fliers. You certainly complained about it enough. Remember how scared you were the night we got chased down the block by a cop?

She smiled in response. Yes, that's true, but when we ran out of flyers, we would share a tuna melt and a beer at our local bar. That was the fun part.

She checked her e-mail shortly after she sent out Martin's

press release and was pleased to see that some journalists were already requesting to be put on Blue Note's guest list.

Good job, whispered Jules.

The cuckoo, the only living witness to her morning's work, jumped out and cuc-koo'd twelve times. Good heavens! Where had the morning gone? Cassandra was going to meet her at the front entrance of the NYU Hospital in thirty minutes. She ran a brush through her hair and threw on a coat while waiting for the elevator to open on her floor.

It opened, but she hadn't expected Carl in it. "You look like you're in a hurry, Marisa. Hope nothing serious."

"A doctor's appointment."

"Are you ill?

"No Carl, I'm not ill." The elevator, indifferent to Marisa's discomfort, took its sweet time descending to the lobby.

Carl had her caged for a few seconds and took advantage of it. "There was a stranger in our lobby yesterday. I asked her what she was doing in our building and she said she was your real estate agent. Are you trying to sell your loft again?"

She glared at him. "You've left me no choice, Carl. As I told you at the meeting I can't afford to live in this building without my tenants."

He blew out air and rolled his eyes and she glanced down at his gold Rolex watch, twice the size of his thin knobby wrist.

"Speaking of your tenants, do they know they have to vacate by the first of June?"

The elevator door opened onto the lobby and she pushed by him out of the door and into the street.

There had been an unusual early April snowfall the night before. Maybe it wasn't so unusual considering the abundance of storms the city had weathered since Hurricane Sandy last November. Marisa rushed ahead blindly through City Hall Park. Her mind was racing through things to do before the Blue Note gig when she heard "Quel beau jour!"

For Marisa, hearing the French language was like hearing a songbird in winter and she stopped to listen. An irate buxom woman crashed into her from behind and shouted, "Look out where you're going!"

She sidestepped through the crowd onto the slushy grass. Triggered by the French phrase, her eyes took in the park's natural surroundings. She admired the sparkling white shawls that the storm had left draped over the black iron benches, now melting under the sun's rays. Caught up in the moment, she snapped photos of the benches with her iPhone and then the statue of Horace Greeley draped in a magnificent white ermine cape that covered his thick metal shoulders and the countless stains from disrespectful pigeons.

You were never kind to pigeons. Flying rodents you called them. You chased them away in the park. But how could they know that Greeley was the first to publish the works of Charles Dickens, Margaret Fuller, Henry James, and Edgar Allan Poe.

She still had Jules's number in her phone, and she sent him a photo of Greeley, typing Miss you!!! before shooting it out into the cosmo.

She jumped back into the flow of pedestrian traffic and rushed down steps to the subway just in time to squeeze inside the #4 express before the door shut. She held onto the metal bar above, trying not to touch anyone, which was impossible. Accustomed to no one getting up for her, even when she was pregnant, she took pleasure in giving the evil eye to young people slouched on the benches; their earbuds leaking out thumping, distorted music that pierced her ears over the sound of the rattling subway cars. She wondered how their eardrums could bear such an assault. She glanced at the obese who took up entire benches as if it were their entitlement for carrying so much weight. She'd stopped giving them the evil eye; the looks they gave back were too scary.

She took the standard urban pose, head bent, staring down at the floor like most everyone else, as humanity crushed her from all sides and the train raged through the tunnels and screeched to a halt at 23rd Street.

When she didn't see Cassandra at the hospital entrance, Marisa hugged her coat against the frigid wind and checked her phone for messages. After five minutes shivering at the entrance, she gave up and found her own way through the labyrinth of hallways and elevators to the Center for BrainHealth. In the waiting room, she signed in, sat down, and checked her phone again. No messages.

An hour passed and no one called her name. She went up to the receptionist and asked if they'd forgotten her. "No, Mrs. Bridges, we were waiting for a family member to join you." She held back her anger and kindly asked to see Enrico. She explained to him that it was her niece who was late and asked him to not postpone the consultation a moment longer. He appreciated the time she'd given to Alzheimer's research, so he decided to bend the rules and ushered her in. It was the same windowless room where she'd taken tests that scored her mental acuity.

"We're here to take a look at your PET scans," he said in a practiced casual manner. He explained to her that the first image showed how her brain used sugar; the second image showed any amyloid plaques growing on her brain, and the last showed any inflammation. Remarkable results would indicate the early onset of Alzheimer's disease. She studied his face but he gave nothing away while he looked over the tests.

Marisa hadn't minded the scans. Lying back on the gurney and being rolled into the donut was like embarking on a jet plane. The humming of the revolving magnet soothed her. She took advantage of those quiet, peaceful moments to breathe deeply and float among the clouds. She felt close to her mother as if she were lying next to her in the tube, whispering in her ear that everything was going to be all right. She wished her mother were there now.

"I don't want you to worry, Mrs. Bridges, but I see something here that needs consideration. I'm afraid we need to retake the second PET scan. The image is showing scattered lucencies that might indicate plaque growth." He looked up from his notes and smiled. "It's probably just a technical error but we don't want to take any chances. Would you mind coming back and retaking your PET scan?"

Yes, she minded. She minded terribly. "Okay," she said, hiding her irritation. Enrico helped her on with her coat. "Now don't worry, Mrs. Bridges. I'm sure it's nothing."

When the elevator opened into the loft, Cassandra was seated on a kitchen bar stool eating sushi from the local Japanese takeout around the corner. The moment she looked up, Marisa could tell from her expression that she'd just remembered their appointment. "Oh my god, Marisa, I'm so sorry. I had a band rehearsal with Martin and then I stopped to get something to eat and completely forgot. Did it go all right?"

"Yes, everything went fine," said Marisa, stiffly. She opened the coat closet and felt her heart crack when she accidentally touched Jules's tweed cap on the shelf above. Somehow she just couldn't part with that cap.

"Would you like to share my California roll?" called out Cassandra from across the room.

"I'm not hungry."

"How did the tests come out?"

"Fine, just fine." Marisa closed the bedroom door a little too firmly behind her.

She fell asleep picturing her brain swelling up into a large balloon and carrying her tired body out the window to whereJules and her mother were sitting on a cloud, waiting for her.

20

Marisa stepped out of the taxi and saw a crowd of young people waiting for the doors of the Blue Note to open. She had to press through the crowd to get to the front door. Surprisingly, the doorman remembered her from years ago and let her in.

Martin, bass player Carlos, and drummer Stuart had settled into one of the two dressing rooms upstairs. Cassandra had been given the larger room with a printed sign hanging on the door that said CICI BELLE. The sign on the other dressing room door said BAND. Marisa felt a flush of fairness rush up her spine. The band was equally important, if not more, and it was her job to make that clear.

CiCi's door was locked. Marisa knocked. "Who is it?" said Cassandra's irritated voice from within.

"It's Marisa." Cassandra cracked open the door wearing a blue silk kimono and pulled Marisa inside by the elbow. She apologized for locking her out, but people kept knocking, and she didn't like to see anyone before a performance. She sat back down at the dressing table in front of an array of makeup spread out like a painter's palette and continued powdering her heavy eyelids in silver blue dust, which was the color of the sequined gown hanging in the open closet.

Marisa thought back to the many times she'd been in this room with other musicians. Cassandra looked up from the mirror with a childlike expression, "I'm so glad you're here. I don't know what I'd do without you."

Marisa smiled back and made room for herself next to

Cassandra's day clothes tossed on the couch. "Is there anything I can do?"

"Actually there is." She smiled and swung a tea bag in front of Marisa. "My parched throat could use a cup of tea." She dropped the tea bag in an empty mug. "I asked a waitress but that was thirty minutes ago and she never came back. Would it be asking too much if you could get some hot water?"

"Not at all. Would you like some honey?"

"No, you needn't bother with that." She looked at Marisa in the mirror's reflection. "But that would be nice," she added as she sucked in her cheeks and rouged her chiseled arches.

"I'll be right back," said Marisa, glad to have something better to do than watch Cassandra paint her self-portrait. She stopped by the manager's office before going downstairs.

At the bar, she recognized Don, the bartender from days past, and asked him if the kitchen could boil her some hot water. Then she went out and bought a plastic Pooh-bear-jar of honey at the corner deli.

Coming back upstairs, she saw the club manager had responded to her request. An 8x10 sign on the band's door read MARTIN STARKS TRIO. A small thing but it made her feel good.

She stood outside Cassandra's dressing room door and listened to her vocal exercises. She admired her impressive low register. She knocked, slipped inside quietly, and was surprised to see that a breathtaking bouquet of flowers had been delivered while she was out. The bright yellow, orange, and purple Gerber blooms with the "Heaven's Door" sticker brought to mind a similar delivery for Cassandra on Valentine's Day.

"How lovely," she exclaimed. "Who are they from?"

"Just a fan," mumbled Cassandra as she penciled in her lips.

Martin burst in before Marisa could extract any more information. "We go on in ten minutes. We'll do three numbers and then I'll call you up on stage. Be ready, okay?"

Cassandra turned to him, "Martin, I've done this before you know and I've never missed my cue."

"Sorry, I guess I'm just a little nervous. There are no empty tables in the house and people are crowded up against the bar."

Unruffled, Cassandra returned to filling in her lips. Martin put his hands on her shoulders and looked at her reflection. "Wow." He leaned down to kiss her but seeing the thick makeup and the sticky gel on her spiked hair he decided against it. "See you on stage, Diva. And don't break a leg, please." He turned to Marisa. "You'll walk her down, okay. She could easily slip on the staircase in those spiked heels."

"Not to worry. I'll be right there."

Cassandra took the silver-blue satin gown off the hanger. A bit of overkill for the Blue Note, thought Marisa, but she hadn't been asked. And she had to admit that Cassandra's orange-spiked head and the viper winding down her long, bare arm were in striking contrast to the elegant gown. A journalist's photo opportunity that would show up online immediately.

Marisa stood on the staircase that overlooked the stage. She assessed the audience listening to Martin's opening number; he was facing a tough New York audience. They considered the Martin Starks Trio as merely a warm-up band for CiCi, who now appeared by Marisa's side. She was poised and alert, a professional, confident performer.

The third funky jazz number received a more rousing response and Martin approached the mic stand. "Thank you. Thank you very much. Now we are going to ask our guest vocalist to come up on stage. She really needs no introduction." He smiled. "I'm sure you all know her. Let's give it up for the one and only the amazing CiCi Belle."

The audience leaped up, clapped and shouted excitedly and made space for CiCi to walk between the crowded tables to the stage. She smiled at Martin, took the mic he offered, and then waited for the audience to settle back down in their seats.

"Thank you. You're very kind. Thank you." She pressed her hand against her heart. "And let's give another hand for these wonderful musicians up here on stage with me." Another applause.

"For those who know me"—another burst of applause and shouts of "We love you, CiCi." She took it all in and clapped her hands together in silent thanks, humbly bowing. "I'm so excited to be here with you tonight and to receive such a generous welcome. After my breakup with The Belles, I didn't know if I'd ever have the courage to perform on my own and now here I am." She opened her arms wide, her gown, and eyes shimmering. More applause.

A fan shouted out "In the Dark," a well-known tune she'd sung with The Belles. "Not tonight," she shouted back. "Tonight I want you to hear some different material. I chose these songs to give homage to those singers whose courage inspired me to return to the stage, singers who gave us all they had to give and performed graciously in spite of their personal losses."

She turned to Stuart who counted off the first tune. After a few bars, she started singing Amy Winehouse's "You Know I'm No Good." The new CiCi strutted across the stage and left no doubt that her powerful voice had healed. She commanded the stage on her own and delivered the same sensuous and lush phrasing known by her fans that thought they'd lost her.

Next she slowed things down with Nina Simone's "Where Does the Time Go." Several teary faces looked up at her from their seats and they weren't all women.

While she was singing Whitney Houston's "Didn't We Almost Have It All," Marisa began drifting away to Jules's burial site on a sloping hill in upstate New York. She had visited the site this afternoon on the anniversary of his death. The morning sun had heated a bed of soft, new spring grass, and she'd laid down on his grave and slept.

Marisa opened her eyes onto the stage and thought she saw Jules at the drum set where he had sat that last night. Feeling faint she gripped the balcony staircase railing. Jules whispered in her ear, *Here I am, my dear, don't cry*. She didn't dare turn around, so she shut her eyes again and leaned back into the shadows of his arms.

CiCi received a standing ovation after her last song, and after many sweeping bows, she moved to the sidelines. At first the audience kept looking over at her, even calling her back, but she kept her attention fixed on the trio, her hips swaying to their music.

Martin finished the set with a riveting guitar solo and showed that he too had a voice as resonating and as soulful as CiCi's except he expressed it through skilled, sensitive fingers.

The audience demanded more and called out to CiCi, as Stuart and Carlos left the stage. The stage lights dimmed to a single amber spotlight and the audience sat back down. Martin picked up his acoustic guitar, pulled up two bar stools, and sat next to Cassandra. Without introduction, they began "Peggy Blue."

As her voice and his guitar weaved together the story of a dying child's bittersweet love, a communal sadness fell over the hushed audience. Even the brisk and business-like waitresses stopped to listen.

When the tune ended, Marisa realized she'd been holding her breath and gasped for air. She'd lost herself in the music and when she turned around Jules wasn't there, but her sadness had lifted. She joined in the enthusiastic applause as CiCi and Martin bowed to the shouts of "Bravo!" Stuart and Carlos rejoined them on stage and they finished out the set with a rousing funk tune that had the audience dancing in their seats. The applause followed the band upstairs where they stood at the dressing room doors in awe of their own stirring performance.

Martin wrapped his arms around Marisa and lifted her off her feet. Everyone was hugging and slapping high-fives as if they'd just scored a goal and won the World Cup.

The second set was as powerful as the first and Marisa held back a rush of autograph seekers while the band squeezed into CiCi's dressing room. Marisa told CiCi's fans they'd have to wait downstairs and locked the dressing room door behind her.

The club manager said he was very pleased with the ticket sales, and Marisa had the sudden thought she should have asked for a percentage over the guarantee. Oh well, next time, she told herself.

What do you mean by next time? You're just playing manager for one night, remember? Jules whispered teasingly.

Yes, she answered, silently. But I'm having so much fun being back on the scene. I'd forgotten how much I missed the thrill of success when you know you have a hit show on your hands, like it used to happen with your band.

Rufus Winckle, an international festival promoter that she'd often worked with back in the day, sent a note to Marisa in the dressing room and asked her to meet him downstairs.

As she made her way toward Rufus, she wondered which of them had aged the most, and she regretted not stopping in the bathroom to freshen her lipstick. She'd last seen this heavy-set, full-bearded German at a dinner party for festival promoters in Cannes. His bear hug was still the same, she thought, as he engulfed her in his arms.

"Dearest Marisa, the years just fall away when I look at you. Has it really been that long since the last time Jules played on one of my festival tours with you there in the wings watching over him? What a team you made." His face fell with his voice.

"I was so sorry to hear of his passing. And it was right here. I can't believe it. His name comes up a lot when we talk of the great players who have left us. He was one of the best."

Marisa was taken back by her old friend's sentiment and it took a moment before she could say, "Thank you, Rufus. Sometimes I fear Jules will be forgotten. It makes me feel good knowing that's not true." She laughed. "At least not while you old guys are still running the show. And I hope you're not quitting anytime soon." Her head tilted. "Are you?"

Rufus shook his head. "Only a few of us, like you, ever leave this business alive." Then with sudden enthusiasm and that glint he got in his eye when he was really excited about a new band, he said, "Wow, Marisa! Where did you find this guy Martin Starks? He's a monster. I haven't heard anyone play guitar like that in a long time. You know I don't usually stay for two sets, especially when I have an early morning flight, but after that mind-blowing first set I couldn't leave. How did you make all this happen?"

"The kids pulled it off, not me."

"Oh that's so like you not to take any credit." He leaned toward her. "Marisa, I want to book this band. I know it's a bit late for a full European tour this summer, but I think I can pull some venues together for a couple of weeks." She knew when Rufus paused that he was gearing up to lay a big surprise on her. "Even a date at Montreux."

"Montreux!" She was stunned. "No way. That's still in early July, right? We used to book that festival a year in advance and Martin doesn't even have a record out, let alone a following."

He laughed. "I forget how long you've been out of the scene. You don't need a record release anymore to book a tour. CDs are just promotion freebies at gigs. They don't really mean anything because fans can download their songs for free. We just need some product to promote on Internet and you've already taken care of that."

She tilted her head, wondering what he meant.

"The club's soundman said you asked him to record both sets, including a video. Smart move, lady. We can use that to promote the dates. And "Peggy Blue" will be a sensation on YouTube. Just say, yes, and I'll get right on it."

"But Montreux?" she stated again and swallowed the last drop in her martini glass. She couldn't believe it could be that simple. Bands often waited years for a gig at Montreux. "Rufus are you telling me everything?"

He gave her a wide toothy smile. "Oh Marisa, you never did let me get away with anything, did you? All right. Here's the truth: The key is CiCi Belle. The Montreux Festival would love to have her back. The Belles have played the festival several times and always draw a huge audience."

She waited.

"When the Impresario—and you know whom I mean when I say the Impresario?" Marisa smiled. "Well, when you invited me to come tonight, I called him. He loved hearing that CiCi was staging a comeback and wanted to showcase her at his festival. And if her trio is available, they'd be the perfect backup band."

Marisa pulled herself up very straight, feeling that righteous buzz shoot up her spine again. "Look, Rufus, I appreciate what you're proposing but I have to make it perfectly clear that Martin invited CiCi to join his band for one night at the Blue Note. That's all. So if I could interest Martin in a tour, and may I add, if he was available, he would only do it if all venues were billed as the Martin Starks Trio with special guest CiCi Belle. Just like tonight."

Rufus laughed. "You haven't changed a bit, have you, Marisa? You were always one to protect the integrity of your musicians. That's why you managed some of the best, like Jules, but you're not being realistic. This would be an incredible opportunity for Martin. He's just starting off. And to be honest, as good as he is, the tour won't happen without CiCi headlining. I know how these festivals work."

Dan put down fresh drinks and said the second round was on him for old times' sake. Marisa thanked him, picked up her glass, and stood up.

Rufus was the one now taken by surprise. "Wait a minute. Don't go off like that. You know you're making it a lot more difficult for me to pull this off, but I'm willing to try it your way. As long as you understand that no matter how we advertise it, CiCi will be the draw."

Marisa tipped her glass to Rufus's with a wide smile. "That might be true, but not for long."

"We'll have to see about that. By the way, am I talking to the right person? You are their manager?"

"No. I'm only helping out tonight but I can be your messenger."

"Well, they'd be making a big mistake not to sign with you.

CiCi's lucky to have you here. Does she have any idea who you are?"

Marisa sighed. "No. I think in her eyes I'm an antique. But you know at my age I'm no longer looking for recognition. I'm proud of what I've accomplished and it's a relief not to have to prove myself anymore. But, as I said, I'm helping out tonight. I haven't managed a band in years, and I doubt I have the energy let alone the mental capacity to do a thorough job. I don't know about you but I have to write everything down or I don't remember. Plus the music scene has changed a lot since I was last on the road." She could hear Jules laughing at her excuses along with Rufus.

"What's so funny? Do you really think I could manage this tour … that is if the tour happens?"

Rufus didn't hesitate. "Yes you could. Just to encourage you, I'll throw a road manager into the deal who will handle the details. You can just sit back on your heels and have a good time."

"Yeah right, I've heard that before. Anyway it's up to Martin and I'm sure he'll want someone much hipper than me as his manager."

She thanked Rufus for offering a tour and told him she'd talk it over with Martin and CiCi.

Rufus gave her another bear hug, and said, "Let me know soon. I've got to start working on the dates right away if it's going to happen."

When she got upstairs, Martin was distributing the money, and Stuart and Carlos were packing up. He handed an envelope to Marisa.

"What's this?"

"It's your fifteen percent commission. It's what you deserve for setting up everything and making this gig happen."

"Oh Martin, I hardly did anything. I just got in touch with a few press people. You're the ones who made it happen."

"No, Marisa, he's right," said Cassandra, putting her arm around Marisa's shoulders. "We came down to the bar so we could thank you, but you were in the middle of being hugged by some big bear."

Marisa blushed.

"So?" asked Cassandra. "Who was that?"

"Rufus Winckle. An old friend of mine."

"Are you talking about *the* Rufus? Why he's world famous for making bands happen. I'm impressed. What did he want?"

"Oh, he has this crazy idea . . ." she said, stopping to yawn. "Pretty exciting actually but I've had all the excitement I can take in one night. I need to get home before I drop. Let's have breakfast tomorrow morning at ten and I'll tell you all about it."

"As long as breakfast means Marisa's cooking, I'm there," said Martin reaching down for his guitar case and showing little interest in this guy Rufus who he'd never heard of.

But Cassandra wasn't giving it up until Martin put his other arm around her waist and pulled her toward him. "I'll do my best to keep you distracted until tomorrow."

Marisa hid her surprise. She'd felt the electricity between them onstage but didn't know it was happening offstage, too. When had the flirtation between these two become something more? And where would it lead?

Marisa got into bed that night feeling much richer than the ninety dollars commission she'd found in the envelope. An amount that reminded her of one thing that certainly hadn't changed in the biz—low wages for talented musicians. Next time she'd make sure they got a sweeter deal. Before Jules could tease her again about being a manager for just one night, Marisa told him to be quiet and let her sleep.

21

The bacon was sizzling when Cassandra and Martin came in the kitchen. A basket of fresh croissants that Marisa had bought at the bakery on her early morning walk was on the island counter along with a vase glowing with yellow tulips.

"How do you think it went last night?" asked Cassandra. "Any feedback?"

"First a cup of coffee," insisted Marisa. For Cassandra she chose the green cup with a pink saucer, the color of her flushed cheeks, and for Martin the pale blue that matched his sleepy eyes. She poured the dark Costa Rican java into their cups, topped them off with frothy steamed milk, and passed around the croissants. Perched on the bar stools, the two kids waited like students for Marisa to begin.

She made them wait until she'd had her first sip and then prolonged the moment with a deep sigh. "There's nothing like that first sip in the morning is there?"

"Marisa!" cried Cassandra. "At least tell us what Rufus said."

"Okay. Okay. Rufus is a European promoter who books American bands. Back in the day he booked my artists on the European festival circuit. Besides being a good friend, he's one of the best promoters out there."

"I know that," said Cassandra impatiently.

"You might, but Martin doesn't." She dipped her croissant in the frothy cream. "He loved your concert."

"And?" said Cassandra leaning forward.

"He's interested in booking the band on a two-week summer

tour that would include a date at the Montreux Festival."

"I knew it," called out Cassandra, clapping her hands; at the same time Martin said, "Montreux! You're kidding. Why would they want us?"

"The Impresario who books the Montreux festival is a big fan of The Belles and CiCi's name alone would confirm a booking."

"Oh," said Martin, his enthusiasm fading. "So you're talking about a gig for CiCi Belle, also known to us as Cassandra?"

"No. Not exactly. I made it perfectly clear to Rufus that the only way you'd consider a tour would be if the billing was the Martin Starks Trio with special guest CiCi Belle."

"Thanks, Marisa," he said, appreciatively, "but I don't think that's my decision alone."

Cassandra held her eyes on both of them while she considered her words carefully. "Before last night I might have said, no, but last night was magical. I wasn't sure I ever wanted to perform again, but I loved being back on stage. And I loved singing with Martin's band. I think we've got a good thing going so why stop after one night? That is, if Martin wants me on his tour."

"These are sure good, Marisa," said Martin biting into a second croissant. He picked up another one and put it on Cassandra's pink saucer. "If we're going to tour together you need to build up your strength and put on some weight."

Cassandra lifted the pastry and took a bite. Martin gently reached over and brushed the leftover crumbs off her chin.

Marisa had been right. Something was going on. "Okay, you two," she said, "you better start getting serious about this. Have you thought about getting someone to help you set up the tour?"

Cassandra and Martin exchanged glances. And then he said, "When neither one of us could sleep last night, we talked about what it'd be like to play more gigs together. Maybe even a road tour. I was a bit worried Cassandra might change her mind this morning," he reached across the island and took her hand. "But since she hasn't ... Both of us agreed that if we ever needed a manager, it would be you."

Marisa gasped. "Tell me you're not serious."

"We wouldn't consider anyone else."

"You need someone who is far more hip about what's going on in the music scene today. Things were different when I was managing bands."

"Hip? Who are you kidding? You're a social media wizard," said Martin and broke into a smile. "I'm still trying to get a handle on Facebook and you already twitter and run a blog."

Cassandra laughed. "It's tweet, Martin, not twitter."

"Whatever. C'mon, Marisa, where's your spirit? You've worked these festivals before. There's no reason why you can't do it now."

When she didn't reply, Martin walked over to Jules's chair. "If Jules were here, he'd encourage you to do it."

Marisa looked away and stared down at the unbeaten eggs.

Cassandra laid her hand on Martin's forearm. "Give her some breathing room."

He sat back down.

Marisa perched herself up on a bar stool. "Look, I really appreciate your offer and don't think I'm not tempted to say yes, but there's a reason why I should say no."

Cassandra frowned. "Something to do with your appointment at the Brain Center a few weeks back?"

Marisa nodded, followed by a sigh.

"Wait a minute. What's going on here? Cassandra told me about your mother having Alzheimer's, but no way is that going to happen to you."

"Thanks, Martin. You're probably right. It's just that I won't know for sure until I know the results from the second PET scan. I can't make any plans until then."

Cassandra put her arm around Marisa's shoulder. "I'm really sorry I forgot to meet you. Now I understand why you were so upset with me."

"When will you get the results?" asked Martin.

"Next Friday."

"This time I'll be with you," said Cassandra. "I promise."

"We'll both be there," said Martin, encouragingly. "And if the test comes out okay then you'll be our manager, right?"

"It's been a long time since I've had such an offer." She looked around the room as if expecting someone.

"I don't think we could do it without you," said Martin.

"Well . . ." she smiled, "I guess I'd be a fool to say no. Okay, if the scan is, as they say, unremarkable, I'll do it, but just for this tour."

"All right, Aunt Marisa," said Martin. "Now can we eat?"

Marisa turned back to the eggs and beat them until they turned a pale yellow. Her heart was beating even harder as she considered what she had just agreed to do.

At the table, they talked excitedly about the previous night's gig between bites of scrambled eggs and bacon.

The next morning, Marisa brought her laptop over to the table and sat across from Martin and Cassandra. "Rufus wants to start the tour in late June and end it at Montreux on July tenth. That means you have about two months to decide on material, write arrangements, and rehearse. It would be great if you could also get some practice onstage."

"No problem," said Martin. "I have a short tour on the East Coast booked in early June." He turned to Cassandra, "That is if you want to come with us. But let me warn you upfront, they're small club gigs, and the pay is lousy. No limos. No wardrobe mistress. No roadies. Just me and the band and long days in the van. Are you sure you're up to that?"

Cassandra did one of those defiant tosses with her head. "How do you think The Belles started? Touring in a van is not new to me. It's my fans who will be disappointed finding me performing in such squalor," she said to tease him.

Marisa knitted her brows. "I think you should leave CiCi's name off the billing. You don't want the press or your fans hanging around while you try out new material."

They both nodded. "Sorry to bring this up," said Martin. "I'll have to book a rehearsal studio and I've got to pay the guys something. What are we going to do for money? Can we get an advance from the European promoters?"

"Not a good idea. If we're asking for handouts, it would put us in a weak negotiating position," said Marisa. "In the old days, we'd go to the record company for an advance on royalties. Seeing that's not possible, maybe I can get a short-term loan on the loft and you can pay me back out of the tour profits."

She looked over at Cassandra who stopped scribbling on a piece of paper and looked up. "I can help out, too."

"Then I'm sure we can pool together enough money. After the festival dates, there'll be enough left to pay us back and then some."

Get going! interjected Jules. He always said that to bring Marisa back into focus when her mind was popping like popcorn, or she was obsessing over something that was out of her control or not important. And he was right. Already two weeks had passed since she'd agreed to manage the band's European tour and that's what she should be working on now that her second PET scan was found unremarkable.

At her appointment, when Enrico told her the good news she was surprised. She'd expected to be diagnosed with early Alzheimer's. When she asked Enrico what she could do to keep her memory intact, he advised her to stay mentally and physically active.

Martin had then turned to Marisa and said, "Don't worry. I'll keep you very active because you're going to manage my band."

But in spite of the encouraging test results and Martin's confidence in her work, Marisa knew her mind wasn't as sharp as it used to be. Her ability to do a good job setting up the tour with all its many details was hanging on a thread. She'd never spent so much time double checking her work and she'd already caught herself scheduling flights to Montreux on the wrong date. She couldn't seem to concentrate.

Her fingers hovered over the keypad like a hummingbird searching for nectar. She clicked on her e-mail, clicked onto Facebook, and then clicked onto her portfolio to see if she had lost money in today's market.

She finally opened her blog and answered a widower in his late sixties who had been grieving the loss of his wife for eighteen months and wondered if that was too long. Yes it is, she told him, and gently suggested he seek professional help for chronic depression.

A fatigued cuckoo popped out of his trap door four times and announced that another hour in his life had passed. Marisa checked her e-mail one last time for news from Rufus confirming the club date in Paris, so she could book the transatlantic air tickets. Once she bought the tickets there would be no backing out.

She blushed and looked around the room when she saw a message from Serge and then laughed at herself for being so foolish. After all, Jules wasn't really there, was he?

No, I'm not. You're on your own now.

Serge was responding to her e-mail about Martin's European tour.

What an amazing coincidence. I'll be in Geneva at a conference when you're in Montreux! Do you think you could be available for dinner one night?

Marisa was beaming when she wrote back: Most certainly! She signed off with love but quickly deleted it and wrote à bientôt.

Now in a far better mood, she turned to chapter six of her memoir. She'd left off when her father informed her and her four older brothers and sisters that they were moving to the desert. Within a few months, her family then moved away from the only home she'd ever known; away from the lush rolling hills and enormous shade trees she passed under when she rode her bike to school. She didn't tell her friends she was leaving. She preferred to take the more dramatic way out and just disappear. In the desert there were no shady trees to stand under in the unbearable heat, and she stopped riding her bike because the wheels got stuck in the sand. And her father had been wrong. There were just as many telephone wires blocking his night sky view; he just chose not to see them.

She jumped when the cuckoo screeched six times and stacked her manuscript back on the corner of her desk. Wanting to wear something different to her dinner with Miles and Sheri, she remembered a jacket just right for a warm Spring evening and pulled it out from the back of her closet.

She took a critical look at her reflection. *You're looking good, my dear,* said Jules from behind the mirror, *but you need to go to the gym more often. And cut down on those caloric gimlets, and the wine too, or you won't be able to fit into that new wardrobe you're planning to buy for the tour.*

Marisa stuck out her tongue and then colored her pouting lips with shimmery gloss, regarded herself in the mirror again and sucked in her stomach.

She didn't have to wait long for the elevator. It was coming up from the lobby before she pushed the button.

When the door opened onto Marisa dressed in a rose-wine linen jacket and a matching skirt, Cassandra blurted out, "Hey girl, don't you look hot!"

Marisa was embarrassed. She kissed Cassandra on the cheek, said she was late, said to use her computer, and then switched places just before the elevator closed.

22

Marisa was still blushing from Cassandra's compliment, repeating 'Hey girl, you look hot,' to herself as she strode across City Hall Park and floated down the subway stairs just in time to jump on the #4 uptown subway. She squeezed between rush-hour commuters, their dour faces within inches of her own, but her spirits remained high. She'd been told she looked *hot*, she'd had an e-mail from Serge, she'd worked on her manuscript, *and* her real estate agent wanted to bring several clients to see the loft. What more could life offer?

After one stop she eyed a narrow empty spot on the subway bench and wiggled in between two gloomy middle-aged men with the girth of wine barrels. They grunted at having to shift their weight to make room for her. At 14th street a pregnant woman came aboard and bumped against Marisa while struggling to keep her balance. Marisa remembered her own pregnant days in the City and gave up her seat. The car's digital clock counted off the seconds and her heart quickened. She mustn't be late.

As the wheels screeched to a halt at Forty-second Street, she shoved her way out and rode the escalator up to Grand Central's vaulted lobby. She hurried through the rush-hour commuters to reach the second escalator that brought her to street level, where she pushed open the outside door and weaved through the cars and taxis on Vanderbilt Avenue over to the Yale Club entrance. Its revolving glass door transported her inside, and she imagined embarking on the Queen Mary just before it pulled anchor and moved out to sea, taking her far away from the madding onshore crowd.

Seven chimes rang out as she skipped up the polished marble stairs to the lounge.

Cassandra had been relieved to see Marisa going out. Martin had a gig and she was looking forward to a quiet, private evening at home watching a movie. She had treated herself to a take-out box of sushi, which she now put down on the kitchen counter.

Though she'd quit the Bitter End job, Martin was a tyrant when it came to rehearsals, and she'd had little time to hang out alone. Not that she was complaining; she loved working with him. He was very creative at bringing out the best in her, just like Don did at Pratt. She was still attending his art class and due to his insistence would finish the semester before leaving on Martin's brief U.S. tour. That way, Don said, if she wanted to come back she could.

Cassandra read through a long list of incoming Facebook messages on Marisa's computer and hesitated before opening a message from MiMi. She was afraid of being shaken down for using "formerly of The Belles" in promoting her Blue Note gig as she'd given up rights to the name when she quit. But there was nothing to fear. The message was friendly, too friendly, she thought. MiMi had read the rave reviews of her Blue Note gig and was proud of her. She apologized for the way things had been so messy between them and hoped they could be best friends again now that CiCi had resurfaced in New York.

Messy! thought Cassandra. Is that what she calls it? Isn't betrayal a far more accurate description than *messy*? Where were these so-called *best friends* of mine when I most needed them? While I was trying to get sober, they replaced me with my clone, dressed her up like me, and gave her my songs to sing.

Cassandra signed off without replying to MiMi.

The Belles often appeared in her dreams. They were on stage performing together, and she'd wake up with a happy heart thinking their breakup had never happened, and then would realize it was only a dream. Then she'd go over all the good and bad memories and stir up all the old conflicts, like she was doing now. She reminded herself that she hadn't made a terrible mistake. She'd wanted a new start and now she was singing with Martin's band. But after hearing from MiMi she was once again filled with doubt.

Too depressed to watch a movie, too upset to eat, she put the sushi in the refrigerator and took out Marisa's bottle of Stoli from the freezer and poured a double shot over ice, it would help her get through a night now ruined by MiMi's friendly note.

She fell back on the couch and skimmed through the current *New Yorker* in hopes of finding a good laugh in the cartoons, but nothing was funny. Restless, she lurked among Marisa's archived boxes, which were going into storage while the loft was being shown to buyers, and wondered what was inside them. She'd offered to help pack them a few days ago but Marisa said she needed to do it on her own. Marisa was like that. It was difficult to help her with anything. And she needed help. Always forgetting where she put her keys or her glasses and couldn't make any decisions without referring to copious notes left on every table in the loft or on her cell phone, which she carried everywhere as if it was the only access to her memory. Maybe it was. And if it was, were they taking too big of a risk having Marisa manage their tour? Cassandra had mentioned her concern to Martin and was irritated when he didn't want to hear about it.

On the top of one of the boxes she saw an old photo album and brought the heavy book over to the counter.

A dozen cities were highlighted on a European map on the front page. Cities that Cassandra had also performed in with The Belles. She flipped to the next page. A group shot in front of a concert hall. Marisa's cheerful smile stood out. She wondered if the cute guy holding the drumsticks was Jules. His other hand was on Marisa's shoulder. He was smiling at her while the other musicians frowned into the camera's eye.

Cassandra recognized that they were in front of Albert Hall. The first time The Belles performed there was after they had an unexpected number one hit on the British charts. The song had been written for CiCi, a raw, gutsy solo performance with the other Belles backing her up. For the Albert Hall performance, Ryan convinced her partners that it would work best if CiCi sang it alone on stage without them. Later, he told CiCi how much they resented it and the only way they would agree to it, is if they too could have their own solos on stage. For her first solo performance, Ryan had picked out for her a low-cut, shimmering silk gown that became her stage costume and her identity as a seductive performer.

She smiled remembering the skintight gown and tall stilettos that made it hard to move sensuously across to center stage and take her place under the spotlight. As a little girl, when her hips still stuck out like sticks, she'd borrowed her mother's heels and practiced swaying her hips in front of a mirror. She imitated femme fatales from the forties, like Rita Hayworth, who she studied while watching her movies on television. Often she at home alone, and her mirrored image kept her company—someone she could talk to without having to shout—someone who listened to her.

That night at Albert Hall, after she sang the last note of "If Tears Are Only Water," there was a deafening silence in the dark theatre. And then she felt two thousand clapping hands engulf her, filling her with so much joy that she had to grip the mic to stay steady. From the deep cavern below came shouts of "CiCi, we love you." She inclined forward again and again to take a bow and then with tiny steps walked backward off stage, throwing kisses.

She'd felt the same thrill performing at the Blue Note. Of course, it wasn't as powerful as the thunderous clapping at Albert Hall; there weren't any backstage guards ushering her through stampeding fans to a waiting limo; DiDi and MiMi weren't laughing and squashing their lips against the closed tinted windows, while fans pressed their faces against the passing limo, like donkeys. She knew she would never experience that life again. Unless … unless what, she asked herself. *Well, hadn't Ryan said you could have it all again if you went back to L.A. with him? But is that what you really want? Have you forgotten the cost?* Cassandra traced her finger up the viper's tail to its pink tongue and pinched it.

She sat down at the foyer's piano and played the melody Martin had given her at rehearsal, asking her to write lyrics. It was a hard-hitting tune that fed her increasing bitterness toward Ryan. He encouraged her to leave The Belles for a solo career, but it wouldn't be any different, he'd still be in total control.

The lyrics came quickly. She scribbled them down and wrote "The Woman In Me" across the top of the sheet.

She belted out the chorus, pounded the notes on the piano, and sang the title lyric over and over again, louder and louder until a thunderous bang on the ceiling made her jump and the music fell off the piano. Furious at the intrusion, she glared up at the ceiling but she didn't want Carl to give Marisa trouble, so she picked the chart off the floor and moved into Martin's bedroom. Cross-legged on his bed, she switched on the portable keyboard, put on headphones, and continued to work.

When Martin came home, he found Cassandra asleep on his bed, the keyboard's lights blinking, and an empty glass turned on its side. He picked up the music and smiled as he read her lyrics, especially amused by the chorus: *I don't need your opinion/I don't need your advice/I don't want your possessions/I can take care of myself/So you'd better think twice/I got everything I need/It's the woman in me/Yes it is/It's the woman in me.*

He liked what she had done to his song but wasn't sure he'd like to have been there when she wrote it. Trying not to wake her, he slipped off her shoes, put away the keyboard, and covered her with the comforter. He slipped in next to her warm body, listened to her soft breath, and felt a blissful moment of unspoken tenderness toward her before joining her in sleep.

23

How different it was now. After months of nothing but solitude and grief, active, joyous sounds bounced off the loft's walls and echoed through the rooms. Martin and Cassandra were coming and going at all hours, often joining Marisa for dinner or to just hang out. Marisa knew by the way they looked at each other that she didn't need to look in Cassandra's bedroom to know she hadn't slept in her bed.

Marisa, working on the European tour, was occupied with her To Do list on her smartphone, moaning when she deleted one task and came up with two more to add and panicking when she misplaced her phone and couldn't remember what she had to do. Just this morning she had to call her own cell phone from the landline and follow its muffled ring to under her bed pillow where she'd been working earlier.

How could she really manage a tour when she had only straw for a brain like the Scarecrow in Oz? The Wizard had stuffed the Scarecrow's head with bran, pins and needles to make him smart, but the idea of stuffing her own head with such things gave her a headache.

The tour dates in Europe had been finalized, but now there were the contract riders to negotiate, hotels and flights to book, and each venue needed to be publicized. Rufus's office was a great help. His young crew knew all the right music journalists to contact through their Internet database but it was difficult building any excitement for the unknown Martin Starks Trio. So CiCi's guest appearance was publicized the most.

Marisa finished editing yet another bodice-ripper novel for Random House while her own manuscript sat idle on her desk patiently waiting its turn.

Jules still showed up for cocktail hour and she sensed his presence when she was frustrated with the tour details. He encouraged her to keep the faith, reminding her that she was an old pro, echoing her own sentiments.

Isn't it just like getting back on a bike after not riding it for years?

Well, sort of, but back then she wasn't worried about falling off or getting lost.

When she left the loft to walk to the market or stroll along the Hudson River, she passed the tree planters outside her building and felt badly that she hadn't gotten to her annual spring planting of impatiens. One morning hurrying to the club for an exercise class, she was disappointed to see that someone else had planted the garden and with petunias, her least favorite flower that would wilt in the summer humidity.

The maintenance of the building had suffered too. The lobby needed sweeping and the windows were smudged with fingerprints. She wasn't surprised when an e-mail circulated, stating that a custodian had been hired and her services were no longer needed. She was actually relieved. The loft was on the market. Karen, her real estate agent, brought potential buyers and the upkeep of the building would be one less thing Marisa had to worry about. There'd been a few offers but they were way below the asking price. She held out for a better offer.

Her correspondence with Serge had become a daily affair. He regretted that what with his book promotion and his busy practice in Los Angeles that he'd been unable to return to New York, but he looked forward to their meeting in Montreux.

She didn't text Miles as often as she used to only because she was so busy. He had resigned himself to his mother going on this tour and perhaps Sheri too had helped him to understand how important it was for her to be productive again.

And as far as the first of June, when Cassandra and Martin

were to vacate the building under the new "no-tenant" rule, she e-mailed her neighbors that she needed an extension and, surprisingly, no one had objected. Maybe Carl was consumed at Goldman Sachs with the volatile world markets. And what could he do anyway? Threaten to take her to court? Well by then her tenants would be gone and she just might be gone too.

So when the thirteenth of June did arrive and Marisa was standing in the kitchen with Martin, who had packed the van and was ready to leave on the short East Coast tour, Marisa said, "Can you believe how fast the weeks have gone by since the Blue Note concert?" She was trying to distract him. He was looking at his watch again while waiting for Cassandra.

It was a four-hour drive to Northampton, their first gig, and he was impatient to get out of Manhattan before the traffic started piling up and he still had to pick up Stuart and Carlos in Brooklyn.

"Cassandra. Let's go," he shouted down the hall again.

"Would you like another cup of coffee?" asked Marisa.

"No thanks. I'm too wired already. What is taking her so damn long?"

Cassandra came in rolling a large Vuitton suitcase with a make-up case on top and a matching satchel over her shoulder. After the Blue Note gig, she'd thrown out her gothic wardrobe and was looking more like her former self—the fashionable CiCi wearing a low-cut green satin sundress under a light linen jacket that covered her tattooed arm.

"You're taking all that?"

She looked at him as if his question was ridiculous.

"Cassandra, this is not a Belles tour. At the clubs we're playing at you'll look pretty foolish dressed up."

She continued to ignore him and turned to Marisa. "Do you like my new dress? I bought it for touring in Europe but why not wear it on this tour?" Martin shook his head and they all got into the elevator.

Cassandra sighed and looked plaintively at Marisa. "I do wish you were coming. I don't know how I'll manage without you."

"I wish I was too, but I've got plenty to do here."

Martin wedged Cassandra's suitcase between amps and under a guitar case in his green Odyssey mini-van. He hugged Marisa and got in the driver's seat. Cassandra strapped herself into the passenger seat. With her make-up case on her lap, she waved to Marisa and off they went.

The loft did not welcome Marisa back. It had become a life-sized diorama that bore no relation to her. Her moist eyes fell upon Jules's chair.

When Karen staged the loft for potential buyers, Marisa had held out against his chair being stored in the basement. But she'd given in to painting over the rather brightly colored walls in layers of white-white paint. Karen insisted that was what the young upwardly mobile buyers wanted.

The memorabilia, the art prints, and the knickknacks had been stuffed away in drawers or closets so these unimaginative buyers could easily see their own things there instead. All that remained was Marisa's desk, the dining table, four chairs, two bar stools, and a wall of barren bookshelves.

At her desk, Marisa shuffled through the booking contracts Rufus had sent for her approval. A sudden gust of wind blew through the open window and swept several of her manuscript pages onto the floor. She picked them up, started reading, then spent the next few hours revising the chapter about her family's forced move out of Beverly Hills adding the real reason for the abrupt departure was because her father lost his studio contract.

Tired, but proud of her work, Marisa sat down across from Jules's chair. But this time her heart ached for what he was missing out on, rather than her own loneliness. She was about to read out loud what she'd written when she burst out laughing. "You blew those pages on the floor, didn't you?" She raised her glass and whispered, "Thank you."

Later while washing up at the sink, she wondered how long it'd be until she could no longer conjure up his voice. She sensed his presence behind her, but knowing it would break the spell to turn she closed her eyes. She felt his touch on her moist cheek and then his hand swept across her shoulder as he passed out of the room like a soft breeze.

The sudsy glass slipped through her fingers and shattered.

Martin had picked up Stuart and Carlos. The four of them had made it out of Manhattan before rush hour and were now heading up I-91 in the van to their first gig—the Iron Horse in Northampton, Massachusetts. The GPS calculated two hours and twenty-two minutes. He looked in the rearview mirror at Cassandra crunched in the corner, gripping her make-up case and basically sending out bad vibes.

She had wanted to sit up front with Martin but longer-legged Carlos won out. Separated only by her Vuitton satchel, Stuart tapped drumbeats on a practice pad, ignoring her looks of annoyance.

Martin had toured with Carlos and Stuart before, and except for the occasional dark moods when no one but local drunks showed up at their gigs, they had a good time on the road, but it was a guy's hang. They'd never had a girl singer traveling with them. When he'd asked Cassandra to join them, he hadn't realized how challenging it would be for her and the band to get along in close quarters. And if they didn't get along on this tour, what would it be like in Europe?

He'd seen flashes of her diva attitude at rehearsals when he told her she was out of tune or made her wait while he rehearsed with the band, but shrugged it off. Carlos and Stuart weren't as tolerant. They had already complained about her bitchy moods.

Trying to please everyone, Martin had set the show so the band could play without Cassandra for the first twenty minutes. That way they could warm up and get into a strong groove before she came onstage. She'd sing three songs and then stand off to the side while the band played a few more tunes and then she'd join them for the featured guitar–and–voice closing song at the end of the set. He knew it was risky giving the band that much time to play between CiCi's performance, especially when they got to Europe where the audience would be coming to hear her, but he wasn't about to give up his music to become a backup band for a singer, not even CiCi Belle.

And now seeing how tense the first few hours on the road had been, he felt like dropping her off at the nearest Greyhound bus station. He jumped when Cassandra tapped him on the shoulder and asked him to pull over at a gas station. But, as if she'd been reading his thoughts, this time she thanked him for stopping and apologized for her weak bladder.

He watched her stroll toward the bathroom, her make-up kit bouncing against her right hip, her orange hair ablaze in the sunlight and turned up Lyle Lovett's "Nothing But a Good Ride." Stuart and Carlos joined in on the title chorus.

Cassandra, trying to make amends, returned with icy water bottles and chocolate bars for everyone. The recent tension in the van blew out the window.

That is until the GPS directed them off I-91 into Chicopee and minutes later they pulled into the Motel 6 parking lot behind a McDonalds. "You're joking," said Cassandra from the backseat. "We're not staying here?"

"Yeah, we are. It's cheap and though it's ten miles from the gig it's near the highway we take tomorrow morning toward Buffalo."

"Near the highway? We're *on* the highway."

Stuart and Carlos got out, rolled their eyes, and grabbed their bags. Cassandra waited in the van until Martin checked in and returned with the keys. He gave one to the guys and opened the room next door for himself and Cassandra. She shouted "No!" from the bathroom when Martin asked if she wanted to join them at Denny's to eat. When they came back for her to go to the club and honked, she came out wearing a silk turquoise pantsuit with spiked silver heels, carrying her make-up case. The guys were wearing clean black T-shirts imprinted with The Martin Starks Trio logo in red.

When Martin asked why the make-up case, she said she'd do her face at the club.

"Okay," said Martin, "but I don't know where. There's only a utility closet behind the stage."

Stuart and Carlos gave each other amused, knowing looks in the backseat.

"Don't worry," she said. "I'll work something out."

Martin stood in the hall outside the club manager's office, which had been turned into Cassandra' dressing room. He shook his head in amazement watching the sleazy manager bring her a pot of tea. And when she came out of her "dressing room" with a wide grin on her face, he had to smile back.

As bitchy as Cassandra had been all day, she was a professional performer and when it came time for her to come onstage she was ready and very able. The first set was a little rough with a few miscues, but nothing too serious. The second set was much tighter and the band really developed some strong moments. By that time the 200-seater club had filled up with Martin's fans; he often played the Iron Horse and had built-up a nice following. When CiCi got down off the stage, walked between the tables, and sat down at one while she sang "Who Knows Where The Time Goes" the audience was mesmerized. And when they performed their closing featured song "Peggy Blue," Martin felt their intimacy return and he started to forgive her.

Back at Motel 6 she sat up in bed, her chin on her knees and peered at him in wide-eyed innocence. "Tonight went well, don't you think?"

"Yeah, on stage it did, but not before. Look, you know, it's hard enough being a band leader, responsible for every detail, when everyone gets along, but you gave us a pretty hard time today."

She glared back at him. "What do you mean? I'm doing my job, aren't I?"

"This isn't about you doing your job, Cass. We're a band. All of us are in this together. I know you're used to limos, hotel suites, room service and blah blah blah, but when you tour with me, we're all on equal terms. No divas on this tour, okay?"

She threw off the sheets, stomped over to the bathroom, which wasn't far to stomp to, slammed the door, and locked it.

When she slipped back between the covers, Martin put down his book and folded his arms over his bare chest. He was planning to tell her to go home, but her puffy red eyes under the overhead light melted his resolve, and he pulled her into his arms, comforting her as he would a child.

"I'm sorry, Martin, really I am." She sniffled. "I don't mean to act like such a bitch. But riding in the van today, I felt like I was starting out all over again and it was so depressing. And then staying in this dump I feel like such a loser."

"Well, you're not. You were great tonight. That was so cool when you sat in the audience. They loved it. We all did."

"When I'm performing I forget everything else. But coming back to this suicidal motel room was really depressing."

"I can drop you off at Boston airport?"

She sat up. "No, I want to do the tour." She crunched up her nose and looked around the room. "But do we have to stay in roach motels?"

"Oh c'mon this place is cool."

She pulled the pillow over her face.

"Oh my poor little diva," he said, patting her pillow. "Let me see what I can do." He jumped up on the bed and unscrewed the naked overhead bulb and put a red towel over the desk lampshade. He took the pillow off Cass's face and kissed her shuttered eyes. "Isn't this better?"

She looked around the room and laughed. "Oh great, now it looks like a brothel."

"What's wrong with that?" he asked, unbuttoning her pajama top.

When they rolled apart, sated, and emerged from the depths of giving each other pleasure, they heard Stuart on the other side of the wall practicing drumbeats on his rubber practice pad.

"Is he always practicing?" asked Cassandra in a raspy voice, covering her ears.

Martin laughed. "I'll separate our rooms next time."

"But what about the shower stalls that remind me of the scene in *Psycho* when Norman stabs Janet Leigh through the shower curtain?"

"Man, you're hard to please. I guess I'll just have to take showers with you from now on to protect you from Norman." She smiled and laid her head on his bare chest.

"You better get some sleep. We're out of here at eight. Long drive tomorrow."

She sat up. "Eight! No way!"

"Cass?" he said, warningly.

"Just joking."

He slipped out of the bed, pulled on his jeans and T-shirt.

"Where are you going?"

"I need to stretch my legs after all that driving today."

"You want me to come with you?"

"No, that's okay. I'll be right back."

Left alone in the room, Cassandra got out of bed and snapped open her make-up case. She drew out the cell phone Ryan had given her in New York when he asked her to stay in touch. She saw no harm in that. He was far away in Japan, and after one trying day on the road with the band, she should keep all her options open. She switched it on and texted Ryan, telling him she was doing fine, loved being back on the road, and singing again. She turned it off and stuffed it back down in the bottom of her make-up case.

24

Until they came stumbling out of the elevator like clowns rolling out of a VW bug, Marisa hadn't realized how much she'd missed everyone and how lonely and silent the days had been. Martin, Cassandra, and the band encircled her with hugs and bursts of robust, contagious laughter.

Cassandra had exchanged her gothic makeup for a clean-scrubbed face and her satin sundress for a work shirt worn over a Martin Starks Trio T-shirt. Levis and red hi-top tennis shoes completed her new look.

After the hellos, Marisa invited them to sit down and read the new European tour itineraries, which she had put in multi-colored folders and placed around the table.

"This is great," said Cassandra smiling over at Marisa making coffee. "The Belles manager never gave us such a detailed itinerary and I like the extra personal touch with the colors and our names on each folder."

Marisa thanked her and handed out mugs of coffee. "I'll also send you e-mails with the itineraries attached."

"That would be very cool," said Stuart. "I'll post the dates on the social media links and everyone can follow us."

"Maybe I don't want to be followed," said Cassandra as her smile faded.

"Why not?" he said teasingly. "There must be lots of people who want to know where *you* are."

"Exactly," said Cassandra, looking down at her folder.

"Thanks, Stuart," interjected Marisa. "That's a great idea."

Martin turned over the pages. "Awesome. You and Rufus really know your stuff. Have you guys seen this? We have three festival dates not just one. Hey, Stuart, will your GPS work over there? There'll be a lot of driving."

"Not a problem, dude, I already ordered a European chip."

"And don't forget," said Marisa, "your road manager Damian will do most of the driving." Marisa told Stuart and Carlos that they would all have to meet at the Air France terminal three hours before the flight.

"Three hours!" exclaimed Carlos. "Why?"

"There might be unforeseen delays, long lines going through double security checks. Those kinds of things." Stuart and Carlos exchanged frowns.

"Hey guys you gotta trust me on this. I know what I'm doing with this stuff. When I was managing Jules's tours, I would check in twenty people, crew, and musicians, at the check-in counter. I'd have a stack of all their passports and they would just sit and wait for me to come back and hand out their boarding passes. It's not like that anymore. And don't forget your passports."

"Yes, Aunt Marisa," said Stuart. "Will there be drum kits at the gigs or will I need to bring my own?"

"All the venues will supply drums and amps and they have your specs. Some kits will be better than others but you only need to bring your cymbals."

"That's very cool, Marisa. Thanks." Stuart's knuckle met hers.

While Martin took the guys home for a well-deserved four-day rest, the two women sat down at the kitchen counter to talk. Cassandra admitted that it was pretty rough going back out on the road in a van. She also admitted that she even considered calling it quits and coming home after the first day.

Marisa tilted her head, waiting to hear more from this usually quiet girl.

"Touring in a van reminded me of when The Belles first started out. Eventually we flew or rode in limos and the band and crew travelled by bus."

"So what's so wrong with traveling in a van? The band and crew are far more fun to hang out with than the stars anyway."

Cassandra laughed. "That's because you were hanging out with one of the stars."

"Well, aren't you?"

Cassandra half smiled and got up to put the mugs in the dishwasher. When she returned, Marisa was staring at Jules's chair. "Marisa?" she said, tapping her shoulder.

Marisa looked up at her as if she didn't recognize her. Then she blinked and said, "Sorry. Were you saying something?"

"Are you all right?"

"Yes, I'm fine. I was just remembering the tours I went on with Jules when I managed his band. I guess it's quite different for a singer."

"It's just I'm used to traveling ... you know ... in comfort."

"Then tell me what you miss more, your partners or the amenities?"

Cassandra was offended. "Hey, don't get me wrong. The guys were terrific at encouraging me to give myself up to the music. They're such great improvisers. They'll try anything." She laughed. "One night I even danced with Carlos. Really, I can't remember when I last had so much fun onstage.

Warming to her subject, Cassandra joined Marisa on the couch and said, "With The Belles everything was so precise, so choreographed. We never changed the order of the tunes or tried anything new or different. And the larger the productions became, the farther away the musicians were set-up away from us. In the largest halls, our band was down in the orchestra pit. We couldn't even see them. We might as well have been a karaoke band."

She smiled wistfully. "Martin really is special, but you already know that." She stopped to twist a few strands of hair that were growing out blond. "But I have to say as far as your question about hanging out with musicians, I could've used some time alone. We didn't talk about it but I think Martin would like his own room on the next tour."

She got up, walked over to the window and when she turned back, she said, "Your home certainly looks different from when I first came to see it. I miss the orange walls. Don't you?"

"Yes, now it's like living in a hotel room."

"Is there anything I can do before we leave? What about this half-filled box? Shall we finish packing it?"

"That's the tour box. Mostly contracts. I'll be taking those papers with me." Marisa hesitated. "But there is something you could do. It's an old tradition of mine to get a pedicure and manicure the morning I leave on tour. It would be much more fun if you joined me."

"I'd love to. But isn't that cutting it close, the morning we leave?"

"No, not if you pack the night before."

"Then let's do it." Cassandra yawned. "Well, if you're sure there's nothing I can do for you, I think I'll take a nap."

Marisa put up her hand. "Wait a second." She picked up her phone and looked through her notes. "Ah yes, here it is. Before I forget, I got an e-mail from DiDi asking for your European itinerary. She must have found out somehow that I was managing your tour. Said she'd asked you but you weren't very good at returning messages. Shall I send it to her?"

"No!" commanded Cassandra. Then seeing Marisa's shocked face, she said softly, "Sorry. But you've gone to enough trouble setting up this tour for us. You don't need to be my secretary. DiDi can get it off Stuart's Facebook page like anyone else." She started rolling her Vuitton bags down the hallway and then came back. "Do you want to go out to dinner later? Maybe at Edward's?"

"Good idea. Shall we say around eight? Martin should be back by then. We'll celebrate the end of your New England tour and toast the next one in Europe."

"You always see life as a celebration, don't you?"

"When you love someone who faces death, you learn to celebrate every day."

Marisa had arranged for a car service to pick up the three of them at noon. Stuart and Carlos would take a taxi from Brooklyn and meet them at the airport. Marisa sent another e-mail to the Board reminding them that she was going away with Martin and Cassandra. The loft would be empty while they were away, but Karen would be coming by to show potential buyers. The only response was from Rachel and Charlie, wishing her a great trip.

Miles had come around the last night unexpectedly with a going-away present and joined them at Edward's for dinner. Marisa was delighted to find an iPad in his wrapped gift box.

There's a hidden agenda to my gift, he'd said. She had to e-mail him every night otherwise he'd worry about her. She was quite touched by his concern, which so reminded her of Jules, and promised to stay in touch.

With Marisa's feet snugly wrapped in warm towels, she turned to Cassandra seated on the pedicure throne next to hers. "Doesn't this feel good? I promise to pamper myself more often but I don't do it. I never can justify the indulgence unless I'm going on a trip. My last pedicure was before Jules and I left for Beaulieu."

"Beaulieu?"

"That's where we spent our summers in France."

"How wonderful that must have been," said Cassandra looking down at her own wrapped feet. "When were you last there?"

"Two summers ago."

"You must miss those trips."

Marisa nodded, closed her eyes, and felt the warmth of Provence on her face. She then turned to Cassandra and said, "They were our most creative and happiest moments. We'd work in our studios and then meet for dinner and discuss"—she smiled—"the plusses and minuses of our days. We would have gone last summer, but it just didn't work out that way."

"Will you ever go again?"

Marisa opened her eyes wide at such a naïve question. "Without Jules? Never." She looked up from her drying nails to the crowd of pedestrians rushing by outside the window. "It just wouldn't be the same." She felt her eyes stinging and closed them.

"You were lucky to have someone like Jules in your life. I always fall in love with the bad guys."

Once their nails were dry, they joined the crowd on the sidewalk and hurried back to the loft. When the elevator opened, the cuckoo was screeching his twelfth and last cuckoo. Karen planned to box him up and store him and Jules's chair in the basement after Marisa left. Recent offers on the loft were sparse and Karen thought it might bring good luck to make a full sweep of everything Marisa still held dear. Or that's how Marisa interpreted her agent's requests.

Martin was waiting at the elevator. "Well girls, did you have fun?"

"You should have come," said Cassandra, holding up her manicured hands.

Martin shook his head at the varnished toenails. Marisa's deep red. Cassandra's cobalt blue. "I don't think that's my kind of thing."

The intercom buzzed. The driver was downstairs.

"I just have one more thing to do," said Marisa, looking over at Jules's chair. "You kids go on ahead and take the bags down. I'll be there in a minute."

She jiggled Jules's chair and smiled. "Uh-uh. No way am I going on the road without you. C'mon, my dear, let's get out of this bleak hotel. We've got a plane to catch."

II.

Tell me how am I supposed to live without you?
Now that I've been loving you so long.
How am I supposed to live without you?
And how am I supposed to carry on?
When all that I've been livin' for is gone.

Lyrics by Michael Bolton & Douglas Thomas

25

"Oh, Jules, can you see this?" exclaimed Marisa as she stared out over the Seine flowing below her hotel window toward the gothic towers of the Notre Dame Cathedral.

The band's early morning arrival at Charles DeGaulle had been like a high-speed film. Rufus was waving at them when they came out the arrival door and introduced them to their road manager, Damian, who whisked away the luggage and instruments in his van. Rufus then hailed two taxis that carried all of them to the Hotel Le Notre Dame.

The first concert was the following night so they had the entire day to relax and get over jet lag. Marisa had managed to sleep through the morning until the sun streaming through her window had awoken her. After she got up to see her window view, she was too excited to go back to sleep.

From her room she hooked up to the hotel's Wi Fi service, breathed a sigh of relief that it worked, and e-mailed the band with the next day's schedule: 4 P.M. pick up at hotel for sound check at the New Morning club; 8 P.M. concert. She added on Cassandra's e-mail the two scheduled interviews between the sound check and the concert.

Quel difference, she thought, remembering the handwritten daily schedules, Xeroxed late at night in hotel lobbies and pushed under doors before she went to bed. Maybe Rufus was right: She should sit back and have a good time.

Cassandra and Martin had invited her to join them on a walk

that afternoon but she feigned fatigue—she wanted to be alone with Jules. She wasn't going to let a little thing like him being dead stop them from enjoying Paris together. But she certainly couldn't tell anyone else that. She invited Cassandra and Martin to join her later for dinner.

Marisa dressed quickly. Paris was waiting to welcome her and Jules back. But when she stepped into the frenetic flow of pedestrian traffic outside the hotel, her enthusiasm deflated. Nothing seemed familiar and the roaring traffic and diesel fumes added to her confusion. She turned back.

No Marisa that will never do. Go with the flow.

She cocked her head to the side and reminded Jules that the last time he said that she fell into a river and sprained her ankle. Was it safe to let him guide her from the beyond?

Just take one step at a time she told herself. And if you get lost, you've got your iPad. She reached into her bag to feel its reassuring presence and headed toward Notre Dame's towers. Stopping at a tabac, she bought *Le Monde,* a few postcards, and though aware of Jules's disapproval, added a pack of Marlboros to her purchases.

She scanned several cafés surrounding Notre Dame before choosing the one with the best view. After ordering an espresso, she lit a cigarette, and did what everyone else was doing—watched the human race rush by like Alice's white rabbit, everyone seemingly late for a very important date.

But Marisa didn't have any such obligations, so with the sun wrapped around her shoulders, she settled comfortably into being a Parisian tourist with nowhere to go, and unlimited time to do whatever she wanted … at least for today.

After her espresso she headed for one of her favorite destinations—*La Place du Marché St. Catherine*, the one quiet street in Le Marais where cars were forbidden. On her hectic business trips to Paris it had been her private oasis, and then later she shared it with Jules.

Turning right and left and right again she found herself back where she started and sat down on a bench to catch her breath. She remembered Jules pulling out maps at such moments and laughing at her for having no sense of direction. But she'd never been good with maps and not wanting to draw attention to herself by pulling out her iPad, she'd have to find it on her own.

It was then that she looked up and saw the *La Place du Marché St. Catherine* sign pointing her in the right direction. She hurried toward it. Her favorite restaurant had the same burgundy striped awning and their table under the green-leafed plantain where they'd sat watching children play in the courtyard was vacant. She was no longer lost. A waiter in a white-starched shirt, black vest and red bow tie brought over a blackboard menu and she ordered the moules frites with a small pitcher of rosé wine.

She wrote in her journal that nothing had really changed and closed her eyes as she felt Jules's hand cover hers.

Have I told you lately that I love you? he said softly.

Blushing, she whispered, "Yes, but please tell me again."

The waiter placed a heaping bowl of steaming mussels in front of her and she closed her journal and put it aside. The mussels were as she remembered ... pure pleasure. She finished her lunch with a raspberry tart topped with Chantilly. This was certainly not a day for dieting.

Dropping a cube of sugar in her espresso, she sat back and held her face up to the mottled sunlight peaking through the leaves, creating an umbrella of bright green lace. She suddenly felt very tired and, to fight off the jet lag, she strolled around the square. A couple of similar age to her and Jules made room for her on their bench. But her heart ached hearing their shared laughter: the man's arm around the woman just like Jules's arm had once wrapped around her shoulders in this Square. It was too lonely in Paris without Jules, she thought, no matter how hard I try to conjure him up.

On the other side of the square, she recognized the mansard windows of the apartment building she and Jules had imagined living in someday. Wedged between planters of blooming red geraniums on an iron terrace was a rental sign and she had the sudden impulse to see it.

When she tapped on the door, a tiny elderly woman, her white hair pulled back in a tight bun, smiled and nodded yes to Marisa's request. As they climbed the ancient stone stairs Marisa's spirits lifted.

"C'est parfaît," she repeated as she peered into the petite furnished bedroom and bath. From its second-floor balcony she looked down on the children playing in the square. She wrote down the concierge's number and said she'd be in touch soon.

At Café Hugo on the corner of Place des Vosges, where she and Jules had often sat in the late afternoons, she sealed her future plan of living in Paris with a glass of kir champagne. And feeling confident she crossed over the tip of ile St. Louis, and took a brisk walk along the Left Bank. When she got back to the Hotel de Notre Dame she collapsed onto her bed, exhausted but very pleased with her small adventure.

At eight o'clock she arrived at a small, old restaurant called Le Robe et Le Palais for dinner with "the kids" as she'd fallen into calling them. From a distance she saw Martin and Cassandra in a heated conversation at the bar. Cassandra tossed her head away from Martin and scowled as he stormed off upset.

Marisa went over to her. "What was that all about?"

"He's being ridiculous. I responded to a text message from Ryan and Martin didn't like it. I told him what I choose to do is no concern of his and he said I was crazy and walked off. It's all Stuart's fault."

"Why Stuart?"

"If he hadn't posted our tour dates on Facebook, Ryan wouldn't know I was here."

"I see," said Marisa but she really didn't think Stuart was the only one who had broadcast their tour schedule and anyone could probably find them if they half tried. And why would Martin get so angry about Cassandra texting her former manager?

Unless Ryan was the "R" on the shredded invitation and her former manager was actually more than her former manager.

"So that's why you didn't want Stuart to post our tour on Facebook? You're trying to avoid your manager? Is he the one—"

"Former manager," said Cassandra cutting off any questions and staring down Marisa as if she too was somehow to blame. "I told Martin that I had texted Ryan back and said 'No. I don't want to see you.' But that didn't satisfy him. Now he's gone off to pout."

"Not for long," said Marisa, relieved to see Martin return.

"You picked a great restaurant, Marisa. Let's sit down. They're holding our table."

What with the wine, the delicious food and the amber, old-world ambiance of one of the oldest bistros in Paris, Martin and Cassandra, for the moment, forgot about their argument.

That was until Cassandra's phone rang in the middle of dessert. It was lying face up beside her on the white tablecloth and the screen lit-up before she had time to click it off. Marisa saw a good-looking man who could have been in an Esquire ad for Ray-Ban sunglasses or one of the actors in "Mad Men."

"Hey, don't let me stop you," said Martin with a shrug. "You're right. It's none of my business. If you want to hang out with that jerk, go ahead. But could you at least go somewhere else to do it."

Unaffected, Cassandra dropped the phone into her bag and excused herself to go to the bathroom.

Martin looked at Marisa with a bewildered expression. "Did you and Jules fight very often?"

"Of course we did, but mostly over insignificant things like directions when we traveled. He expected me to navigate and I was awful at reading maps."

"But was he ever jealous?"

Marisa laughed. "My goodness, yes. Aren't we all at some time? But he was good at hiding it. When someone flirted with me,

Jules would just get real quiet and withdraw and not say anything sweet to me until the next day."

She drifted off as her eyes followed a young couple being seated.

"Marisa?" She turned her attention back to Martin and continued. "When Camille's father visited—"

"Wait a minute," said Martin. "Camille isn't Jules's daughter? You were married to someone else before him?"

"Really?" chimed in Cassandra coming back to the table. "And you think I keep things to myself?"

"I was very young at the time. Back then you might say a child-bride. We outgrew each other."

"And was your first husband a musician too?" asked Martin.

She felt her face blush. "Yes, I'm afraid I have a thing for musicians. But they were quite different. The first one played guitar and was much more into being a pop star than a serious musician."

"You were married to a pop star?" asked Martin, even more amazed.

Embarrassed at having opened the doors into her past, Marisa said, "Shouldn't we be getting back to the hotel? Big day tomorrow."

"Are you kidding?" said Cassandra. "We're not going to let you slip away without telling us more than that. Who was this guy?"

"No one you would know. It was back in the Sixties." She laughed. "Before you were born!"

"Try me," said Martin. "My parents might have known of him. What was his name?"

"Johnny Knight."

"You're kidding. He was your husband? He was with the Invictors. That's amazing. Wasn't one of their big hits 'Live for Today'? Now it all makes sense." He broke into Knight's song: "*Sha la la, live for today.*"

"Okay. That's enough. I'd rather we talk about Jules."

"Then tell us how you two met?" said Cassandra.

"At Seventh Avenue South, a musician's bar in Manhattan. It

had two stories. Drinks downstairs and live bands upstairs. It was considered a very hip place to hang out."

"Wasn't that the Brecker Brothers' club?" said Martin. "Where everyone played."

Marisa nodded. "On our twenty-fifth anniversary, Jules and I went to see how it had changed. It was hard to see anything, but when our eyes got accustomed to the dark we found ourselves surrounded by seven-foot transvestites. They looked down on us as if we were a weird species. It kind of felt like the bar scene from *Indiana Jones*."

"And what were you doing at Seventh Avenue South over thirty years ago?" asked Cassandra.

"I had just moved to the City from L.A. and was checking out the downtown music scene with my friend Annie, a wardrobe mistress for one of the bands I managed. A guy squeezed between us at the crowded bar to order a drink and we started talking. I told him I'd just moved from L.A., and he told me that was a coincidence because he was having a drink with his girlfriend who was leaving New York that night on a plane to go back home to L.A."

Marisa smiled into the distance. "He didn't seem very upset about it. And before he left he asked for my phone number. Neither of us had a pen to write it down, so he said he'd memorize it and call me soon.

"Annie told me I was crazy giving out my phone number like that to some total stranger. But when I looked into his eyes I knew I could trust him." Marisa felt a wave of grief coming over her and swallowed it down with the port wine Cassandra had ordered. "We married the following year."

"Wow. What a great falling-in-love story," said Cassandra. "I wonder if that could ever happen to me?" She looked over at Martin. "What about you? Do you have a love story to share with us?"

He shook his head and holding his gaze on Cassandra said, "At least not yet."

"This is awesome," said Martin, standing outside Le Robe et Le Palais. "Paris at night. He looked toward the Metro. "How should we get back to the hotel?"

Cassandra slid her hand around Marisa's elbow. "Are you up to walking?"

"I'll never get to sleep after that crème brûlée if I don't. But I hope one of you has a better sense of direction than I do."

"Not to worry," said Cassandra. "I used to live here."

"Really?" they both said at once. "When was that?"

"I studied at Beaux-Arts." They continued to stare at her, waiting for more. "Let's walk and I'll tell you about my student days in Paris." Arm in arm, they meandered in the direction of the hotel and didn't notice a pinpoint of light radiating off a cell phone held by a man standing under the eaves of a building.

Ryan had taken the chance that CiCi hadn't turned off location services on the phone he'd given her back in New York. He hadn't heard from her since her road tour with Martin, until today when he texted her from his Paris hotel room and invited her over. He didn't like her saying no.

He grinned at the screen's gray pulsating circle as it moved up the street on a Paris map and then he stepped out of the shadows to track her on his cell phone from a safe distance.

26

My, this girl really knows how to paint a face, thought Marisa, when the next morning she saw Cassandra in the lobby flanked by two waiters serving her coffee and croissants. She must have opened up her make-up case before dawn to create such a stunning self-portrait. I wonder how she'd paint my portrait? Blur the wrinkles? Color in my faded lips?

The magazine interviews went smoothly. Cassandra evaded the probes as to why she left The Belles. The journalists from *Le Monde* and *Time Out* told her they had been worried about her when she disappeared from the scene and looked forward to hearing her comeback performance that night. Cassandra raved about Martin's trio and how thrilled she was to be working with such a brilliant composer who had given her the opportunity to write lyrics for his songs. Marisa found it quite ingenious and not at all like a diva when Cassandra suggested they interview Martin after the gig so they could take credit for discovering him.

The band was finishing their sound check when Cassandra and Marisa arrived at the New Morning club on Rue des Petites Écuries in the 10th arrondissement. Marisa hadn't been inside these doors for many years but it felt like she'd just gone out for a cigarette; it all felt so familiar. Though a fairly small venue, the New Morning was known for booking young unknown artists on their way up. If they became famous, they would usually return to the club out of loyalty. Concert posters on the walls testified to that fact.

Marisa pointed out an old poster advertising one of Jules's concerts at the club.

"Wow," said Martin. "That's really cool. And right next to John Scofield and Miles Davis."

"Mark my words, Martin. Someday you'll be on that wall." He shrugged. "Everything okay? All the equipment here?"

"Yeah, no problem. Damian had everything setup and ready when we got here. He really knows what he's doing." He turned to Cassandra. "The backstage dressing room is—"

"I know," said Cassandra, throwing back her head. "I've been here, too. If you haven't noticed there's a framed poster of The Belles in the lobby." She turned to Marisa and said, "Would you mind bringing a pot of tea to my dressing room? My throat's really dry from those interviews." Without waiting for a response, she picked up her make-up case and strode down the hallway, her long linen skirt hugging the contour of her hips.

Martin frowned. "There goes my diva! I learned during our stateside tour that she flips from Cass to CiCi before showtime. Why don't you let Damian bring her tea?"

"Oh, I don't mind. And Damian's busy enough. There's not much for me to do and I prefer to be useful anyway."

"Yeah, I can imagine it can get pretty boring hearing musicians play the same music night after night. I'll try to add a bit of Tabasco tonight."

"Tabasco?"

"Yeah. When I feel we're losing our audience I throw in a few sudden bars of improvised music to get us going again."

"Okay. But don't worry about me getting bored. There's always something that comes up that needs to be taken care of. Did I ever tell you the time—"

"Sorry," he interrupted, pointing over at Damian, "but I need to check on something."

She tried not to show her disappointment and reminded herself that her stories of the old days might not be that interesting to a younger generation. After all, when she started touring with bands, Martin hadn't been born. She shook her head in amazement.

When the New Morning opened its doors to ticket buyers, Marisa counted the tables filling up quickly. She gave up hers to a young group, looked for a back wall to lean against and watched with satisfaction as the crowd rushed for the last empty seats.

Trained from years of leaning against walls in clubs just like this one, Marisa could size up an audience response easily. She could tell this was a strong musicians crowd. They weren't celebrity-seekers; they were here for the music. A noticeably different crowd from the Blue Note; there would be fewer devoted fans shouting "CiCi, we love you."

She was right and both the band and CiCi rose to the occasion without any Tabasco sauce added. After each spellbound guitar solo and vocal feature, Marisa joined the thunderous clapping hands and took in the thrill that comes from representing a group that is really, really good.

After the last set, Rufus invited everyone to a local brasserie to celebrate. Flo's had been there since 1896 and the waiters still wore black uniforms with starched white aprons hanging low from their waists, heavy with the tools of their trade, while carrying immense trays, over-weighted with wine carafes, champagne, and bowls of oysters. The noise was deafening, and they had to push their way through a charged-up crowd to get to Rufus's reserved table.

Rufus was undaunted by the roar and talked loudly above the noise. How much he liked Martin's pacing of the set. His ending on the duet with CiCi was brilliant. But speaking aside to Marisa sitting next to him, he suggested she talk to Martin about giving CiCi more time on stage when they got to Germany. She told him that she had no influence with Martin when it came to things like that. It was his band and he was the bandleader.

After eating a dozen oysters and drinking too much champagne, Marisa excused herself to go to bed and left Rufus holding court, which he loved to do. When she pushed her way through the crowd and got to the street, the paparazzi were snapping pictures of some young musicians. She had no idea who they were. It was the stocky guy in sunglasses ushering them into the limo while holding off the flashing cameras that held her attention. She was trying to place his face when Martin came running out and insisted on seeing her to a taxi.

Cassandra had known immediately who it was. She saw Ryan leaving the restaurant but turned away before he saw her.

Early the next morning, Marisa, Cassandra, Damian, and the band boarded a 9-passenger rental van and headed south for a club date that evening in Lyon, a six-hour drive. After telling Marisa how much they loved Paris and hoped to go back soon, Stuart and Carlos, in the middle row, turned their attention to Martin who was sitting upfront and playing a recording from last night's gig. Cassandra, in the back row with Marisa, stuck earbuds in her ears and effectively shut out Marisa who eventually leaned her head against the window.

She and Jules had driven out of Paris in a similar van with him listening to the previous night's performance, raving over the best moments and moaning over the tunes that needed work. Just like now, there was no place for her in the conversation.

The Lyon applause was similar to the one at New Morning; the audience on their feet at the end of each set, stomping for more music. The group was starting to hit their stride. Marisa absorbed the applause, acknowledging to herself that Martin could become quite successful if his manager took all the right steps. But that wouldn't be her job. She'd be more than satisfied to just get them through this tour. She had other things she wanted to do.

Really, Marisa, what things?

"Don't you worry, my dear, I have plans. First there is the memoir to finish."

Good. When are you going to do that?

"I don't know!"

The group got a few extra hours of sleep before driving the next day to their first important festival date that night at Cannes where the international press would be largely present. It was a thousand-seat concert hall, which put a lot more pressure on the band; they were accustomed to playing only club dates. They piled into the van and headed for the A7, l'autoroute du soleil; the main artery flowing down to the Mediterranean coast from Paris to Provence.

Every summer, year after year, she and Jules had taken this route to their summer retreat. And would have this year if—

Say it, Marisa. It's okay to say I'm dead.

She leaned her head out the window and let the sweet, balmy air brush away her tears.

Time, Marisa, it takes time.

She felt Jules's fingertips touching her cheek or was it just the wind?

Marisa smiled at the band's stunned expressions when they pulled up under the yellow awning of the Majestic Hotel facing the Mediterranean in Cannes. Only Cassandra remained nonplussed as bellboys in red jackets and matching caps opened their doors and started taking out the luggage.

Re-remembering when she was last here, Marisa jumped when Martin called out, "Hey, are you sure this is the right hotel?"

"Not to worry. The festival is covering the rooms."

"Yeah, but what about the twenty dollars for java in this joint?"

Rufus had asked Marisa if the band might prefer a cheaper hotel around the corner for that very reason, but she'd said no. A selfish decision; she wanted to stay at the Majestic and she dragged the others along. She told Martin about a cheap café a few minutes away but now they needed to check in and get some rest before tonight's concert.

At the front desk, Marisa handed out keys and told the group they'd be picked up at six to go to the sound check. In rusty French she explained to the bellman that the guys would prefer to take their own instruments to their rooms. Cassandra left her baggage with the bellman and headed for the elevator.

Rufus had warned Marisa that the Majestic had been renovated since she was there five years ago. But standing under the remaining chandeliers, she found it easy to turn back the chapters of her life story and let the vivid memories come flooding in.

Not wanting to face an empty hotel room, Marisa took a stroll along La Croisette, the old seaport. Yes, she agreed silently, the hotel had changed but La Croisette was remarkably untouched by current styles. Like an old postcard, French men and women were still walking their bejeweled miniature dogs and the same old men were parading their young paramours.

Restaurant hawkers motioned to Marisa to come in and taste their fresh crustaceans, but she shook her head at the beckoning men in oyster-stained blue overalls and walked on.

At 6 P.M. Cassandra floated down the hotel lobby staircase and slipped into the first car. Marisa got in after her and the band followed in the second car.

In the festival hall's lobby, Cassandra, with make-up case in hand and clothing bag hung over her arm, strode off to her dressing room, telling Marisa to call her when needed for the sound check. Does that girl ever *not* know where she's going? wondered Marisa. She took Martin, Carlos, and Stuart down the theater's center aisle, passing rows and rows of empty red velvet seats and climbed the steps onto the stage.

She felt giddy imagining what it must be like for these three young musicians to look out over the empty seats soon to be filled with a thousand people coming to hear them play.

"Aunt Marisa, do you really think we can do this?" whispered Martin.

"Just play like you have been playing up until now. The rest will take care of itself."

And it did. The concert was more than they could have hoped for. The audience and the promoter were ecstatic. After the concert, the promoter couldn't wait to escort them to dinner at a secret, celebrity restaurant.

One could easily drive by the Cove's humble, black-painted shack without any idea of what delights were behind its dimly lit entrance. The host and hostess, Philippe and Carole, greeted their guests with Kir Royales. "A million bubbles and hand-picked Cassis grapes," said Marisa, clinking her glass against Martin's. "A gift from the gods."

A table for eight had been reserved for them against a glass-plated wall that looked down on the Mediterranean surf. A hundred candles reflected in the windows as waves hurled against the glass and then pulled away leaving behind a foamy brine, giving one the sensation of being at sea, unanchored and adrift.

During a four-course meal, their hostess Carole strummed an acoustic guitar and sang folk songs from her Rumanian homeland. Martin was invited to join her but he demurred politely. For dessert, crêpes Suzettes were set ablaze with cognac. Everyone thought this was the final dramatic touch of their evening when they were surprised by a sudden blare of light spotlighting a rocky precipice outside the window.

The host, Philippe, had changed out of his three-piece suit and was now standing on the edge of the precipice wearing only a black Speedo, his muscular, bronze torso glowing in the light. He stretched up on to his toes and froze.

Cassandra gripped Martin's hand. "Oh my god, he's not going to . . ."

The host, transforming into Superman, took a flying leap up into the starry sky and plunged headfirst into the crashing waves below. It wasn't until his head emerged from the black sea that Cassandra released Martin's hand and joined in the applause.

In the lobby of the Majestic, everyone thanked Marisa for a wonderful evening. Cassandra got into the elevator with Martin's baseball jacket draped over her silk pantsuit. He'd given it to her at the restaurant when he saw her shivering after the diver dropped into the sea.

Now it was Marisa's turn to shiver. Five years ago she rode up the same elevator with Jules after dinner at The Cove to celebrate their thirtieth anniversary. She hadn't mentioned that to anyone; some things are better left unsaid.

The next morning Cassandra and Martin were banging on Marisa's door until she let them in. Martin spread the international morning newspapers on the floor, opened to the reviews of last night's performance. "Look, Marisa," Martin said, "We're a hit!"

The headlines in the music journals and dailies were unanimous. *Exciting new band featuring CiCi Belle's extraordinary comeback. — Martin Starks is an exceptional new guitar virtuoso.* The online music reviews were the same; reviews that Marisa hoped would go viral across the Internet cloud.

And thinking of viruses, she picked up the phone and asked Stuart, Carlos and Damian to join them in her room for breakfast on the balcony. Then she called Dr. Jazz, the in-house doctor. He arrived an hour later and gave everyone B12 booster shots. Marisa was taking no chances on anyone getting sick during the grueling tour in front of them. Too much at stake to take chances.

27

It was a short flight from Nice to Munich. After showers at their hotel, the group arrived at Jazzclub Unterfahrt to see a crowd lined up around the block. A thrilled club manager, Ina, rushed out to inform them that a third set had been added after the scheduled two sets sold-out. Proof that the social media cloud Marisa had hoped for had reached Munich. This free, spontaneous publicity still amazed her. Back in the day, bands were popularized through the press and the radio airplay, strategically coordinated with a new record release. It took months to build an audience and now she was witnessing an overnight success.

And what lifted her spirits even higher (while leaning against the back wall of yet another dimly lit music club) was watching the audience's enthusiastic response to the group. CiCi received top billing on the posters, and her fans had come to hear her sing, but they were soon swept up in the trio's sophisticated and powerful instrumentals. They listened and clapped hard after every solo. And for good reason. The band's confidence level was responding to the groundswell of appreciation, which was starting to happen around them. They gave another rousing performance.

The only person who wasn't happy after the gig was Cassandra. When they all got back to the hotel lobby she turned on Martin. "The opening instrumental numbers are too long and you're all taking way too many solos. I'm the featured singer in this group and not somebody standing ogle-eyed in the wings waiting for permission to perform."

Martin kept cool but anyone could tell he was seething

underneath. "I haven't changed the set order. You get the same amount of time on stage as you've had on the other gigs."

Cassandra rushed off to her room without saying good night to anyone. "Just ignore her," said Martin. "She'll get over it."

Marisa wasn't sure that was true. She knew that problems could fester when groups didn't talk things out.

Cassandra wasn't the only one she was concerned about. Stuart was always late for the "lobby call" (the time they agreed to meet in the morning to leave in the van for the next gig). Everyone would sneer at him, even groan, but he didn't notice. Marisa decided they must have a group meeting, but didn't see any free time for several more days.

Munich was the first of seven consecutive cities on the German club tour, with a routine as predicable as a metronome: Wake up. Check out. Pack van. Get in van. Drive. Check in to next hotel. Play gig. Sleep. Wake up. Check out. Pack van. Get in van. Drive. Play gig. Sleep.

Established since Paris, everyone knew their places in the van. Martin sat shotgun or switched with Damian and drove; Marisa and Cassandra shared the "girls" backseat; Stuart and Carlos commandeered the middle seats. On the backseat, Marisa read books she'd saved on her Kindle and Cassandra withdrew behind her earbuds or wrote in her journal. The musicians listened to music on their devices or texted their friends or leaned forward in their seats and listened to last night's gig.

Marisa saw that Cassandra kept her cell phone in her bag and never answered it when it rang. When she asked why, Cassandra mumbled something about it being a gift from Ryan and she only kept it for emergencies. Marisa wanted to ask what emergency could possibly happen on this tour, but Cassandra had put her earbuds back on and turned to the window. The last time that Marisa felt any real warmth from Cassandra was at the nail salon in Manhattan and after the concert in Cannes. The girl had done a turnaround and only talked to Marisa when she needed her help. Marisa was unfazed; she'd been through this before with singers.

By the third day out on the drive between Mannheim and Frankfort, Marisa felt road fever in the air when the band didn't listen to the Mannhiem gig. Instead, they squirmed in their seats and demanded more stops to stretch cramped legs and to buy snacks. Everyone felt the strained relationship between Martin and Cassandra. Since their argument in Munich they avoided each other and slept in separate rooms.

Frankfort's Jazzkeller was a small intimate basement club, like the Unterfahrt in Munich. When CiCi came up on the small stage wearing a satin gown, even she had to agree she was overdressed. She gave a solid performance but the fun on stage had stopped. Her only comment as they drove back to the hotel in the van was that she hoped the next venue was not in another damp, seedy basement.

Stuart glared at her. "God, you are so out of it, Cassie. You have no idea how great it is to be playing these famous jazz clubs. We're playing in some of the same places as Monk, Mingus, and Chet Baker. This is as good as a gig at the Village Vanguard in New York. And Marisa and Rufus went to a lot of trouble to get us into these clubs." Cassandra ignored him and a heavy silence followed.

The next morning everyone was in the lobby waiting for Stuart as usual but this time Martin had lost his patience. He wanted to get to Berlin in time to rehearse an instrumental he'd composed on the road and, if it felt right, wanted to add to their set.

When Stuart strolled into the lobby, Marisa, worried about a fight, got between him and Martin. Stuart apologized, said he forgot to set his alarm, and promised not to do it again, but Martin was still angry.

He wasn't the only one. Cassandra was at the front desk grilling the receptionist about some letter she found under her door. She wanted to know who dropped it off and when and how did he know her room number? The poor clerk had just come on duty and his English was obviously not up to Cassandra's fast-clipped demands with an American accent. When she got no intelligible answers to her questions, she stomped out of the hotel and took her seat in the van. If anger steamed, it would be rising from her ears and nostrils. No one wanted to get near her.

The usual banter between the guys was on hold. Just like yesterday everyone kept to themselves as much as they could in such close quarters. They were just pulling out of their second pit stop, when Cassandra leaned toward Stuart and startled everyone when she yanked off his QuietComfort Bose headphones. Stuart twisted around in his seat and said, "Hey! What are you doing?" All eyes were on Cassandra.

"I have something to say to you, Stuart, and I want to make sure you get it. I've asked you nicely before and now I'm telling you. Take our itinerary off your Facebook page. I'm being harassed and bothered by fans because every move we make is reported on your page."

He smirked. "You got that wrong, little diva. After you got so pissed off, I took the hotels off my page. But as far as the tour dates, I have no control over social media. News on our tour is everywhere. So get over it."

"Liar!" Cassandra hissed. She yanked his headphones off and threw them out the window.

Martin slammed on the brakes and Marisa grabbed on to Cassandra just before she hit her head as the van lurched off the road, throwing everyone forward. Martin jumped out of the van and jerked open the side door. "Get out!"

Cassandra shouted back, "No!"

"Get out or I'll come in there and drag you out."

The guys stared straight ahead and even Marisa kept quiet. This was between Cassandra and Martin now and it wasn't her place to interfere. They needed to do this. The tension had been building and was starting to affect the group's performances. There was a dead silence.

Without Marisa stepping in, Cassandra knew Martin would pull her out of the van. She got out. Stuart slammed the door shut behind her and shouted out the window, "Go get my headphones."

Martin came back around the van, got in, and sped back onto the autobahn.

"Wow, dude, that was serious," said Carlos, who hardly ever spoke. Marisa could see Martin's angry eyes in the rearview mirror and kept quiet.

Stuart had once told Marisa that Martin was the nicest guy in the world until someone pushed him too far and then watch out—you don't mess with Martin Starks. Now she knew who could push him too far. She remembered what Miles had found out on Facebook about Martin's temper. Certainly he wouldn't strand Cassandra on the autobahn for too long. Or would he?

She looked at Cassandra's empty seat, relieved to see she had taken her purse. This might be just the emergency when she'd need her phone. The make-up kit had fallen on the floor. It stared up at Marisa like a puppy abandoned by her mistress. She was about to tell Martin he had to go back when Stuart leaned forward, "Hey dude, what about my headphones?"

Martin spun off at the next exit, circled over the overpass, and headed back.

Cassandra stood right where they'd left her. She held Stuart's headphones in one hand and her cell phone in the other. She dropped the phone in her purse when she saw the van. Marisa opened the door and offered her hand. She was surprised when Cassandra accepted it.

In an uncomfortable silence they arrived at the Berlin Hilton and everyone rushed off to their rooms. Marisa sighed with relief to finally be alone. She pulled up her messages on the iPad and opened an e-mail from Rufus: Warsaw festival offer. Other band cancelled. All expenses paid. Plus $2000 fee. Fly tomorrow to Warsaw. Play one night and then fly to North Sea. Holding date so let me know asap if you accept offer. It could be fun for the guys.

She wanted to ignore the offer but the choice wasn't hers. She didn't want to rely on text messages so she called Cassandra and the band and asked them to come to room 203 for an urgent meeting. There were lots of groans but everyone trudged in a few minutes later.

Carlos and Stuart sat on the couch facing Cassandra, who sat holding a notepad and a pen. Martin stood at the window and looked out on Berlin's industrial towers. Marisa told them about the offer and aired her concerns. "I've scheduled the tour so we could arrive at the North Sea Festival in Holland on Friday afternoon and have a long overdue night off. You'll be able to hang out, hear other bands, and meet up with your musician friends. If we add the gig in Warsaw, it means nine performances without a break plus two extra flights."

Stuart and Carlos still loved the idea. They'd heard there was a hip jazz scene in Warsaw and wanted to check it out. And though they didn't say it, they had to be thinking it meant not getting in the van tomorrow with Cassandra for another six-hour drive. They promptly voted yes.

Martin joined the guys on the couch. Cassandra scribbled furiously on her notepad and held it up: NO WAY!!! THROAT RAW. CAN'T TALK. AIRPLANES DRY CAUSE MORE DAMAGE. MUST REST BEFORE FESTIVALS.

"Oh c'mon, CiCi girl," said Stuart. "You singers are paranoid. You need to let up on your anxieties. Warsaw's gonna be fun." Cassandra put down her notepad and crossed her arms over her chest.

Marisa wondered if Cassandra was as miserable on the Belle tours as she was on this one. And did she always use her voice as an excuse to avoid confronting things she didn't want to do, not even willing to talk about it.

Marisa shook her head at the memory of a past tour she had managed behind the Iron Curtain in Poland (back when it was still called the Iron Curtain). She remembered a Polish girl taken from the bass player's hotel room by the police and then forced to walk home in a snowstorm. The band's saxophone player was arrested for buying souvenirs on the black market, and the diva's passport stolen, which meant Marisa had to spend an entire thankless day at the American consulate working things out. And then, exhausted, she stayed up until dawn and drank vodka with the Polish promoter as they counted out and exchanged Polish zloties for U.S. dollars. Everyone on the tour, all fifteen, stuffed black market dollars in their money belts so they could get it through customs and out of Poland.

She was curious to know what it was like now but not curious enough to actually go there … there were more pressing needs. She looked up to see everyone staring at her.

"Marisa," said Martin, as he shook her shoulder. "We're waiting for your vote?"

She looked over at Cassandra. "I vote we pass on Warsaw. There'll be other chances for you guys to play there."

Martin then voted no.

When Cassandra left, she held up the notepad to Marisa: THANKS.

28

The Quasimodo gig in Berlin had ended with standing ovations but the next day as they drove the three-hour drive to the next gig in Hamburg, there were no high-fives given, no laughter, and no words spoken.

The Fabrik, previously a huge machine factory whose steel-girded architecture remained intact, was a huge club, and already a thousand tickets had been sold. The Belles had even played there, which should have made Cassandra feel at home, especially when she saw above The Martin Starks Trio's marquis sign, in larger letters, special guest CICI BELLE.

But in the dressing room, she complained that the club manager should have brought the pitcher of water she'd asked for and asked Marisa to get it. Marisa was heading out the door when Martin stopped her and said he'd take care of it. He brought back a full pitcher, smiled, and poured Cassandra a glass. Marisa was relieved to see he wanted to patch things up.

Cassandra must have thought the same thing and looked up from brushing on her face powder to smile. That was when he anointed her head with ice water. She jumped up, screaming and flailing at him but he grabbed her wrists. He yelled into her dripping wet face, "Don't you ever ask any of us to go fetch anything for you again. Where the hell do you get this idea that we owe you something? Did you put the band together? Set up the tour? Plan the sets? Work out the music? No. If it weren't for Marisa and me, you'd be mopping up puke at the Bitter End. And do you thank us? No. You do nothing. Nothing but bitch.

We're all sick and tired of it. Do you hear me? Sick and tired of it."

He stomped out of the room and slammed the door behind him.

Cassandra collapsed into a chair and buried her face in her hands. Marisa handed her a towel and tried to put her arm around Cassandra. "I'm so sorry. Martin shouldn't have done that." Cassandra pushed her away and sobbed into the towel. "Please, just leave me alone."

Marisa hesitated but the door opened and Damian stuck his head in, "Marisa, I need you up front." She promised Cassandra she'd be right back but Damian was having trouble balancing the sound and she had to stay out front.

The band played Cassandra's entrance cue several times before she finally made an appearance. On her way up to the stage, she grabbed a drink off someone's table. She took hold of the mic in her other hand and introduced the musicians as her karaoke backup band. When she finally did sing, Stuart covered up her voice by playing loudly on the drums. She threw down the mic and walked off stage seemingly unaware of the shouts and boos from the audience.

Marisa rushed backstage but couldn't find Cassandra in the dressing room. The band continued to play without her and when the audience started up a chant and demanded her return, Martin invited them to stay on for the second set when she'd be back. Many of her fans walked out and asked for ticket refunds.

Martin didn't let it faze him. He and the band laid into a blistering funky groove. The audience got into the music and was soon up dancing on the wooden floor.

Marisa found Cassandra at the bar, ushered her back into the dressing room and locked the door after ordering a pot of coffee.

"Don't do this to yourself. You're not getting back at Martin, you're damaging your own reputation," said Marisa. "You'll regret it later. I know you're tired. We all are." Cassandra leaned into her and they walked back and forth in the dressing room. There were many knocks on the door but Marisa told everyone to go away.

When she was sure Cassandra could be left alone to redo her make-up, she went out and found Martin. He looked at her and shrugged. "Whatever" was all he said when she told him Cassandra was sober enough to do the next set.

Cassandra's voice was hoarse. She couldn't hit the high notes and tripped several times on her gown. She stayed in the wings for most of the set and Martin didn't call her out to perform their "Peggy Blue" duet.

After the gig, Martin came to Marisa's hotel room expecting a sympathetic ear. He didn't get it. Yes, she understood his need to set things straight with Cassandra but not before a performance and not with a jug of water. This was an important venue and they had barely avoided a disaster.

Marisa wanted no more backstage dramas. From now on he was to stay out of Cassandra's dressing room. The two most important dates of the tour were yet to come and she told Martin he needed to focus on the music not his personal feelings. She assured him that once they got to the North Sea Festival everything would work out. It was one thing for Cassandra to make a fool of herself at the Fabrik but she wouldn't dare do that at a festival. No. No. Not at a festival.

Martin sank down in a chair. "I know I got out of hand tonight but what was I thinking when I asked her to be in my band?" He shook his head. "What was I thinking? Never get hooked on a beautiful woman with a beautiful voice, especially when you have no idea who the real person is behind that voice. I have to say it felt so good to play out tonight without being concerned about *her* vocal numbers. The band was jammin' really good. Like before we joined forces with little ole Miss CiCi Belle."

Marisa thought Martin had fallen for more than a voice but didn't think this was the time to say so. She did try to explain that, yes, Cassandra was difficult to work with, but her fear of throat fatigue was real. One inflamed nodule could crack her voice for several days. And if she wasn't careful, damage her voice permanently.

"Okay. I get what you're saying but I still don't feel sorry for her. I promise to stay away from her, but Montreux is my last gig with CiCi Belle."

Martin wasn't Marisa's only visitor that night. She had just gotten in between the cold sheets with her iPad when she had to get back out and open the door to Cassandra.

"After all you've done for me," she rasped, "I wanted you to be the first to know that I'm leaving the tour. I've made arrangements for someone to pick me up here. I can't take this abuse, my voice is raw." Her eyes brimmed with tears that could melt anyone's heart except, perhaps, Martin's.

"You're shivering," said Marisa. "Come get under the blanket." She handed Cassandra a glass of water and a pill. "Take this."

"What is it?"

"It's great for morning hangovers. And I think you're going to have a whopper. Do you want to tell me what took you over the top tonight?"

"Ice cold water for a start. I felt so humiliated, so hurt … this tour has been a horror. I bought a fifth of Jack this morning and put it in my make-up kit. And once I start … I don't stop."

Marisa half smiled. "I see. So your make-up kit doubles as a first-aid kit."

"I guess you could say that. I thought I had my drinking under control, but when Martin threw that water on me, I lost it. He's not my only problem, not by a long shot." She swallowed the pill and gulped down the water.

Marisa hoped Cassandra would speak about her other problems but when she didn't, Marisa said, "Look, about quitting … are you sure you don't want to sleep on it? It's been a rough day and you might see things differently tomorrow. Have you considered your loyal fans and how disappointed they'd be if you didn't show up? If you leave now, tonight's performance will be a black mark against you, but it'll be forgotten when the international press reviews come in after your festival performances. You have a brilliant career in front of you, Cassandra, don't give it up over

Martin's misbehavior. I'm sure tomorrow he'll tell you he's sorry."

Marisa put her arm around Cassandra and held her until she stopped crying.

"I'm okay now," said Cassandra, sitting up on the edge of the bed. "And you're right. It wouldn't help me at all to leave now. But I can't imagine anything other than a miracle that would put Martin and me back on the same stage after Montreux."

You're probably right, thought Marisa, after Cassandra left. But at the same time there was another miracle taking place. She'd kept it to herself because she didn't want to make Martin nervous, but the groundswell that had started in Cannes hadn't stopped. The gig at the Fabrik was a further example of what he could do on stage. The audience went wild and not because of CiCi. Video clips of the band's performance were climbing the YouTube hit charts and there was incredible anticipation over the Martin Starks Trio at the upcoming festivals; the festival dates might even sell-out, which was almost unheard of for a new band.

Cassandra paced her room after leaving Marisa's, arguing with her other self.

She stopped to pour Courvoisier into a plastic snifter she carried in her make-up kit and brought the rim to her lips, swallowing the amber liquid like a spoonful of honey. The pleasurable warm sensation flowed down her raw, aching throat.

But moments later her mind raged again, not leaving her alone: *They've forgotten who you are. You're the star here. There'd be no tour if you hadn't come along on this joyride. You're the one who's at risk. It's your reputation on the line.*

She stared at the empty snifter. *Oh, go ahead.* She poured another shot and tossed it down her throat. Slapping her arms against her thighs, she paced the room again.

Martin was deluded in Munich when fans started fawning on him backstage and he thought he was the star. You never should have fallen for his act back in New York when he told you how much he loved your voice. Loved your lyrics. Even loved you. What a laugh. He was just trying to pull you in, use you, like everyone else.

She sat on the bed, pressing her hands against her ears, but the voice was relentless.

And now because he suddenly has a minor following, and let me repeat, minor following, he thinks he can drop you. Does he really think you don't know he gives the band more solos, cuts into your time onstage? Gloating while you're stuck in the wings. And then to throw water in your face like you were some whore.

Well you got back at him didn't you. All you needed was a little courage. The next shot spilled over. *Only Ryan can help you now. What a fool you were to think you could make it without him.*

Cassandra picked up the cell phone. Her link to Ryan. That's how he knew Marisa and the band had mistreated her—knew how she dreaded getting into that horrid little van every day. She'd texted him from the dressing room after Martin had drenched her. He texted right back, promising to come for her after the Valentino's performance in Bremen, or he'd send his driver, Mike.

It's all Marisa's fault. She talked you into staying with that crap about disappointing your fans. What about your voice? What if it cracks in Montreux? Then it'll be too late. Just like it was with The Belles when they abused your voice and had to cancel dates because you couldn't sing. Then they were sorry.

Cassandra turned the phone on. There was a message from DiDi. They were finishing their tour in Geneva and wanted to know how her tour was going. They'd heard nothing but good things and wished they could see her perform with her new band.

Hell, why not? She tapped: Can you come to montreux after geneva? We can talk then. I miss you and mimi.

She had just sent the text to DiDi when the phone beeped and lit up: Cannot get away. Mike there tomorrow afternoon. Will drive you to paris. Love you madly.

She wrote back: Change in plans. Finishing tour. Fans counting on me. Don't be too angry.

She turned off the phone and dumped it in the wastebasket. But she couldn't turn off her raging mind: *Who's going to help you now? Marisa? Ha. We know where her loyalty lies.*

But maybe I can change that, she thought. Appeal to her as a woman. Take her out to lunch in Rotterdam. Tell her the truth about Ryan. Ask her to be my manager.

No, girl, you're on the wrong track. Only Ryan can help you now. Without him you'll soon be back wiping up the bar at the Bitter End.

She picked the phone out of the trash and texted Ryan again: Sorry. Can you come to rotterdam? I have tomorrow night off.

Cassandra woke up on the floor with the phone vibrating and ringing inside her aching head. She crawled around until she found Ryan's face staring up at her from the lit screen. The empty bottle of cognac lying next to him.

She moaned, turned it off, dropping it back into the wastebasket.

Unable to pull herself up on the bed, she curled up on the floor and rocked back and forth, crying out, "What have I done? Somebody please help me."

29

The next morning they were on the road to Holland's North Sea Festival. After North Sea, they would fly to Geneva for the last festival concert. No one in the van was talking. But there was an exciting edge to the silence. Marisa peered over the others' heads to see out the front window as if she were in a drive-in and didn't want to miss a scene.

Hours later, when the van took the Rotterdam exit, she was startled out of her nap. "Where are you going, Damian? This isn't right."

"Marisa, where have you been?" he teased. "The festival's been in Rotterdam ever since the concert hall in den Haag was torn down seven years ago. Don't you read your own itineraries?"

"Oh dear." She smiled at the curious looks. "Sorry. I must have dozed off and forgot where we were." Everyone continued to stare at her, so she fumbled in her purse and pulled out her iPhone and pretended she had to look at an important text message.

Ten minutes later, Damian pulled up to the front entrance of the Best Western ART Hotel, the band's home for the next two nights. It was an architectural wonder. It had an enormous bottom floor with a narrow tower on top where the rooms perched. Cassandra jumped out, ignored everyone, and headed for the hotel lobby with just her make-up case. Martin looked at Marisa and shrugged his shoulders as if to say, we won't have to deal with her much longer will we.

Cassandra had already checked in and left the lobby. I understand, thought Marisa. I can't wait to be alone in my room either. This well-deserved night off will do us all good.

Marisa handed out swag bags to the band: North Sea T-shirts, baseball caps, festival programs. All-weekend passes to the halls, wristband identities, and free beer coupons, which pleased the guys the most.

Marisa went to her room, closed the door behind her, and collapsed on the bed. *Good job*, she told herself. *Two weeks on the road and you didn't forget anything—yet anyway. Well today was a bit of an embarrassment. No, you're not senile. You just need some rest.*

She opened her iPad and was happy to read several e-mails from old friends who'd seen her name on the list of managers present. Everyone was pleased to hear she was back on the road again. There was also an e-mail from Rufus. He would arrive at the hotel at six and had made dinner reservations for just the two of them. What fun, she thought.

Before a much-needed nap, she sent off text messages to the band and told them to have a good time on their free night but not to over indulge. Then she sent a message to Cassandra and reminded her of the four interviews the next morning. It surprised her when Cassandra wrote right back: Thanks for my luggage. Had to go bathroom. Marisa smiled. She'd often used that same excuse herself to get away from everyone quickly.

The house phone blared like an alarm clock and woke her up bleary eyed from her nap. She thought she was at home and reached across the bed to answer it and nearly fell between the two beds onto the floor.

She heard Rufus's voice when she grabbed the receiver. "Did you forget our dinner tonight? I'm here in the lobby."

She pulled herself up straight to turn on the light. She squinted at her watch but couldn't read it and had no idea where she'd put her glasses. She feigned alertness and said brightly, "I'll be right down. Just give me a few minutes to freshen up."

Dinner with Rufus was always delightful and delicious. As she used to say as a complimentary joke, he gave great dinner. Somehow he always knew the best restaurant wherever they were on the road. Her New York exercise program had paid off and she liked what she saw in the mirror when she shimmied into her slim, silk dress. So did Rufus by the look he gave her when she walked toward him in the lobby.

"The road has done you wonders," he said as he looked her over and then gave her one of his memorable bear hugs. They always made her feel well loved and appreciated. She could do with more of those hugs. "You must have had a great time with those youngsters."

Someone stopped them on the way out who looked vaguely familiar. "Marisa? Is that you? Great to see you. You look just the same! Are you back on the road?"

"No, just a visit. I wanted to see if North Sea was still as good in its new location."

"I can tell you. It's not. But let's get together later."

They walked on and she asked Rufus who that was but he couldn't remember either.

Seated at a table by an open window that overlooked the Rhine, she felt Jules's caress in the soft warm breeze and didn't hear Rufus when he ordered their drinks and dinner. Jules would have wanted to be there with Rufus, his old friend.

The wine arrived and after the traditional tasting, they touched glasses. "Santé."

"So tell me about the tour."

She relaxed in the leather-cushioned booth and told him how successful the tour had been and, as they had planned, the band was really tight after the German club dates.

"Good! Then let's film both festivals. We'll get some clips we can put out on YouTube and build on the group's momentum."

"Well, I said the band was doing great but that doesn't mean they're doing great with CiCi Belle."

"Oh? That's bad news. What happened?"

"Both Martin and Cassandra have told me separately that they don't want to work with each other after Montreux. Just between you and me, it's Cassandra who's going over the deep-end. She worries constantly about her voice and she really hates being with the guys in a van."

"So it's true, what I read about Berlin. She was drunk onstage."

Marisa nodded yes. "Unless something extraordinary happens to bring them back together, Montreux is the last gig."

"You don't seem very upset about it."

Marisa sighed. "Actually, I'm not. She's definitely difficult to work with and she doesn't know how to work with the band. They like to change things around and they're improvisers. She's used to a precise set list."

"Isn't that a bit harsh? She's probably not used to the competition on stage from musicians. She's used to a well-paid back-up band that's there for her and gives her what she wants."

"Well, that's just not possible with this band. They've really tried hard to support her on stage, particularly Martin. If she would at least meet them halfway, like she did in New York and at the gigs in France. Now she's being an ice queen on stage and off ... hardly speaks to any of us ... says she has to protect her voice."

Rufus shrugged. "She's a singer. What do you expect?"

She laughed. "Now you sound like Jules."

"Ah yes. Jules avoided singers, if he could, didn't he?"

"If she'd just let go a bit."

It was easier to talk about Martin. "Martin has a sound like Scofield—blues infested, forward driven grooves—but still a style all his own. You have a major artist on your hands."

"*I* do?"

"I guess I should tell you." She took a sip of wine. "The truth is, Montreux is going to be my last gig. I don't know how you keep it up year after year, Rufus. I need a place to hang my hat and it's not in a hotel room."

"But have you figured out where that is?"

"No. But I will figure it out. I just don't want to think about it until the tour is over."

"Marisa, that's only a couple of days from now."

"I know." She smiled. "It'll come to me. But as far as what happens next to Martin, he's seen what you accomplished on this tour, and he wants to work with you."

"Have you talked to him?"

"Not yet. I plan to at the end of the tour. But, mark my words, Martin will be a major player in the music scene. I see it every time he plays to a live audience. They just love him and he loves them. They can't get enough of each other. He just needs the right team—and that includes you, Rufus."

"Thanks, Marisa. I've never known you to be wrong about your artists, but I'll have to see for myself tomorrow night when they play in front of two thousand people."

"Two thousand! But I thought the band was booked in one of the smaller venues."

"It was. But the festival director saw the strong online presence and he saw how fast the tickets sold with CiCi Belle as the featured singer. When another band cancelled, he thought it was worth the risk to put our band in the empty slot … the Congo stage."

"Did he increase the fee?"

"Ah Marisa." He tipped his glass against hers. "Don't worry. I'm looking out for your band. Three thousand dollars was added to the contract and there's a guaranteed percentage from the ticket sales."

"Wow. That's good news. But the program and posters were printed weeks ago. How will anyone know where they're playing?"

He laughed. "You have been away for a while. The Internet has transformed the way we advertise artists. Any band changes are posted on the festival website and on Facebook and Twitter."

She shook her head in amazement.

"I still want to video tomorrow night. If CiCi leaves, we can just cut out her songs. That is, if there's enough material without her."

"No problem. Martin just added another tune he wrote on the road. Now that they're more confident, the band is taking on more instrumental solos. That's part of the problem between Cassandra and Martin."

A waiter set down a steaming plate in front of her. She gasped. "Rufus. How could you possibly remember that I love Peking duck?"

"Bon appetit," he said with that roguish twinkle in his eye that she remembered from years ago.

She hadn't expected it when he told her that he'd remarried. She'd known his wife. The four of them had spent good times together when she and Jules visited them at their house in Munich after their tours.

"And you, Marisa? I can't imagine you being a widow forever nor do I think Jules would want you to be."

Serge came to mind but she quickly decided to keep him to herself. "It's too soon, Rufus. That's the furthest thing from my mind right now. Maybe in the next season of my life I'll go it alone."

Rufus confided in her that he was thinking about retirement or at least he wanted the youngsters in his office to take on more responsibility. "It's really not my thing anymore. It's all business now. My company still turns a good profit with the festival tours but the big money is in merchandise."

"Merchandise! Martin wants to be paid for playing his music not selling T-shirts."

"And he will. As long as there are talented, creative musicians, there'll be a venue to play their music and a live audience to listen. They've sold seventy thousand tickets to one hundred fifty performances on thirteen stages at this festival. The record companies had to find new ways to profit from their artists now that recorded music can be downloaded on Internet."

Marisa, suddenly worried, put down her fork. "But how will Martin survive if there are no royalties from record sales?"

"Don't worry. He can still make money from his performance fees and when he gets a record deal he'll get a percentage from the merchandise they sell at his concerts."

"My things have changed since my heyday in the music biz. I think it was more fun back then."

"To tell you the truth, I've never understood why you left this business. You were so successful. Why stop doing what you're really good at?"

She laughed. "I took too many bands to the top and then they broke up and I was left empty-handed. I got tired of renting my life out to artists who were having more fun than me, so I became one myself." She paused. "And quite frankly, Rufus, there just isn't an unlimited amount of time ahead for me. When Jules was diagnosed with terminal cancer, I learned to treat everyday like your last and do what you really want."

"Good idea," he said patting his large belly while reading the dessert menu. Then he turned his attention back on Marisa. "Is that why you became a writer? So you could have something you could call your own?"

"You got it. I haven't published yet, but I have a real passion for writing. And Martin needs a manager who has a passion for this new style of management and that isn't me."

Rufus frowned. "It's not me either. That's why I've hired these young kids to help out. They did a terrific job on your tour."

"But I never met anyone from your office."

Rufus ordered profiteroles and turned back to Marisa. "No you didn't. They were too busy in front of their computer screens creating a media buzz. Why do you think there were so many people at your gigs? Go online and search for Martin Starks. He'll come up at the top of the page every time. Tour schedule. Biography. All the reviews beginning with the New Morning. And, more important, the video clips from the concerts have gone viral on YouTube."

"I didn't see anyone with recorders."

"Marisa, you're showing your age … not a good thing in this business. Fans can video performances on their devices and upload them to YouTube instantly. My office links those video clips to our huge base of concertgoers and we buy banner ads in the venue markets."

"Stop, Rufus. My head's spinning with all this tech stuff." She bit into a profiterole. "I forgot how good this dessert is."

"I've got something even better. Martin was on the A-list for the Paul Acket Award: Artist Deserving Wider Recognition."

Marisa's hand stopped in mid-air and the chocolate dripped on the tablecloth. "That's impossible. This is his first European tour."

"I didn't say he won. It's enough that he was considered. That almost guarantees a gig here next year." Rufus looked at his watch, gulped down his second espresso and asked for the check. "One of my bands will be onstage in a half hour—want to come?"

"No thanks. All I want to do tonight is get lost in a really good book and forget about the techno music biz."

"That doesn't sound like you, Marisa. You used to be the last one to go home to bed."

She smiled. "I'm a little older now and I didn't just have two double espressos."

As Marisa walked toward the hotel elevator, mulling over all she'd just learned from Rufus, she sensed someone staring at her from across the lobby. Even without her glasses, she recognized Ryan from the picture she'd seen briefly on the screen of Cassandra's cell phone. Good-looking devil, she thought. But why is he here?

She went up to her room, got into bed with her iPad, and searched for Martin Starks on Google. Rufus hadn't exaggerated. She even recognized herself dancing in the wings at the Berlin concert. She opened her e-mail and she felt like she was the one who had had a double espresso when she saw a message from Serge. She'd started to think he'd forgotten her.

Hi there. In Geneva. I can be in Montreux on Sunday. Dinner? Let me know where you're staying.

She suddenly tingled all over and sheepishly looked around the room for Jules before she wrote back: Good to hear from you. Yes to dinner on Sunday! I'm at the Grand Hotel overlooking the lake.

She'd just sent her message when the phone beeped with another message. This one from Cassandra. She confirmed the interviews for the next morning and invited Marisa to join her for lunch after. That's a surprise, thought Marisa. She's never invited me to lunch before and the way she's been acting toward me on the road I never expected that she would.

Oh don't be so suspicious, Marisa. She just needs a friend.

"Jules?" The curtain stirred in the breeze. "Are you reading my e-mails? You're not jealous, are you? Is that why you're here?"

She waited a few seconds and when he didn't reply, she said, "His name is Serge and, no, we're just friends. It's just nice to have someone to talk to other than a ghost."

30

CiCi Belle glided across the lobby of the ART Hotel at 10 A.M. as if she was modeling on a Parisian runway. People gawked, many stopped her. One fan waved one of the CDs she recorded with The Belles in her face and said her replacement was a real disappointment. CiCi opened her fountain pen and signed CDs and programs until she saw Marisa across the room at the coffee bar. She broke away from the admiring crowd and hugged and kissed Marisa's cheeks as if she were meeting an old friend. This sudden affection came as a surprise. It was as if she had metamorphosed overnight from the angry, depressed Cassandra in Hamburg to an exuberant, confident CiCi in Rotterdam. Was it all show or was something up? Marisa didn't have a clue. She only hoped Cassandra/CiCi's new found happiness had nothing to do with Ryan's arrival the night before. The way he had glared at her from across the lobby had given her goose bumps.

"You smell good!" exclaimed Cassandra. "What is that?"

"You like it? It's called Pomegranate Noir."

"Nice." Cassandra looked around the lobby. "So where's our first interrogator?" As if on cue, a middle-aged man in a crumpled suit with a PRESS badge swinging from his thick neck, approached. "Hi. I'm Deke Burke from the North Sea office." He looked Cassandra up and down, from the bodice of her low-cut dress to her ankles, rather too freely, thought Marisa. He turned his red-eyed gaze on Marisa's badge. "And you're Marisa Bridges." He did a double take. "Wait a minute. I know you. Didn't you manage that really funky, crazy band? And then there was that fabulous singer. Whatever happened to her?"

Marisa took a sharp breath. "You have a good memory. That was quite a few years ago."

"Shall we sit this one out? I just ordered a pot of coffee. If you partied nearly as much as I did last night I thought you might need some java."

"Actually I'd prefer tea," said Cassandra, making it clear she was not one of the party animals he was referring to. She and Marisa watched him from across the table while he set up his phone to record the interview.

Cassandra passed over the usual mundane first questions. She knew his game and said she didn't have a favorite color. Or a favorite book. Or a favorite band. Then he got down to what he really wanted to ask but Cassandra answered in the same cool fashion as if they were still talking about colors. "I left The Belles for artistic reasons. I wanted to be more challenged."

Without wavering she answered the next battery of questions. "Yes, Martin's a terrific collaborator and a virtuoso guitarist." "No, we're only friends." "No, we haven't made any plans beyond this tour." "Yes, I miss singing with The Belles but it has been a wonderful experience playing again in small intimate clubs where I can connect with the audience." She smiled sweetly. "It's important for a singer to do that occasionally so they don't forget why they wanted to sing in the first place. So, no, I have no plans to get back with The Belles." And "No, they haven't asked me."

"Do you want—"

"No. I don't have time to work with anyone else now. I'm going into the studio to record a solo album."

He was as surprised by this news as Marisa and was about to ask for more information but Marisa said they had run out of time.

He shrugged, snapped a few photos, and packed his bag.

Marisa and Cassandra were looking around for the next journalist when Deke asked, "Is that why you were in the bar last night with Ryan Peters, to talk about your next recording? I thought you two were on the outs. I won't write about it, of course, but is something heating up again between you two? It certainly looked like it last night."

Marisa told Deke the interview was over. Cassandra put her hand on Marisa's. "It's all right. I don't mind answering. Last night was the first time I've seen Ryan since I left The Belles. We spoke briefly, and then I went up to bed ... alone. Sorry to disappoint you, Deke, but there's nothing more to it than that."

After he walked off in a huff, Cassandra smiled when Marisa asked her if she really was going into the studio. "Not exactly but I do plan to record a solo album, I just don't know when."

The second journalist was more interested in Cassandra's new musical direction than her private life, which was a relief. There was no mention of Ryan.

By the fourth interview, the news had spread that CiCi Belle was in the lobby. Another crowd of autograph seekers swarmed around her. Devices flashed. Cassandra turned to Marisa and said in a low voice, "Let's get out of here. I know a quiet local bistro where no one will bother us."

In the cab, Marisa thought her phone was vibrating but when she plucked it out she saw that it was the wrong color. "What the—?" she looked at it curiously and then remembered. "I'm sorry. I completely forgot to give this to you. You left it in your hotel room in Hamburg and the maid came running up to me with it when I was checking us out."

Cassandra looked at it like it might bite her. "Here take it," said Marisa, "I might need to reach you." Cassandra ignored the lit-up screen, clicked it off, and dropped it in her purse. She was about to say something when the cab pulled up to the restaurant in downtown Rotterdam.

When Cassandra sat down and immediately picked up the wine list, Marisa thought it her duty to remind her that she had a gig that night. "Don't worry," snapped Cassandra. "I can handle it."

There was an uncomfortable silence after this heated exchange and both women studied the menus. After the waiter took their orders, Cassandra removed her sunglasses and sat back.

Marisa was checking her messages when Cassandra said, "You probably were wondering why I invited you to lunch today?"

Marisa put her phone away. "Actually, I was. I don't know what's come over you on this tour, but you haven't been much of a friend."

Cassandra looked out the window and when her eyes returned to Marisa, they were moist. "I'm sorry. It's nothing personal. I just don't like touring like this. The performances yes, but not in between." Marisa kept herself from saying that performances were less than ten percent of touring, and if that's how she felt about road tours, she should consider another profession.

Cassandra went on, "I had hoped this tour might be different, what with Martin and me hooking up, but that didn't work out, did it?"

"No, it didn't." After the waiter uncorked the wine, Marisa asked, "Are you disappointed?"

"Yes I am. But that's not why I asked you to lunch. I wanted to apologize for my—my inappropriate behavior toward both you and Martin." The waiter placed a bowl of steaming mussels in front of them.

Cassandra continued, "I should have known better. I can count on one hand the singer-musician couples that stay together. We were statistically fated to break up before we even met." She laughed bitterly. "It's ironic that 'Peggy Blue' keeps getting tighter and tighter as a duet, while Martin and I get further and further apart." Her face saddened. "I guess Montreux will be our swan song."

"And whose fault is that?" said Marisa sharply.

"Is that really fair, Marisa? Have you forgotten it was Martin who threw a pitcher of water in my face and it is Martin who has been slyly cutting down my time onstage"— Cassandra stopped. Marisa seemed more interested in eating her mussels than listening to her moan. Cassandra changed her strategy.

"Look, I'm really sorry I was such a bitch on this tour but you're wrong when you say it was my fault. I thought Martin was different, someone who would love me for myself and not because I used to be famous or could still be famous, but it didn't work out that way, and when he turned against me, I turned into my bitchy old self. I know that didn't help you any either."

Marisa had put down her fork. "I know it hasn't been easy for either of you on the road. And I don't know how it's going to get any better with Ryan here. If I remember correctly, back in Paris, Martin didn't even want you to answer his text message. I don't know what he's so riled up about when it comes to Ryan, but it would be better for all of us if he doesn't see you two together."

"He won't," she snapped angrily.

They both ate in silence, until Cassandra said, "What I told that press guy, Deke, is the truth. Ryan insisted that I join him for a drink. Everyone was watching us at the bar. If I'd said no … well let's just say he has a rather nasty temper and it's best to go along with him when he's in one of his moods."

"You said Ryan was your manager. You didn't tell me he was also your boyfriend."

"Former boyfriend! Former manager!"

Marisa winced and looked around the room, surprised that no one had heard Cassandra slap her hand down on the table.

With the same hand, Cassandra covered Marisa's. "There I go having to say I'm sorry again. I asked you to lunch to apologize and here I am yelling at you. You're right, I haven't been totally honest. But now I am. Last night I finally set Ryan straight. He wanted me to sign a new management contract. I tore it up and told him we were through and to stop—"

Marisa cut her off. "So it's not by accident that Ryan is here, is it? He's the one who left messages at the hotels. He's the reason you didn't want Stuart putting our tour on his Facebook page. Is he stalking you?"

"Stalking me? Why of course not. Why would Mr. Ryan Peters stalk me when he could have his pick of any artist?" Her hand shook as she refilled their wineglasses.

Marisa asked, "Is Ryan the *R* on the florist card you dropped in my trash?"

"You should have been a sleuth, Marisa."

"And I saw you get into a limousine. So tell me, please, what is really going on between you and Ryan?"

Cassandra put down her wineglass and stared openly at Marisa through misty eyes. Between sniffling and wiping away tears with her napkin, she told Marisa about that night and the other nights with Ryan that led up to the horrible night at the loft.

She told Marisa that Ryan had tracked her ever since they left Paris and that he would have had her picked up in Hamburg if Marisa hadn't talked her out of leaving the tour. She told Marisa that she'd thrown away the phone in Hamburg to stop herself from contacting him. That, yes, she was afraid of him, but she couldn't break away, because, in spite of every awful thing he'd done and as crazy as it sounded, part of her still loved him. And she apologized for asking Martin not to tell her about Ryan.

Marisa took this all in without saying anything, but she felt betrayed and was about to lash out at Cassandra for deceiving her when she heard Jules say, *This is not about you. She needs your help so give it to her.*

Marisa looked down at her dark glasses and put them on. It would make it easier to say what needed to be said. Something that might help Cassandra break away from Ryan.

"Before I met Jules I worked in the film industry. My 'Ryan' was an up-and-coming Hollywood producer. Absolutely charismatic. Bon vivant. He made my life look dull in comparison. I'd never been with a man like him. You might say he swept me off my feet when he took me to dinner on the rooftop of Caesar's Palace and waltzed me across the ballroom floor, holding me close when I lost my footing and whispering in my ear, 'Don't be afraid. I'll catch you if you fall.' That night I gave myself over to him completely. I'd never known such passion." She stopped to clear her throat with a sip of water.

"We collaborated on a film script. He was confident it would be a blockbuster. I believed him and devoted every moment of my life from then on to make that happen … besides cooking for him and cleaning up after him and . . ." she looked down at Cassandra's hand gripping hers, ". . . being his sex object."

Marisa took a deep breath and continued her story. "After we sold the script, he didn't need me any longer and abandoned me, stripping me even of my screenwriter credit. But I still loved him."

Cassandra let go of her hand and sat back in the booth.

"I don't know if I was jealous or really wanted to warn his new girlfriend when I sent an anonymous letter telling her that he beat up on women when he felt like it. A few nights later he banged on my door. I wouldn't let him in. He told me not to be afraid. He didn't come to hurt me. He wanted to work things out. Once inside, he put his arm around me. Kissed me tenderly. Invited me to take a drive up in the hills to see the full moon. Parked the car in a deserted canyon. Turned to me and said, 'This is your night, baby. You're going to get what you deserve. I'm going to kill you.'"

Marisa held her eyes on the white tablecloth, her voice was barely audible. Cassandra had to lean forward to hear her. "He beat me with his fists. I was too afraid to fight back and rolled up into a ball. He punched me again and again. Then, suddenly, he stopped, pushed me out of the car and took off."

Marisa looked up into Cassandra's shocked face. "The awful thing was that while I lay facedown in the dirt, I actually pleaded for him to forgive me. I blamed myself for what he did to me. Can you imagine that?"

Cassandra nodded. "Yes, I can."

Marisa brushed away a tear falling down Cassandra's cheek. "You have to break away from Ryan."

Cassandra smiled through her tears. "But don't you see, Marisa?" She broke into a laugh. "That's why I'm so happy today. *He* broke away from me. When I wouldn't sign that contract he told me that he didn't want anything more to do with me. He said, 'It's over.' I am finally free of him."

Marisa suddenly felt very tired; too tired or too unwilling to put a hole through Cassandra's fleeting joy. She looked past her at the empty tables, surprised they were the only ones left. She ordered an espresso.

Cassandra drank down a full glass of water. Then she fidgeted in her purse until she found her wallet and asked for the bill.

Marisa dropped a sugar cube in the demitasse and waited for it to cool off. "You know, Martin didn't betray you, but when you flipped back into a diva, you turned him away. I think he's totally confused by you but he still cares. And if he sees you with Ryan, I don't know what he'll do."

"I told you. He won't. Ryan is leaving tonight after his band's performance. He doesn't fly, so his driver will take him to Geneva by car. Imagine that, a guy like Ryan being afraid to fly."

"I'm not surprised. Underneath their bravado, men like Ryan are cowards." Marisa was about to get up when Cassandra pulled her back. "Before we go, please tell me, did your dark prince ever come back again?"

"Oh yes. He had another idea for a screenplay and wanted me to work with him on it. But by then I no longer needed him to color in my life." She smiled. "I'd finally realized I could have a deep, satisfying career without him. So for the first time ever I was able to say no to him and mean it. He didn't believe me. He kept raising the ante with money and other bonuses, wanted to be lovers again. When he finally got it, finally heard me saying no, he went into a rage, but this time I wasn't scared."

"Why not?"

Marisa smiled. "We were talking on the phone. Honestly, I don't know if I could have said no to him in person. He was a very scary guy when he didn't get his way."

"Marisa, will you come with me to the sound check? Ryan might see me there."

"But I thought you said—"

"I did. But you never know with Ryan. I'm sure it was like that for you with your prince."

Marisa nodded in understanding and then asked, "What are you going to do after Montreux?"

Cassandra sighed. "I don't know. I need to go off and figure things out. My dad says I can come stay with him in Maine. But I need a few days in New York to gather my art supplies from school and your basement." She hesitated. "Would it be all right if I stay in your loft? It'd be just a few days."

Marisa turned to the window wondering if this was the real reason she was invited to lunch, then remembered what Jules had said about her helping the girl. "All right. But if you see Carl or anyone else from the building just tell them you've come to pick up a few things you left in the basement. And keep the loft neat. My agent might show it to a buyer at any time."

"Thanks Marisa. Please believe me when I say that in spite of Martin hurting me like he did, I want him to succeed just as much as you do. And I'm going to do my best to make that happen. I promise." She smiled sadly, "It'll be my going away present to both of you."

31

Marisa was waiting in the lobby to accompany Cassandra to the sound check when someone grabbed her from behind. She swung around to find Martin with a wry smile on his face.

"Martin would you please not do that again. You scared me half to death."

"Sorry, Marisa, I didn't mean to frighten you. Are you ready to go? I was going to walk you over." He frowned when she told him to go on without her. He'd been at the concert complex last night and it was a massive labyrinth.

"Are you sure you'll be able to find the Congo stage?"

Marisa told him she was waiting for Cassandra and they would come together. He looked surprised and she added, "Cassandra took me to lunch today. She wanted to apologize ... to both of us."

"Yeah, right" he said bitterly. "She makes both our lives miserable for two weeks and now she decides to apologize. What else did our sweet diva have to say?"

Taken aback by Martin's anger she hesitated before saying, "She told me all about Ryan and what happened that night at the loft."

He shook his head. "She should have told you a lot sooner, or I should have. At the time I thought she was just embarrassed, but now I think she was protecting him."

"You may be right." Marisa looked around the lobby expecting to see Ryan lurking in the shadows. "I thought you should know that Cassandra had a drink with Ryan last night in the hotel bar."

"Oh god, don't tell me he's here?"

"Yes. Their meeting was mentioned in this afternoon's festival newsletter, hinting they were getting back together, but that isn't true. They broke up last night for good. She only talked to him because she was afraid he'd cause a scene if she didn't"

"My, the poor defenseless girl. C'mon Marisa, I hope you weren't fool enough to believe that story of his hold over her like I once did."

"Martin, where's your compassion? Do you have any idea what it's like to live for what feels like eternity in a small cage with an animal and be so afraid of him you can't move, let alone escape? Well that's what it's been like for Cassandra with Ryan. I think you need to be a little more understanding. She needs our help."

"No way, Marisa. She's trouble and she's trouble I don't need. And neither do you. As far as Ryan, I'd prefer not to see him anywhere near me but not because of Cassandra." He clenched his fists unconsciously. "I just have a thing about men beating up on women. If I do run into him—"

He flinched when she touched his forearm. "Forget it, please, Martin. Someday Ryan will get his due, but you're not his avenger." Marisa had never found the right opportunity to ask him what made him snap in that incident at Juilliard that led to his expulsion but she could see now that it certainly could have been nasty if Martin felt justified.

He shook out his hands, shifted his feet, and took several deep breaths, letting the air out slowly. He looked around the lobby and settled his eyes back on Marisa … the intensity of the moment lifted. He saw Carlos and Stuart motioning at the exit. "Look, I've got to go. You're sure you'll be all right? Do you remember the name of the stage where we're playing tonight?"

"Of course, I do. The Congo stage. Martin, please, I can take care of myself."

He smiled. "I'm sure you can, Aunt Marisa. I just like taking care of you." He leaned down and kissed her cheek. "See you at the sound check."

She waited another fifteen minutes and then called Cassandra's room. There was no answer so she took a courtesy car to the concert complex.

Dammit, she muttered to herself, standing in an empty theatre. Now I've gone and done it. I thought for sure this was the Congo stage. I'm going to miss the sound check if I don't find it soon and then Martin will be right to think I can't take care of myself.

The hallway was crowded with concertgoers rushing to performances. She looked around for help but everyone ignored her until she held out her hand like a traffic cop and yelled, "Stop!" She almost collided with a young man wearing an official North Sea badge around his neck.

"Please tell me where the Congo stage is?" she asked, trying not to appear like a confused old woman.

"Certainly," he said with a cultured English public school accent that surprised her, considering the tattooed arms and spiked vermillion hair. He looked down at her backstage badge. "Marisa Bridges? Aren't you here with CiCi Belle and her band?"

She pulled herself up to his chin. "No, Hans," she said, reading his badge, "I'm actually here with the Martin Starks Trio. CiCi is their guest artist."

"Oh, I see. Sorry. I must have misread the program sheet for tonight."

"Yes, you must have. Hans, can you please point me in the right direction."

"I'll do even better. I'll take you there myself."

Marisa tried to keep up with her guide but it was like following the very-late white rabbit down into an underground tunnel to Alice's tea party. Marisa arrived exhausted under the Congo marquis and, without stopping, Hans waved good-bye and rushed on.

She waited until she could breathe normally, and then pushed the door open just as Martin was shouting "Testing" into the mic.

Damian was at the soundboard making adjustments on the dials. Marisa snubbed Cassandra waving at her from the stage and sat down in an aisle seat wondering why she had even bothered to come. Damian had everything under control. She laid her head back and closed her eyes.

"Marisa, wake up," called out Martin, shaking her. The band and Cassandra were looking over his shoulder with concern. "We were starting to worry about you when you didn't show up earlier."

She was embarrassed to be found in such a compromised position, "I got a bit lost."

He turned to Cassandra. "I thought Marisa was coming with you?"

"She was. But something came up. Didn't you get my text message, Marisa?"

Marisa shook her head.

The group dispersed except Cassandra who stayed with her until Martin brought her a glass of water.

"I must have taken the wrong corridor and the nice young man who led me here walked very fast. Do you have everything you need? Is the sound okay?"

Martin smiled. "Everyone's been incredible. I'm really spoiled. I'd like to take Damian back to New York with me."

Finally left on her own, Marisa pulled out the night's contract from her briefcase, but the small print was way too small and she searched in her bag for her reading glasses.

"Are you looking for these?" asked Damian who was walking up the aisle. "They were on the floor. They must have fallen out of your briefcase."

"Thanks. Is everything going all right?"

"Couldn't be better, Mrs. Bridges. It's going to be a great night for the band. I can feel it."

"Damian, could you stop calling me Mrs. Bridges. After all, we did just spend two weeks together in a van."

He laughed "Okay. Marisa it is."

While she waited for Martin to finish the sound check, she

pulled out her phone and saw the text message that Cassandra had sent earlier. She had an unexpected errand to do and would meet Marisa at the venue. But that's odd, thought Marisa, this is coming from a different number than the one I have for her.

Martin returned and they walked slowly back to the hotel and enjoyed some quiet private time together. Neither one of them mentioned Cassandra who had run off after the sound check.

After a nap and shower, Marisa felt revived. Especially after receiving a message from Serge reconfirming their plan to meet in Montreux and how he looked forward to seeing her again. She dressed carefully, taking time with her makeup before slipping on a pale blue, silk summer dress. She checked herself in the mirror, pulling up the low-cut bodice as if she heard Jules saying she should.

In the lobby, she saw the band but no Cassandra. She'd left a message at the desk saying she'd meet them at the venue. Martin was pissed off. He was nervous enough about the night's performance without worrying whether Cassandra would show up.

"It'll be all right, Martin. Cassandra promised me that she'd do you a solid tonight. You'll see."

"I hope you're right."

He took in her dress and told her she looked fantastic. "Can I be your date tonight?" he asked, taking her arm. She squeezed his arm and smiled up at him. "I'd like that very much."

The festival's music director had made the right decision when he decided to change venues. By the time Marisa took her traditional stand against the aisle wall, in a good position to rush backstage if needed, the hall was filled to capacity. Martin had added another tune to their opening set before their featured singer came onstage and Marisa saw the audience fidgeting in their seats between songs. She'd have to ask Martin to cut it back to two opening numbers in Montreux where CiCi was even more popular and the audience might not be as polite.

When Martin finally called CiCi to the stage, the audience jumped up and started calling out "We love you, CiCi."

She walked toward center stage, took the mic from Martin, and thanked every one for coming. She said it was great to be back at the North Sea Festival. She announced Martin's band, and got the audience to acknowledge each of the musicians with rousing applause. The lights dimmed and she began singing "Didn't We Almost Have It All."

From where Marisa was standing, she felt chills when she saw Cassandra and Martin performing together. No one would have ever thought they were on the outs. As she'd promised, CiCi gave it her all, her fear of straining her voice forgotten, and Martin answered with his guitar, their hips undulating rhythmically like lovers until the set was over. The audience went wild and shouted for an encore.

When Marisa arrived backstage, Martin had his arm around Cassandra and they were both talking at once, still feeding off the energy they'd generated onstage. But suddenly Cassandra whispered in his ear and broke away, stopping briefly to hug Marisa on her way out.

"Where is she going?" asked Marisa.

"She said she promised to meet up with some old friends," said Martin.

The band wanted to stay at the concert hall and hear John Scofield so Marisa reminded them to be in the lobby at 8 A.M. sharp for checkout and she left with Rufus. He walked her to the accounting office, while raving how good the concert had been. "Are you really sure Cassandra's leaving? You could never tell it by their performance."

Marisa reaffirmed that Montreux was their last gig together.

"What a shame," said Rufus. "They work so well together."

After they picked up the money, Rufus hesitated, "Shall I take you to the hotel?"

"Rufus, I'm fine. Just point me in the right direction" She hugged him good night. "Will I see you in the morning?"

"Not if you're leaving at eight! And don't forget to leave the cash in the hotel safe tonight. There've been some robberies in the rooms."

"Good idea," she said, patting her bloated handbag full of cash. The most money the band had made on the tour. "Thanks for suggesting it. Good night, Rufus. See you in Montreux."

Marisa took off brusquely toward the taxi stand and let the fresh night air revive her after the stuffy, overpopulated concert venue. She pulled up short when she heard shouting and looked in the direction of an unlit park. She could barely make out a man leaning over a woman and pressing her against a tree.

She was about to yell for help, when the man pulled the woman away from the tree and wrapped his arms around her in an embrace. From where Marisa was standing it looked like they kissed. Just a lover's quarrel, she decided, and stepped into a waiting taxi.

She remembered to remove the money from her purse and deposit it in the hotel safe before going upstairs to bed and thankfully slipping between the sheets.

Early the next morning Marisa and the band were in the lobby. This time waiting for Cassandra and Marisa was nervous. They were catching a flight to Geneva and there was no room to be late. She telephoned Cassandra's room. No answer. She rode the elevator up to room 350. Ignoring the Do Not Disturb sign, she rapped on the door until she heard Cassandra shout angrily, "Go away!"

"It's Marisa. Have you forgotten you have a plane to catch?"

Marisa heard a lot of rustling on the other side of the door and tapped again. "Cassandra, are you all right?"

The door opened a crack—wide enough for Marisa to see smeared mascara under puffy red eyes. "I overslept. I'll be right down."

"Do you want me to help you?" Marisa said, keeping the door open with her foot.

"I'll be quicker on my own. Five minutes."

Before the door shut, Marisa was certain she heard someone else speak.

Out in the parking lot, she said, "You guys look like you had quite a night and I guess Cassandra did too. She'll be down in a few minutes." They all shuffled into the van to wait, too sleepy to complain.

Marisa returned to the lobby just as Cassandra stepped out of the elevator, wearing her wide-rimmed hat and oversized dark glasses. "Sorry, Marisa. I overdid it last night. God! What a hangover. Can I have one of those special pills you gave me in Hamburg?"

"I'll give you one in the van. But are you sure you're all right?"

"Nothing that your little pill won't cure." She forced a smile. "What a night! I'll never drink again."

32

The plane was sitting on the tarmac waiting to take off for Geneva when Marisa realized she'd left the gig money from the North Sea Festival behind in the hotel safe—the most money they'd made for a gig from the entire tour. She looked around guiltily at the group and sent a frantic text message to Rufus: Help! Forgot money in hotel safe. Can you bring to Montreux? I hope. I hope. Call me if problem.

Years ago she left a briefcase containing a large envelope filled with 100-mark Deutsch bills at a venue in Hamburg. She'd handcuffed the briefcase handle to her wrist, an old roadie trick, but had unlocked it to wash her hands and forgot it. Fortunately her briefcase was right where she'd left it by the toilet, with the money still in it.

By the time the short flight screeched to a stop in Geneva, her anxious thoughts had built up to a fever pitch.

An announcement blared over the PA that there was to be a delay getting off the plane and everyone was to remain in their seats. No explanation was given. Two uniformed customs agents boarded the plane and paged Marisa Bridges.

"What the hell is going on here?" said Martin waking up next to her.

"I'm not exactly sure," she said, "but fix your collar and run your hands through your hair so you don't look like a druggie or the over-protective Swiss authorities will never allow you into their straight-laced country." She didn't have to prepare Cassandra who was sitting across from them. She apparently knew the routine as she brought out her makeup kit and gave herself a face-lift. Marisa saw a bruise on her left cheek that, as good as Cassandra was at putting on makeup, it was going to be impossible to cover-up.

Customs officials escorted Marisa and the group off the plane. They were ushered through customs barriers without any questions being asked and released into the arrival hall. A rush of journalists flashed cameras in their faces and called out questions. Martin looked back at Marisa and Cassandra as they hurried down the hall. "Is this for her?" he asked.

"Just keep going," said Marisa, shepherding him along with the band. "Damian will get the luggage." Suddenly the Montreux festival staffers appeared with ID badges hanging from their necks and led the group out on to curbside and into a Mercedes limousine waiting with opened doors. They jumped in and the limo took off. The guys looked at each other in amazement and broke out laughing.

"Dammit, Marisa! What's this all about?" said Martin. "Did they have us mixed up with somebody else?"

"No, the customs officials assured me that the fanfare was for you and Cassandra. The Montreux festival office called me this morning and told me your North Sea gig had created quite a media blast and the press would be here to photograph your arrival. They wanted to be the first to get it out on Internet. That's why customs wanted to get you out of the airport before the exits got blocked."

"Man," said Martin, "that was kind of scary. Promise me you won't let that happen again without warning us."

"I thought it was cool," said Stuart. "Is this what happened to you, diva girl, when you toured with The Belles?"

Cassandra kept her face to the window and mumbled, "Yeah, and it wasn't fun."

The limo pulled out onto the highway. "Wow! Look what we have here?" said Carlos, opening a small refrigerator door and pulling out a beer. "I could get used to this real easily." Martin and

Stuart did the same. Marisa handed Cassandra a Perrier before opening one herself.

"When we get to the hotel, there might be a few journalists hanging out in the lobby," said Marisa, "but don't talk to them. Interviews have been scheduled with Cassandra for tomorrow morning and, Martin, they requested that you be there too."

"Can't Cassandra do them for both of us? I want to work on the set list for tomorrow's concert. And she's much better at that kind of stuff than I am. Right, Cassandra?" He nudged her but she ignored him and leaned against the blacked-out window.

"It's important or I wouldn't have scheduled them. One of them is for *Rolling Stone*." Martin raised his eyebrows. "I'll keep them brief," Marisa said, trying not to worry about the money left behind. "Damian will be in the lobby at six tonight and he'll take you over to the convention center to hear tonight's concerts. Your IDs and Festival programs will be in your rooms with a list of all the concerts and the performing artists. Take your ID badges. They'll get you in for free."

"Damn, Aunt Marisa," said Martin, "you think of everything." Almost, she thought, looking at her phone screen. No word from Rufus. "What would we ever do without you?" He turned to the group at large as the limo cruised along. "Hey everyone, I'd like to make a toast to the best manager in the world." Cassandra turned away from the window and half smiled as she lifted her Perrier to Marisa.

"Hey, how long is our set tomorrow night?" asked Martin. "I need to know before I write up the set list. We got short-changed last night, not that I'm complaining about having to get off the stage for Scofield."

Marisa looked at her notes. "Seventy-minute set including encores."

"Cool," said Carlos. "That'll give us more time to play out and take a few more instrumental solos. Right, Martin?"

Martin looked over at Cassandra who had returned to staring

into the black window. "We'll see. For now I just want to sit back and enjoy my beer."

The limo slid to a stop at the elegant front entrance of the Hotel Grand. Marisa informed the journalists waiting in the lobby that there would be no interviews until the next day. Even so, one young man with a press pass came up to Cassandra and started, "Don't you have a couple of minutes you could give me? I've been waiting all day." Marisa put a protective arm around Cassandra's shoulders and led her to the elevator.

Marisa handed her a few more hangover pills in front of her room, and asked her if there was anything else she could do. Cassandra shook her head. "I'll be all right. I just didn't get any sleep last night."

"I can see that," said Marisa. "Do you want to talk about it?"

"Not right now. Maybe later."

Cassandra was about to close the door when Marisa added, "Call me if you need me. I'm right down the hall."

Marisa's phone vibrated. She quickly grabbed it and made a wish when she saw it was from Rufus. Yes! He had picked up the money. Marisa shook her head thinking of all that time in the plane she had worried needlessly. With a lighter step, she headed down to her room but Martin stepped out of his and stopped her. "Marisa, what's going on with Cassandra? She looks really down. I thought after last night's performance—are you keeping something from me?"

"No. She just needs to be on her own right now. She wants to rest up for tomorrow night's concert."

"Damn, I hope she doesn't blow it again."

She was starting to get cross. "Martin, don't you think you should be a bit more concerned about her rather than about the concert?"

"I'm sorry, Marisa, but she's been driving me insane. Switch on. Switch off. Last night she was so awesome on stage I thought I could forgive her anything. I even thought maybe we could work things out but today she's an ice queen again. What's her problem?"

"I don't know Martin. But we're not going to figure it out standing here. I've got to get some rest before the party tonight."

"What party?"

She sighed wondering if she'd ever get off her aching feet. "The Montreux Festival's Impresario, the man who runs the festival, is having a party at his chalet and has invited you and the band and lots of other musicians. It's an event not to be missed, even if it's just to see the snow-tipped Alps in the moonlight from his terrace. Damian can bring you after the concert. There should be an invitation in your room."

"That must be the envelope on my bed."

"Can I go to my room now, Martin?"

He smiled. "Have you seen the amazing view from your balcony?"

"No, I haven't. Instead, I'm standing in this dreary hallway talking to you."

"Okay, I got it. By the way, how are you getting to the party?"

Marisa put the key in her door, but before she could step into her room, he said, "Aunt Marisa, is there some other guy in your life besides me?"

She smiled and closed the door.

A warm stream of sunlight fell over her as she flung open the French doors and stepped out onto the wrought-iron balcony. She'd been there before and the familiar alpine view brought back strong, sentimental feelings. She spun back into the room to tell Jules to come look at the view, but he was his usual invisible self. She shook off her disappointment and said out loud, "Okay, be that way, but you could have told me not to worry about losing the group's money. I'm sure you knew it would work out."

She uncorked a miniature bottle of Dom Pérignon from the mini-bar and stepped back out on the balcony to toast herself and the many successes and failures that had gotten her here so many times in the past. And now here she was again, so many years later.

She went back in the room to stretch out on the couch and had barely closed her eyes when the house phone rang.

"Hi. It's me."

"Oh . . ." she said, almost dropping the phone as she slid off the couch and onto the floor in astonishment. Yes, she'd expected his call, but to now actually hear his voice ...

"Marisa, are you all right?"

Embarrassed at her schoolgirl behavior, she recovered and said, "Yes. I'm just a little out of breath. I was out on the terrace taking in the mountain air. For me it's like a cure."

"For me, too. Can you see the Alps reflecting on Lac Leman?"

"Yes. Can you see them from your hotel?"

"I'll go look. But what's your room number?"

"What's my room number? You're here? At the Grand? I don't believe it. Hold on." Marisa rushed around the room looking for her key and finally found it under her briefcase, "I'm in three-ten."

"Perfect. I'm two floors above you in five-twelve. Go out on your balcony and look up."

She looked and saw Serge waving down at her. Their laughs met in the air. He shouted something indecipherable.

She got back on the phone. "Can you be ready by seven?" he asked. "The restaurant has a terrific view and I don't want to miss the sunset."

Marisa felt her pounding heartbeat. Trying to sound normal, she said, "I'll meet you in the lobby."

"Marisa?"

"Yes, Serge?"

"It's wonderful to hear your voice and to see you even from afar."

After the click, she called out "Ohh la-la la-la," and hugged herself to make sure it was all for real. She twirled into the salle de bain and drew a bath in an enormous tub. When it was full, she soaked in the rejuvenating bath oils as if she had finally discovered Ponce de León's Fountain of Youth.

33

Marisa saw Serge first. He was wearing khaki pants and a forest-green plaid shirt that drew attention to his emerald eyes. A well-worn brown leather jacket was slung casually over his shoulder and a few rogue locks of silver-streaked hair had fallen down onto his bronze forehead. She'd forgotten how thick his eyebrows were and still black as if defying his age. A smile spread across his face as he strode toward her.

"It's really you," he said kissing both her cheeks, his bristly beard tickling her skin and sending shivers all the way down to her red-polished toes.

The hotel-parking valet pulled up in a red Porsche 911 and Serge opened the door for her.

"Is this yours?" she asked.

He laughed. "No, not on my salary. A colleague of mine in Geneva insisted I borrow it when I told him I was coming to Montreux to meet you. Are you all right with the top down?"

"Absolutely," Marisa said.

He laughed again. "How did I know you'd say that?"

They drove along the lake toward Lausanne, then turned off toward Vevey and climbed up into the mountains. A long enough drive for Marisa to put a cap on such unexpected giddiness, or at least she tried, but the warm feelings she'd felt for him at the Yale Club months ago rushed in. Because they'd been e-mailing back and forth for months, it made it easier to talk to him now and by the end of the scenic drive she had calmed down, almost.

They walked up a steep staircase to the restaurant, and Marisa took in the tables with red-checkered tablecloths on a terrace that was perched high on a precipice overlooking the lake below. Serge had reserved a table with a panoramic view of the lake and, to the south, the Jura Mountains.

Oh my god, thought Marisa, I've been here before. Decades ago when she really was a teenager she went to school in Lausanne for a short while. Back then, she'd imagined bringing someone special to this very spot, because it was so romantic. She'd tried to bring Jules several times but they could never fit it into their schedule. She didn't tell Serge. She didn't want to take away his obvious pleasure in being the first one to bring her there.

The sun, as if having waited for them, began its slow slippery descent behind the western ridge of the Alps. They sat in silence and watched it disappear. Its orange afterglow was a brilliant light show, illuminating the sky in shades of purple, rose, and orange. When the black curtain was finally drawn across the spectacle, the temperature dropped and Serge, seeing Marisa shiver, wrapped his leather jacket over her shoulders.

"Do you want to eat inside?" he asked with concern.

"Are you kidding? First the sunset and now the night sky. This is a spectacle not to be missed. And isn't that a full moon? I've been so busy with the tour, I have no idea whether it's coming or going."

"It's full tonight." Their eyes met briefly. "You know, I've been imagining what it would be like to bring you here, and now that you're actually here … I know this is crazy to say, seeing we've only known each other a short time, but the truth is I feel like I have the woman of my dreams sitting across from me."

Embarrassed, Marisa turned to watch the torches surrounding the illuminated turquoise pool being lit. Their reflections in the water quivered from the soft breeze caressing the surface. She didn't look back at Serge until the food arrived.

Marisa told him about the tour while they ate foie gras on

toast. The problems. The solutions. She even told him about Cassandra and Martin's breakup. He listened attentively and asked questions.

She was still talking when she noticed he'd finished his magret de canard and she'd only taken a few bites. She picked up her fork. "Sorry. I'm talking way too much. This is so delicious. Isn't it an amazing coincidence that we're able to be here tonight?"

"Marisa, it's not exactly a coincidence," he said, fidgeting in his chair. "It's true that I'm giving a lecture at the International Society of Mental Health in Paris next week . . ." He looked through his wineglass into the candlelight.

"And?" She tilted her head and waited.

He smiled. "Isn't it obvious? I do have a lecture in Paris next week but I came here a week early because ... well, because I wanted to see you."

Marisa almost swallowed a whole French fry and coughed into her checkered napkin.

"Sorry, I probably shouldn't have said that."

"No. No. I'm ... well I don't know what to say." She took a drink from her water glass. "Actually, Serge, I'm quite flattered. But can we slow this down a bit?"

Serge looked out at the dark night and Marisa stared at her hands in her lap, wishing she hadn't said that. Why couldn't she just enjoy the evening for what it was? A flirtation. A wonderful flirtation.

Serge gazed into her eyes. "You're right. I'm not handling this very well, am I? It just feels so good being here with you." He looked out at the shimmering pool and for the first time, she saw sadness in his eyes. "When we first met I didn't expect to see you again and it didn't seem necessary to tell you about my personal life but now I think I should. I was once married too."

"Oh. Are you a widower?"

"No. Divorced."

"Was it long ago?"

"Long enough but it still hurts when I think of her and all we once had."

"I understand," Marisa said gently. "Was it—"

"Hell? Yes it was. But that's all in the past. I'm okay now." Marisa nodded but wondered if that was really true.

He took her hands in his. "Your hands are icicles. Are you sure you don't want to go inside?"

She shook her head.

"I feel like you're going to get up and leave at any moment. Please don't. I don't want to rush into anything, believe me. But if you feel at all like I do, we should give us a chance. Even if it's only for brief moments like tonight."

Marisa spoke from her heart. "Since Jules's death, I've never really considered being with another man. But at this very moment I feel an undeniable impulse to wrap my arms around you and hold on and it's not just because I'm freezing. I could blame it on the full moon or the magic of the Alps or the wine but it's really just … you. It's how I feel about you."

She stood up from the table and Serge started to get up. "No don't. I just need to go to the ladies room. I promise I won't bolt. It wouldn't be practical. We're too far away from the hotel to walk back." She smiled. "I'll be right back. I promise."

He smiled back at her. "I certainly hope so. You're wearing my favorite jacket."

Marisa, along in the bathroom, gripped the cold sink and took several deep breaths. She studied her reflection shocked by how old she looked compared with how she felt. "Tell me that didn't just happen," she said out loud. "A man I hardly know just told me he wants to have me in his life. I'm just not really ready for this." Her face brightened. She let out a yelp. "Oh yes! I am!"

"Are you okay?" asked Serge when she returned to the table.

"I'm fine. Really. Quite fine."

"Do you still want me to take you to the party?"

"Absolutely!" She smiled and said teasingly, "I'm looking

forward to showing you off to my old friends who think I became a recluse when I left the music biz."

He put his arms around her and held her for a moment before whispering in her ear, "You're beautiful."

She hiccupped and their shared laughter filled the night sky and the full moon smiled down upon them.

34

Marisa asked Serge to leave the top down on the Porsche. She didn't want a ceiling over the joyous mood she was in. They were going to climb up a steep windy road to the Impresario's chalet and she wanted to feel the wind on her face.

Before they drove out of the parking lot, Serge put the chalet address into the GPS while Marisa checked her messages. She was hoping there'd be one from Cassandra. Nothing. "Oh dear."

"Anything wrong?"

"Do you mind if we stop by the hotel? I'm worried about Cassandra. She's not answering my text."

"All right. Looks like it's on our way." He put down the GPS and turned to look at her. "But, on the other hand, Marisa, are there ever moments when you consider your own happiness first?"

She laughed and put her phone back in her purse. "No. At least, not as often as I should. An old habit, I suppose. My life has always been about taking care of other people. That's what managers do, and when I wasn't managing someone, I was being a wife and a mother. But you're right. Let's not stop at the hotel. I'll just sit back and enjoy myself."

He didn't start the engine as if waiting for her to do something. "You must have been a hippie," he said, amused.

"You're right, but how did I give myself away?"

"For one thing, hippies like to enjoy themselves orbiting through space with the top down. But the real giveaway is that you don't fasten your seatbelt. Here let me do it." He leaned over and belted her in. "I don't want any harm to come to you."

"Thanks. Now that I'm buckled up, can we go? I don't want to miss the party." She realized she sounded rather brisk but as much as she was enjoying their flirtation, she felt he was getting too familiar and it made her uncomfortable.

Halfway up the mountain, Marisa had to admit she was chilled to the bone, and while Serge pulled into a turnout to put up the top, she couldn't resist checking for messages again. She frowned.

"Still no word?" asked Serge. "Look, we can go back down and check on her if you want."

"No it's all right. Really."

"Tell me more about Cassandra," said Serge. "Maybe I can be of help."

She hesitated but he was looking at her so earnestly, she thought, maybe he could help.

She told him what Cassandra had told her about Ryan at their lunch in Rotterdam. Then she told him about Ryan showing up at the festival and how Cassandra appeared in the hotel lobby with a bruised face the next morning.

"I can certainly understand why you're worried."

"She'd deny it, of course, but Ryan definitely has her on a leash, a long one for the moment, but that's because he's confident he can pull her in whenever he wants. I'm afraid of what might happen to her when he does. I don't know him personally, but from what Cassandra has told me, he could be dangerous. Men like him think nothing of hurting a woman when she doesn't do what they want her to do.

"But why am I telling *you* this? You wrote the book on it."

"I might have written a book on abusive relationships, but it sounds like you have some firsthand knowledge."

Marisa stared up at the night sky. "Yes, well, I was in one. Fortunately, I got away."

He squeezed her hand. "You're one of the lucky ones. Many of these kinds of relationships only come to an end by violence or suicide."

She turned to him with her face tightly drawn. "That's not

going to happen to Cassandra. At least not while I'm around. If only I could make her realize she doesn't need Ryan. That she's the one with the talent, not him."

"I'll do anything I can to help," said Serge. She thanked him and told he'd already been a great help by just listening.

The headlights flooded the road and they drove on in silence.

The parking attendants motioned with their flashlights for Serge to pull up to the gated entrance of the chalet. "Wow. Who is this Impresario?" asked Serge. "Have you known him long?"

"Philippe? Yes, but I haven't seen him in years. I doubt if he'll remember me."

An attendant helped Marisa out of the car and Serge took her arm. The chalet jutted out on an overhang like a falcon's nest.

They walked through the opened gate and down a steep flight of stairs. Serge turned to Marisa. "Between the mountains, the hairpin turns, the full moon, the starry night and being with you, life suddenly seems very thrilling." He laughed, and wrapped his arms around her. "You've bewitched me, haven't you?"

Before she could answer, the door opened onto a large living room teeming with laughter and animated conversations shouted above a blasting PA system playing music from last year's festival. Young male waiters dressed in Speedos and black-leather vests, left unbuttoned to show their muscular, oil-rubbed torsos, and shod in high-heeled black patent leather boots trimmed in sequins, welcomed Serge and Marisa with trays of caviar and other delicacies. Another lowered his tray of champagne glasses filled to the brim.

"Shall we?" asked Serge. "Oh why not?" answered Marisa, quickly forgetting her earlier intention to abstain.

Seeing Martin over in the corner by himself and looking quite miserable, she brought Serge over to meet him.

"I'm certainly glad you're here," said Martin, his face brightening. "Carlos and Stuart met some good looking girls and deserted me. They're outside dancing by the pool. This is just not my thing and I'd just as soon go back to the hotel."

"Marisa just wants to say hello to some old friends and then we'll take you back with us," said Serge.

"If there are any left that still know me," added Marisa.

"Aunt Marisa, everywhere you go you meet someone you once knew back in the day."

Serge looked surprised. "Is Marisa your manager *and* your aunt?"

"No," Martin laughed. "It's just a little wishful thinking. I'd like her to be my aunt and she's still hesitating about being my manager." A waiter appeared with Martin's Scotch on the rocks. Marisa had only seen him drink beer and hoped he could hold his liquor, which wasn't easy high up in the Alps.

A short man in an all-white leather suit with red owl-shaped glasses perched on the tip of his nose rushed over and kissed Marisa's cheek. "You're here, ma chérie! How wonderful. And isn't it just like you to make a grand re-entrance with a sensational new band. This must be your protégé, Martin Starks. Hello, Martin." Philippe shook Martin's hand and held on to it like it was a valuable treasure. "I don't know if Marisa's told you, but the guitar is my favorite instrument, second only to guitarists themselves."

"Do you play?" Martin asked, feeling uncomfortable.

Philippe let go of Martin's hand. "Used to until I found out my true calling was producing music festivals." He turned to Marisa. "And speaking of favorites, where's my girl CiCi?"

"She wasn't feeling well," said Marisa. "She said she was going to stay in tonight."

"That's odd. You know, they were expecting to meet her here." Marisa gave him a questioning look.

"DiDi and MiMi." He scanned the room. "They so much want to meet you, and Martin. CiCi's told them wonderful things about how you've both helped her come out of retirement." He winked at Martin.

"Really?" said Marisa. From what Cassandra had said about

her former partners she couldn't imagine them saying anything that nice. She assumed, if anything, they'd be jealous. But had Cassandra told the truth about her past?

"Oh there they are," said Philippe, enthusiastically. "I'll bring them over."

Philippe crossed the crowded room and brought back two elegant, tall beauties that could have been Cassandra's sisters, one on each arm. They both had large, wide eyes, full lips, arched cheekbones, and pale powdery complexions. Their faces were framed by thick silky hair, one auburn, the other jet-black, which cascaded down to their bare, thin shoulders. Their little black dresses showed off narrow waists and sensuous hips, with firm breasts swelling underneath.

Marisa yearned to be young again and, looking at Serge taking in the new arrivals, he seemed to be having similar thoughts.

Martin was stunned when he realized The Belles were the same two women Stuart and Carlos had been dancing with.

Philippe made quick introductions and scurried off as he recognized someone else who had just arrived.

"Where's CiCi?" asked MiMi after the introductions. "She was going to meet us here."

"She was?" said Marisa, still finding that unbelievable. "You've been in touch with her?"

"Yes, several times. Didn't she tell you we were coming?"

"Oh that's so like her to keep everybody in the dark." interjected DiDi.

MiMi continued, "We just played the last date of our tour in Geneva last night so how could we say no to her invitation. You were only an hour's drive away and Philippe had his driver pick us up. He's so nice to us."

"This is our favorite festival," said DiDi, the more animated of the two. "Philippe treats us like royalty when we're here. And his parties are to die for!"

"Quite honestly," said MiMi, "we were jealous that CiCi was playing the festival this year and we weren't." As if suddenly realizing how bad that might sound, she added, "But don't get me wrong. We're thrilled that she is."

"CiCi raves about you and what a terrific job you're doing," said DiDi. "And not many of us can say that about our managers, can we MiMi?"

MiMi tossed back her hair just like Cassandra often did without hair, and added a sharp "No, we can't."

By now it was getting a little late. Marisa was tired of standing, the girls were speaking way too fast, and the throbbing bass coming from the PA was giving her a headache.

"Well if she said she was coming I'm sure she is. Why don't we wait for her outside on the terrace where we can hear each other without competing with Whitney Houston? It's a great song but the volume is killing me."

Serge arranged a row of chairs and everyone sat down, but now that the music was muffled, there was an awkward silence.

MiMi looked at her watch and seemed annoyed. As if reading each other's minds, which Marisa thought they probably did often, DiDi said, "Mimi, I'm sure she's coming. Someone said they saw them leaving the hotel and Ryan would never miss out on Philippe's party."

"Ryan?" said Martin—the first word out of his mouth since he'd been introduced. "What's he doing here? Doesn't he have anything better to do than follow us around, or I should say follow Cassandra?"

"You call her Cassandra? How dear," said DiDi. She smiled sweetly. "I haven't heard anyone call her that since high school."

"As to CiCi being followed by Ryan," said MiMi, "let's just say he's extraordinarily attracted to her." Her lips curled up. "But you seem to have the power of attraction yourself. I hear that you and CiCi communicate really well together onstage. Actually a showstopper. I'm looking forward to seeing it."

If Martin wasn't so angry with Ryan being there, he might have blushed. "Look I'd really like to get this straight. Did she break up with him or not?"

"To tell you the truth, we were also surprised. After she left Los Angeles, they were no longer an item. But I guess at North Sea somehow he convinced her to give it another try. At least that's what Ryan told us in Geneva. He showed up on the last night of the tour, as he always does, to collect his commission."

"Oh," said Marisa, who didn't know Ryan was still managing The Belles. "So Ryan's your manager?"

Mimi was just about to answer when DiDi interrupted. "Look!" she said, pointing inside. "There they are!" Martin took one look and shot out of his chair. He stomped through the living room with his fists clenched. He glared at Cassandra and brushed against Ryan, but to Marisa's relief he kept walking and went to the bar.

Cassandra didn't seem to have noticed. She was leaning up against Ryan while she searched the room as if looking for someone. When she saw DiDi and Mimi she broke away from him and rushed over.

It was lovely to see these three old partners reuniting. There was really something special about the three of them together. A special magic.

"Well, well," said Ryan stepping onto the terrace into the middle of their teary reunion. "What a wonderful surprise, girls. When did you cook this up?" CiCi stood between her two friends with her arms around their waists as if forming a protective wall against Ryan. Ryan's smile never left his face but his piercing eyes targeted on Cassandra made Marisa shudder.

"She wanted to surprise you," said MiMi, defensively. "Isn't it great that the three of us are here together?"

Ryan kept his eyes on Cassandra, who was looking down at her feet. "I don't want to disrupt this touching reunion," said Ryan, "but don't you think you should introduce me to your new friends?"

Cassandra released her grip on MiMi and DiDi and put her arm around Marisa for support. "This is Marisa Bridges … the girls you already know well … and the guy who just left is Martin

Sparks, I mean Starks." Then turning a blank stare toward Serge, she stammered, "And who are you?"

Marisa introduced Serge to Cassandra. "Nice to meet you, Cass—or should I call you CiCi?"

"Whatever." She held out her hand unsteadily and Serge caught her as she tilted dangerously over the balcony.

"Here, I'll take her," said Ryan, pulling her to his side. "Don't worry about her. She's just having one of her migraines, right CiCi?"

"At the hotel I did have one … then Ryan gave me something that's made me rather dizzy."

Ryan called over a waiter carrying a tray of full champagne glasses but he was the only one who took a glass.

Cassandra looked up and smiled brightly. "C'mon girls, let's go find somewhere to talk. We have lots to catch up on."

"Wait a minute," said Ryan, holding onto her waist. "Isn't this my reunion, too?"

"No," said Cassandra, shaking his hand loose and moving nearer the girls. Ryan knew he was outnumbered. "All right, baby. I've got some business with Philippe. But don't wander too far away. I want to get you home early tonight. Tomorrow's a big day for you." He kissed her cheek and sauntered off.

Arm in arm the girls hurried off to the other side of the pool and left Serge and Marisa staring at each other. Martin came back from the bar with a fresh drink in his hand. "What's going on, Marisa? Why are they all here?"

"As you heard the girls tell us, Cassandra invited them. But why Ryan is here, I have no idea." Then more firmly she said, "Martin please stop looking at me as if I'm somehow to blame. I didn't know anything about it. Sit down. We need to talk about Cassandra."

"Hey, I don't need to talk about her." He turned to leave.

"Please, hear me out. I told Serge about Cassandra's problems on the way up here. He's had some experience with women like her in abusive relationships. I thought you could fill him in with what you know. We should all be trying to help her."

Serge explained that he was a psychologist.

"Cassandra doesn't need a psychologist. She needs to get a grip on her life."

"Martin, I don't think you understand what's going on here. It's not that easy for her. She needs our help."

"Not from me. I'm sorry but I've had it up to here with her. If she wants to make a mess of her life and go back to that jerk, that's up to her. The less I have to do with CiCi Belle after tomorrow night the better."

Marisa was about to say something when Serge interrupted. "Look, we don't have to talk about this tonight. But can we talk tomorrow?"

Martin looked over at Cassandra laughing with her friends and his voice lost its edge. "Okay. But not tomorrow. I don't want anything getting in the way of our concert tomorrow night." He turned toward the house. "Look, I feel like joining the guys and trying to have some fun of what's left of the party. And my glass is empty. Come find me when you're ready to go."

Cassandra left MiMi and DiDi and came across the terrace to Marisa. She called out, "Martin," but he ignored her. "He's angry with me, isn't he?"

"Shouldn't he be?" said Marisa. "We're both rather disappointed to find you with Ryan after you told us it was all over. Why is he here anyway? And why is he giving you drugs?"

"Oh Marisa, you ask too many questions."

Marisa frowned with her lips drawn tightly.

"Oh, all right. Just like I told you. In Rotterdam he offered me a contract. When he insisted I sign it, I said no. He ripped it up and said that was my last chance. There'd be no more offers. When he knocked at my door after the concert, I told him I had a terrible migraine and to go away. He gave me something to help me sleep. And it sure did. I didn't wake up until you were banging on the door telling me I had a plane to catch. I'm just as surprised as you are that he came to Montreux."

"Is that who was in your room when I knocked?"

Cassandra ignored her and said, "So now here we are, one big happy family." She raised her arms, smiled, and made a sweeping bow.

When she came up from her bow, her smile disappeared. Ryan was leaning against the living room doorway, slowly curling his index finger several times in her direction. Then he pointed his index finger at the ground. A smile never left his face, and one could have thought it was all in good fun. Marisa knew otherwise. Though unsure how they could fit both Cassandra and Martin in the backseat of the Porsche without taking the top down, she said, "Why don't you come back to the hotel with us? We're going to leave now."

"I can't do that," she said turning her back on Ryan. "Don't worry about him. I'll go back to the hotel with MiMi and DiDi." Marisa looked unconvinced. "I promise."

"Okay. But don't forget you have to be in the lobby at ten for interviews."

"Hey, I have an idea," said Serge. "Why don't we have breakfast together?"

"Sure," mumbled Cassandra as she walked unsteadily back over to MiMi and DiDi.

In the meantime, Ryan had slipped back into the house. Marisa didn't like leaving without Cassandra but she reasoned with herself that the house was full of celebrities and the people who represented them—managers, lawyers, accountants, promoters, and record company execs. Very important people. Ryan was a lot of things but he wasn't stupid. He wouldn't do anything to jeopardize his reputation as a well-respected manager. Not here at Philippe's party. As long as Cassandra left with MiMi and DiDi she'd be okay. She looked around for Damian to ask him to drive the girls back to the hotel but she didn't see him.

She left Cassandra with Serge and went to find a bathroom. She was about to enter the half-opened door when she heard MiMi and DiDi's distinctive American accents. She stood off to the side and listened.

When they came out, Marisa made sure the girls returned to Cassandra. Then she stood at the front door waiting for Serge and Martin. Ryan appeared out of nowhere and lunged toward her. "So, Marisa Bridges, are you behind the girls' reunion tonight?"

"No. I'm not." She tried to move away from him but he had her pinned against the wall.

"Did you know the girls were planning to sing together tomorrow night during CiCi's set?"

"No. I didn't." That was a lie. She'd heard about that and a lot more while eavesdropping on MiMi and CiCi a few minutes ago. But she was certainly not going to share that with Ryan. Not until she had a little more time to think about it.

He put his right arm against the wall and leaned closer. "Philippe heard about it and he thinks it's a great idea. I don't. And I'm sure your boy Martin doesn't think it's a good idea either. What are you going to do to stop it?"

Marisa wasn't going to let him intimidate her and she glared back at him. "It's not up to me. If Martin's into it, then there's nothing we can do."

She felt his hot breath on her neck. "C'mon Marisa, you can't be serious. I thought you were a smart manager. Don't you realize that The Belles will upstage your wonder boy?"

Inside she was trembling, but she said firmly, "I doubt that. Anyway, why are you so opposed to it?"

"Isn't it obvious? I'm about to launch CiCi's solo career. Getting back on stage with The Belles would be a very stupid move. Her fans might think they were getting back together."

Ryan was so close now that she could see one eye twitching and his tongue licking his Mick Jagger lips. He was really upset about the girls getting together and now she knew why. Suddenly, no longer afraid of him, she smiled. "I'd like to hear the girls sing together as The Belles."

"You're not listening to me, Marisa. If you don't stop this from happening, then I will."

At that moment she hated him intensely but she said calmly, "Are you threatening me?"

Ryan tossed his head back and snickered. "Of course not. We're just having a friendly chat."

Just then, Serge came over and put his arm around her, protectively. "Are you ready to leave, Marisa?"

"Yes. Ryan was just saying good night. Weren't you Ryan?"

The sudden sound of a glass breaking made everyone turn in the direction of CiCi, who had dropped to her knees to pick up the shards. Marisa saw MiMi and DiDi trying to pull her away.

Ryan stood by watching them.

35

Serge and Marisa gave up waiting for Cassandra and had breakfast by themselves out on the sunny terrace. Behind them, yachts with billowing white sails glided across the shimmering blue surface of Lake Leman under the influence of a forceful breeze.

A brief ping had Marisa scrambling in her purse for her phone. She read the message out loud to Serge: Sorry. Overslept. Lobby at 10.

"Not to worry," he said, putting his hand over hers tenderly. "We'll work this out together after I've talked to her and Martin. I'm sure he'll understand once he realizes what she's gotten herself into." Marisa wanted to believe him but she knew it would take more than talking to get through to Cassandra. There must be something else she could do.

The phone lit up again with a message and she reached for it reflexively. "Please don't," said Serge. "Just take a moment to breathe in this view. It's such a perfect day. How about taking a hike with me up to a restaurant I know that's famous for fondue and local Alsatian wine?"

"Oh, that would be nice," said Marisa sighing deeply. "Cassandra and Martin have interviews and then there's the sound check, interviews and . . ."

He folded his napkin and threw up his hands. "Okay. I understand. I'll leave you to it."

"Right," she mumbled, looking down at her messages and not hearing the disappointment in his voice. He was half way across the terrace when she looked up and called him back. He stood behind her chair and put his hands on her shoulders. "Don't worry, Marisa. I know this is your big day."

"I'll leave a backstage pass for you at the front desk. We'll meet there."

He kissed the back of her neck and whispered in her ear, "Try to do something nice for yourself today."

When Marisa finished looking at her messages she went back into the lobby and stopped short. Ryan was arguing with Cassandra at the front entrance of the hotel. He had a tight grip on her arm. When he saw Marisa approaching he let go of her and walked off.

"Is that man ever happy?" said Marisa, when she came up to Cassandra.

"Not when I don't do what he wants." Cassandra rubbed her arm. "Look Marisa, I've got to talk to you about something."

"It's all right, dear, I already know."

"You do? How? Are you sure we're talking about the same thing?"

"I overheard the girls talking about it last night. They were thrilled when you asked them to join you on stage tonight."

"Aren't you upset that I didn't ask you first?"

"No, not at all. I think it's a splendid idea. Wish I thought of it myself. The perfect ending to a great tour."

"Really? I can't believe you're saying this. I tried to talk to Martin about it a few minutes ago but he just walked away."

"Let me talk to him."

"Thanks so much. Look, I'm sorry I missed breakfast. Anyway you both seemed quite happy on your own without me." She looked around the lobby. "Where did he go?" Marisa pointed out the door where Serge was folding back the ragtop on the Porsche. "Fancy car! You're so lucky, Marisa! Where did you ever find him? I thought tall, dark, handsome gentlemen only existed in old black and white movies. He's so cool looking."

Marisa smiled. "He's a bit too old for you, don't you think?

C'mon we'll be late for the interview." Cassandra flinched when Marisa took her by the arm.

"Sorry." Marisa said, looking down at Ryan's red fingerprints on her bare arm. "I guess he has a pretty strong grip."

The interviews were uneventful. Cassandra and Martin spoke to each other genially in front of the journalists. No one would have guessed that that night was going to be their last concert together, or that privately they weren't even speaking to each other.

Marisa had accomplished everything on her To Do list before the performance, except for one last meeting that wasn't on her schedule, she thought, riding up the elevator.

Martin was packing up his guitar, when she arrived near the end of the sound check. She asked if she could have a few minutes to talk to him. She told him about Cassandra wanting the girls to join the band onstage. He was firmly opposed to the idea until she told him that Ryan was even more opposed. She explained that he was trying to lock Cassandra into a contract for a solo career and this reunion with her old group was definitely not the impression he wanted to send to her fans nor the international music journalists who would review the concert.

When Martin still hesitated, she played her final trump card. "Martin, I've never asked anything from you, but this is very important to me."

"But why?"

"I can't really say. You'll just have to trust me on this one."

"All right, Marisa. I'll do it for you, but not until the encore. One singer is hard enough to deal with onstage. I'll come up with a tune that would work well for all of us. But who's to stop Ryan from keeping them offstage? He is their manager, right?"

She smiled, confidently. "Don't worry. I've got that all worked out."

Marisa left the Convention Center and took the palm tree promenade through the lakeside gardens back to the Grand. A familiar walk. She'd taken it before at other festivals with other bands and then later with Jules. As she walked, she considered that her entire history in the music business had started and was now ending in Montreux. Not a bad finish, she thought, feeling quite pleased about the plan she conceived after Serge told her to do something for herself today.

And what about after tonight? she heard Jules say. She lifted her face up to the sun to feel his caress in the balmy breeze and whispered. "If you must know I really have no idea what's going to happen next."

It's just like you to say that but don't you think you've procrastinated about the future long enough?

She nodded in agreement and hurried back to her hotel room.

She sat at the desk and hovered over her iPad until her nimble fingers performed a brief, sprightly sonata on the keys. First, she cancelled the next day's flight to New York. After studying the next day's train schedule, she booked the local train from Montreux to Geneva and then the TGV from Geneva to Montélimar, arriving by mid-afternoon. She e-mailed Bridget with her arrival time and asked to be picked up at the station. Then she snapped the iPad cover closed with a heartfelt, "Good job!"

Moments later, snuggled in the hotel's thick, white, terry cloth robe, she lay down on the terrace for a short siesta. Only to jump back up again and send off a text message to Serge, hoping it would bring a smile to his lips as he dipped his fork into the melting fondue at the restaurant he went to in the mountains.

Thanks for the good advice. I did something for myself today!!!

An hour later she woke up to her beeping phone. She immediately checked her messages to see if Bridget had gotten back to her. No, but there was a message from her real estate agent.

"Oh my god!" she shouted. "Oh my god! I can't believe it." She read it twice for the sheer joy of it: Cash offer on your loft.

Her mouth opened wide. $10,000 above asking price. Shall I accept?

She wrote back feverishly: yes! yes!! yes!!!

Marisa danced around the balcony in her terry cloth robe not caring that down below the tight-lipped socialites were staring up at the madwoman on the balcony with undisguised disdain. She was tempted to open the robe and expose herself but it was time to get dressed.

In the long hotel room mirror, Marisa admired herself in the silk crepe de chine dress she'd brought specially for tonight's concert, relieved that it still fit after the hi-cal desserts she'd been unable to say no to. The summer dress was a simple affair but the light blue silk brought out her eyes and the skirt draped nicely around her hips. It would please Serge, she thought, and then blushed guiltily at her reflection in the mirror and wondered if it would have pleased Jules too.

Marisa put her painful stilettos in a bag for later and slipped on some comfortable shoes to walk back along the lake to the concert hall. Halfway down the hall, worrying about whether MiMi and DiDi had received the backstage passes she'd left for them at the front desk, she heard a familiar voice in her head and braked abruptly.

Marisa! You've forgotten your own pass!

"Oh Jules," she said aloud, as she would have done if he were alive. "What would I ever do without you?" She ran back to the room.

Not only had she decided to stay in France and visit her old friend in Beaulieu, and then almost immediately afterward had a generous offer on her loft, but now she was going to hear Martin perform at his first Montreux festival. It was way too much to happen in one day, she thought. And filled with such joyous expectations, she rushed through the lobby, reached the lakeside promenade and opened her arms wide to embrace the Mediterranean and breathe in the balmy air and, yes, to feel Jules's light caress. Then, shaded by the shimmering palms, she spent the brisk twenty-minute walk going over the details for the tour's grand finale.

Relieved not to see Ryan hanging around backstage, Marisa saw two dressing room doors with signs on them. One said CICI BELLE and the other MARTIN STARKS TRIO. She smiled. She hadn't had to ask this time. Things were certainly looking up for Martin.

She tapped on CiCi's door and found her seated in front of the vanity, brushing on matte powder. She turned to look at Marisa and said, "Wow! Girl! Don't you look stunning!"

Pleased with the effect her entrance had made, Marisa sank down on the couch to catch her breath. She needed to put a lid on her euphoria before she burst.

Then, as she watched Cassandra put on her makeup an unexpected memory entered her mind. When her daughter, Camille, lived in New York, she used to apply Marisa's makeup before they went out together to have fun. It worried her that she hadn't had her heart to heart talk with Camille about Alex. And now that she wasn't going home after the tour, she suddenly missed both her children a lot.

Cassandra called her name, which drew her back into the dressing room to hear Cassandra say, "I'm scared about tonight. As you suggested, I promised Ryan that The Belles wouldn't join us on stage and he calmed down … considerably. But when he finds out I lied to him, I don't want to be anywhere near him."

"Don't worry. I've got that all worked out."

"But how?"

"You'll see, my dear," said Marisa, and winked.

Cassandra went back to filling in her thin eyebrows with liner. The Goth look was gone, only the viper tattoo remained. "At least tell me how you ever got Martin to agree?"

"I told him he owed me a favor and when he found out Ryan didn't want it to happen that cinched it. But only one song, and not a Belle tune. He'll bring out the girls during the first encore. He didn't tell me what the song would be."

"But there's still Ryan to deal with."

Marisa came up behind her and massaged her tense shoulders. Cassandra studied her in the mirror and looked up. "Would you like me to do your face tonight? Your dress is gorgeous but I think your face could use a little something."

"I was just going to ask that very thing," said Marisa, sitting on the stool. "But you'll have to hurry. MiMi and DiDi are going to be here in a few minutes."

Cassandra looked at her suspiciously.

"You'll see. I met with them earlier and they wanted to see you before the show," said Marisa, looking down at her phone for messages.

"At least try and sit still while I do this," said Cassandra, holding Marisa's chin up while she brushed mascara on her lashes. She had just colored Marisa's lips when there was a tap on the door. Both girls were wearing black sequined gowns like Cassandra's and Marisa wondered if they'd planned that in advance. She was just about to tell them how beautiful they looked together when DiDi turned the tables and said, "Marisa, you look terrific. CiCi has the Midas touch, doesn't she? I've missed her not putting on my makeup before our shows."

"I'll do it now if you want," said Cassandra. "Going against Ryan's wishes has me spooked and I'd rather keep busy."

Marisa said, "Let's have our little talk first."

"Wait a minute. What talk?" said Cassandra, knitting her brows and frowning at Marisa and the girls standing behind her, who were all looking back at her in the mirror.

"We've got to get a few things straight here," said Marisa.

DiDi and MiMi sat down on the couch and Cassandra turned away from the mirror and said, "I don't know what you're all up to but this better be good. I don't need to have anything more to worry about tonight."

"Where shall I start?" said MiMi who was the eldest and seemed to be the least nervous.

Marisa sat down on a chair and said, "Why not start when CiCi was in rehab? Tell her why you didn't come to visit."

"We wanted to come," said DiDi, defensively. "But Ryan told us you didn't want to see us."

"That's ridiculous," said Cassandra. "Why would he say that? Of course I wanted to see you. He knew how depressed I was when you didn't show up and how I kept hoping you would. You were my family."

"We still are," countered DiDi. "You've got to believe us. We didn't come because Ryan told us you left strict orders for us not to visit. He even sent back the flowers we sent you."

"No, that can't be true," said Cassandra. "It makes no sense."

DiDi turned to MiMi who continued for her. "At first, we thought so too. Why would you not want to see us? But Ryan can be very convincing. As you well know that's one of his many talents." Cassandra nodded. "After you left rehab, he told us you were quitting the group because you were upset about the way we treated you. That you even accused us of stealing your solos. That you wanted to go out on your own so you could decide on what you really wanted to sing without us browbeating you."

Cassandra shifted her eyes from MiMi to DiDi. She was having a hard time accepting what they were saying, but she had complained to Ryan about her partners getting on her nerves and that maybe she'd be better off as a solo act. She never thought he'd repeat what she said to MiMi and DiDi. What could he have to gain doing that?

MiMi cut into her thoughts. "Then we got really pissed off

at you. We'd postponed the tour and held off the record release while we waited for you to get better, and then for you to suddenly quit—"

"And not tell us yourself," chimed in DiDi. "The tour that we all worked so hard on was starting in four weeks. We couldn't believe you could dump us just like that without any warning."

"No!" Cassandra shook her head violently and put her hands over her ears. "No. This is crazy." She stood over her former partners. "When I got out of rehab I told Ryan I'd be willing to wait until after the tour to make my final decision about leaving, but he told me that wouldn't be necessary. That you were already working with my replacement. What you're saying now just can't be true."

"Listen to them, Cassandra. There's more," said Marisa.

Cassandra crossed the room to her gown hanging on a makeshift wardrobe pole. "No, I need to get dressed now."

Marisa took her hand and brought her back over to the couch and sat her down between the girls. "This is more important. You'll have plenty of time to get dressed."

MiMi continued. "Yes, we did have a replacement but it was Ryan who'd set that up. Said it was insurance in case you did something stupid and quit. He auditioned the singers, not us, until he found one who had learned the songs and practiced our dance routines by watching videos of our live performances. When he told us you had quit, he took credit for having your replacement ready to go on tour with us.

"We went into an intense rehearsal schedule and left on tour four weeks later with new publicity shots. All the time thinking you had screwed us."

"Ryan told us you'd left L.A.," added DiDi. "He said you were drinking heavily again. He said he even hired a detective to find you and blamed himself for letting you get away. He sounded so hurt, not like his usual bombastic self." She laughed. "We actually felt sorry for him.

"When we read on Facebook about your comeback

performance at the Blue Note, we should have been furious at you for not letting us know first and not keeping us in the loop, but we were so pleased to know you were singing again we forgave you."

She turned to MiMi, "Didn't we?"

MiMi nodded her head. "We reached out to you after that but you never answered our messages."

Cassandra blotted the smeared mascara running down her cheek.

"That's why we were so surprised when you invited us here," said MiMi. "And then to ask us to join you onstage tonight, wow, that was totally unexpected." She glanced at Marisa. "Marisa overheard us in the bathroom saying we were so glad to be back together again, even if it's just one evening. She was surprised that you had invited us after telling her how awful we'd treated you. She asked us to meet with her this afternoon so we could sort things out."

Cassandra squeezed their hands and turning from one to the other, said plaintively, "I've missed you so much. But I couldn't forgive you after you abandoned me in rehab."

The girls put their arms around her shoulders. "You still don't get it," DiDi said, choking up and brushing back her own mascara-stained tears.

"We didn't abandon you," said MiMi. "Ryan manipulated all of us. He had a huge investment in you and was afraid he was going to lose it. So he figured out a way to keep us on his hook and you too. If he hadn't told us all those lies, we would have talked things out like we always did.

"My god, CiCi, we weren't happy with the direction Ryan was taking us on either but we couldn't get you to talk about it. We wanted to break our contract but were afraid you'd never agree to it."

"But he's still your manager."

MiMi turned to DiDi and she nodded her head and said, "You tell her."

"He's history, after tonight," said MiMi. "Actually we'd already planned to leave him before you invited us to Montreux. He never listens to our ideas and goes way over the top with expensive theatrical productions that make him look good and we end up paying for. It comes out of our royalty advances, as you know. And now that we know what a conniving son of a bitch he really is, we're definitely canceling our contract as soon as we get back to L.A."

Cassandra tossed back her head and laughed bitterly. "Yeah, right. No one breaks with Ryan. Don't you think I've tried?"

"Well, we're going to do it," said DiDi, standing up abruptly with her long manicured hands spread across her wide hips in defiance. "Our lawyer says there's an indentured servant clause we could use. You explain it, MiMi. You're better at that stuff than I am."

"It appears Ryan's gone way past the legal term of our contract without renegotiating. I'm surprised he didn't notice but he's been busy with his other artists. Our lawyer thinks we can cancel our contract without going to court or paying Ryan off."

"And listen to this," said DiDi, staring wide-eyed at Cassandra. "Our lawyer said that the agreement Ryan wrote and we signed, cutting you out of The Belles is bogus. Ryan negotiated for you and for us and even charged us a legal fee." She laughed. "His big fat ego got him in trouble on that one. It's illegal. Our lawyer says we can sue him for conflict of interest."

Marisa looked up at the wall clock. "We don't have much time now before curtain call and there's some choreography involved, so let's get to work." She smiled broadly at their confused looks and tear-stained cheeks. "First off, fix your mascara."

Fifteen minutes later there was a tap at the door: "Five minutes, Miss Belle."

"I've got to warm-up," said Cassandra. "Sorry DiDi. I'll have to do your makeup the next time we perform together."

In the stage wings, Marisa found the band gaping out at the packed Miles Davis Hall. "Awesome," said Stuart. "All those people out there have come to hear us play. How cool is that. Cassandra, too, of course."

"Let's give them a strong blast-off, shall we?" said Marisa, her spirits high.

"But where's Cassandra?" asked Carlos. "She's still in the band, isn't she?"

"Do I hear someone calling my name?" Cassandra said, coming up behind Martin. "You guys met DiDi and MiMi before, right? Does anyone mind if they join us in our blast-off."

"Fine by me," said Stuart, opening up just enough space for DiDi and MiMi to squeeze in on each side of him, hip to hip. Martin explained to the guys that The Belles were joining them for the encore. He asked if they were all right doing a new tune; one Cassandra had written lyrics for. "No problem," said Stuart. Martin handed out the sheet music.

Marisa put her right hand out to start the pre-concert ritual and everyone stacked their hands on top. They started humming together until they reached a vibrating energetic peak, threw their hands in the air, and yelled, "Whoosh!" Marisa could have sworn the whole stage shook or was it just her.

"Break a leg, guys," said Cassandra. She stopped Martin with her hand, "Thanks."

He looked into her eyes briefly, seemed about to say something, but strapped on his guitar and walked onto the stage to a roaring welcome from the crowd.

36

Marisa hurried into a jam-packed house and took her place against the aisle wall. She was looking forward to the show just as much as the audience. The house lights dimmed and the band was illuminated by ninety-six multi-colored lights controlled by Damian, who was working the sound and lights from a booth in the back of the theater.

As the band launched into their first tune, she searched the audience for Serge, hoping his height and silver-peppered hair would stand out in a crowd of young people. After she heard the start of the second tune, and was satisfied with the balance of the instruments, she returned backstage.

Ryan was in the right wing with DiDi and MiMi flanking him on either side. Marisa froze in her tracks. She almost changed her mind. She hadn't expected to be so afraid.

He looked quite the celebrity in a black pin-stripe suit, gray polka-dot silk scarf, and black fedora. She'd imagined him in an open-collared, half-buttoned Hawaiian shirt, showing off his hirsute chest and gold chains, but soon realized that sleazy managers of the past had learned how to look more sophisticated and didn't give themselves away so easily.

"Sorry, Marisa," he sneered with pleasure, "but my girls will not be joining CiCi on stage tonight. It would've been *fun*. But that's show biz, isn't it?"

You can do this, Marisa, you can do this.

She walked up to him with her eyebrows knitted and her mouth shaped in an 'oh' to feign her disappointment. "But why not?" She turned to MiMi and DiDi. "I thought you wanted to sing with CiCi?"

Ryan put his arms around MiMi and DiDi's waists and pulled them close to him as if they were his puppets and he was pulling the strings. "Tell her, girls."

"Ryan doesn't think it's a good idea. If we'd known before last night we could have had time to rehearse," said MiMi. "He's afraid we might make fools of ourselves." Ryan didn't see her wink.

Marisa turned and faced the band to hide her involuntary smile. The band was now several tunes into their set and the sound system was amplifying the music pretty loudly.

"Shouldn't CiCi be onstage by now?" shouted Ryan coming up next to her.

"Five minutes."

"Five minutes. Why so late?"

"She's the band's guest singer not the main act."

"*That's* a big mistake. Those are CiCi's fans out there, they didn't come to hear some unknown jazz guitarist," he snarled.

The audience gave a thunderous applause and Marisa turned to him. "Really, Ryan? Evidently the audience doesn't agree with your assessment. Maybe you should let me decide what's best for my band."

"Hey Marisa, come on now, don't be so tough on me. I know what I'm doing. Just ask my girls."

DiDi removed his wide-brimmed hat so they could both kiss his cheeks and ruffle his slicked-back hair. "He's just the best, isn't he?" they said in unison.

"Oh yes, he is," said Marisa. "And now that you're CiCi's manager again, her share of this tour money should probably go to you." She smiled and patted her thick money belt.

She looked around backstage. "Let's find somewhere private, so you can count it. The girls can come along if they want. It'll only take a few minutes."

Ryan looked doubtful. "All right. But let's be quick. I don't want to miss CiCi's performance."

"Hey Ryan," said MiMi, "where's your backstage pass ID. You know how finicky the Swiss security guards are."

"I lost it. I don't need it anyway. They all know me by name and, if they're new, Philippe will vouch for me."

They headed down a long corridor with dressing rooms on either side. "Hey, where are you going?" said Ryan, stopping at Cassandra's door. "Let's do it in here." He banged on the door. No answer. He jiggled the door. It was locked.

"We must have just missed her," said Marisa walking on. MiMi and DiDi took Ryan's arms and ushered him forward. At the very end of the corridor through a heavy door they stepped into a storage room crowded with shelves of old amplifiers, mic stands and boxes of sound equipment. "This'll do just fine," said Marisa.

She was handing Ryan an envelope when Cassandra rushed in breathlessly. "I thought I'd never find you. Come quick! Martin's collapsed on stage."

Marisa gasped. Cassandra retreated, the girls fast behind her. Ryan looked confused holding the envelope in his hand and in that instant Marisa shoved him back and jumped outside before he knew what was happening. Cassandra swung the heavy metal door closed. The four women pressed their bodies against it from the outside with all their strength as Ryan shouted from the inside to be let out. Marisa struggled with the sliding steel lock, but with one final push from the girls, she was able to slam the bolt home. They gave each other high-fives and hurried back to the stage.

Martin announced CiCi and called to her to join him onstage. Her fans called out "We love you CiCi! We love you CiCi!" Illuminated by a yellow spotlight, she approached center stage, bowed several times, and opened her arms as if to embrace each and every one in the audience. She then turned and stretched out her hand to each of the musicians in the band. As she mentioned their names and said she was proud to be performing with them the audience applauded enthusiastically. She smiled at Martin and started to sing "Didn't We Almost Have it All."

That night Cassandra and the Martin Starks Trio gave their

best performance of the tour. That night, after weeks of playing on the road, they were a fine-tuned ensemble. Cassandra strutted back and forth across the stage, raising her powerful voice above the beat of Carlos's drums and the rhythm of Stuart's bass and the cries of Martin's guitar. The electrified audience rose from their seats and danced in the aisles.

At the end of the set, the stage went dark. Carlos and Stuart walked off. Marisa radioed Damian to spot the center stage in blue and Martin and CiCi walked into it. The audience hushed while Martin picked up his acoustic guitar. Then without an introduction they performed their duet, "Peggy Blue."

When they finished, the house was silent. Martin put down his guitar and took Cassandra's hand. Together they bowed. The applause shook the rafters. CiCi reached for the hands stretching up to her. Martin pulled her back and they ran off stage and brought back Stuart and Carlos. The audience stomped their feet, demanding an encore.

CiCi ran offstage and brought back MiMi and DiDi. The audience chanted "DiDi, MiMi, CiCi; DiDi, MiMi, CiCi; DiDi, MiMi, CiCi." The band didn't wait for them to quiet down before starting up with "A Woman in Me." The girls strutted back and forth across the stage to the band's rhythmic pulse, bending down over the edge to shake as many hands as they could. They backed off for CiCi's lead vocal, but came together on the chorus: *I don't need your opinion/I don't need your advice/I don't want your possessions/I can take care of myself/So you'd better think twice/I got everything I need/It's the woman in me/Yes it is/It's the woman in me.*

Marisa was dancing in the wings. She was so caught up in the performance, she hadn't noticed Serge standing behind her until he spun her around, pulled her into his arms and whispered, "Bravo, Marisa!" Then Philippe, the grand Impresario, was shouting at her above the din. She could barely hear him but heard enough to know he was telling her they must come back next year. She was so thrilled with the band's success that all she could do was shake her head up and down joyously and keep clapping.

Philippe shouted, "Where's Ryan? He's usually here to take all the credit."

He didn't wait for an answer and walked onstage to take the mic and congratulate The Belles and the Martin Starks Trio on their performance. He took the final curtain call with them. The audience didn't want them to leave the stage and kept shouting for "More."

Marisa was still looking on from the wings when a security guard approached her. "Sorry to bother you but we found some crazy guy screaming his head off in the storage room. He said you locked him in." An amused smile spread across Serge's face.

"That's ridiculous," said Marisa. "I've been right here."

"That's right, officer," said Serge, putting his arm around her, trying to be serious.

"He says his name is Ryan Peters and claims he's their manager." He pointed to the stage. "I asked for some ID or a backstage pass but he didn't have anything on him except an envelope filled with a wad of newspaper clippings. He says you cheated him. We've got him in the security office. Do you think you could come and identify him?"

Marisa thought long and hard before saying. "No. Sorry. I need to be here when my group comes offstage."

"Then do you know where Philippe is? The guy said to find him." Marisa pointed to the stage. "I don't think Philippe would want you to interrupt him right now."

The officer shrugged. "Personally I think the guy's nuts. I guess we'll have to put him to the security holding cell until someone can identify him. When Philippe comes offstage ask him to call us." He tipped his hat. "Sorry to bother you."

Marisa picked Ryan's hat off the chair where DiDi had put it when the girls took it off while standing beside him earlier. A perfect souvenir for a magical evening, she thought.

The band and singers gathered at the Hotel Grand's bar to unwind after the show. Marisa left Serge with the band and joined the girls, drawn to their harmonious laughter that sounded like church bells.

CiCi turned to Marisa, "Wow, Marisa. I always said you'd make a good sleuth. When did you figure out what Ryan was up to?"

"At Philippe's. Why was he so upset to see the three of you hanging out together and why was he so violently opposed to you performing together? Any manager would love a free publicity stunt like that. Then when I overheard DiDi and MiMi in Philippe's bathroom saying how shocked they were when you asked them to join you onstage, and saying how much they'd missed you, that didn't add up. If MiMi and DiDi were telling you the truth then someone else had been feeding you lies; and who was in a better position to do that than your manager? As long as Ryan could keep you apart, a common divisive strategy managers use to control their bands, he could have what he wanted ... The Belles *and* CiCi ... which meant twice as much money and fame for him and he got to keep a hold on you personally at the same time." Marisa stopped to catch her breath.

"While he had you sequestered away at that lux rehab hotel, he moved ahead with his plan. He convinced you that The Belles didn't want you in the group and he convinced the girls that you hated them. As long as he could keep you apart, it would work. But he hadn't counted on you running away and living incognito in New York City or on you eventually contacting your former partners and inviting them to Montreux."

Stuart called over to MiMi and DiDi, "Your drinks are getting warm."

They went to the bar and Marisa turned to Cassandra. "So what are you going to do now?"

She shrugged. "I have a plane ticket to go to New York tomorrow. After that my dad invited me to stay with him for a while at his summer cabin in Maine, so I think I'll take him up on it. We could use some time together. The girls and I are probably going to go our separate ways but at least it will be on friendlier terms this time. And I need some time to work out the next steps in my career."

"Well, just don't disappear again. It'd be a shame to waste all that talent."

Cassandra hugged her. "Thanks Marisa for everything. If I ever do decide what I'm going to do when I grow up and need a manager again, might you be interested?"

Marisa smiled and shook her head no. "The last thing I want to do right now is manage anyone other than myself!"

They draped their arms around each other's shoulder and rejoined everyone at the bar. Marisa gave her last managerial instructions: "Cassandra, be in the lobby at seven. Serge tells me that you're flying out of Geneva tomorrow at nearly the same time, so he offered to drive you." Serge and Cassandra exchanged smiles that made Marisa feel a tiny bit jealous. "Don't be late!"

Damian showed up and said Philippe had gone to his chalet to party with some of his buddies and left instructions not to be called. So they're going to keep Ryan in the security cell until tomorrow morning. The girls giggled.

Marisa turned to Martin. "Damian will pick you guys up in the van at ten. Here's the itinerary Rufus faxed to me. I don't know how he managed to get these dates together at the last minute but he did. I envy you a week in southern Italy."

"You can come with us, Aunt Marisa," said Stuart, squeezing her waist. "I'm not sure how we can go on without you."

"Thanks for the offer but you guys have worn me out. I need a break."

"And where are you going to go for a break?" asked Martin.

She looked over at Serge. She had wanted him to be the first to know of her plans but everything had happened so quickly and now everyone was waiting for her answer.

"Tomorrow I'm taking the train to visit a girlfriend in southern France."

"Wow, Marisa," said Stuart, " you don't let the weeds grow under your feet, do you?" She didn't correct him, thinking it must have been an expression his parents used and he'd mixed up grass with weeds. And at that moment she was more concerned about the unhappiness that had just fleeted across Serge's face before he turned and smiled at her.

No one really wanted to be the first to break up their farewell party but someone had to, so Marisa got off the bar stool and reached for Ryan's fedora on the table. His leather bag with his passport was in the hotel safe. DiDi had grabbed it when she ran out of the storage room. Marisa planned to call Rufus later and ask him to mail it to Ryan's Malibu home.

Just to be doubly safe, Cassandra was going to stay with the girls for the last night. They said it would be like old times in high school having a sleepover. And her early morning flight would take her safely away before Ryan was released. Marisa calculated that it would take Ryan a couple of days to get a new passport at the American Embassy. By then he'd have heard from The Belles's lawyer and would have a lot more on his mind than tracking down CiCi.

"Hey, that's a cool hat," said Carlos.

Marisa smiled. "It's yours. It'll look much better on you than me."

Serge put his jacket over Marisa's shoulders and walked her to her room. He seemed distracted. As if reading his mind, she said, "I didn't decide to go to France to visit my friend until this afternoon or I would have told you. I need some time to just take it all in. As I also got a message from my real estate agent in New York saying there'd been a serious offer on my loft. If it goes through, and it should, there's just no reason for me to hurry home. Most of my things are in storage anyway and my lawyer has power of attorney to handle the sale transaction."

"You have everything worked out, don't you?" he said ruefully.

She sighed. "Not really. I hadn't expected to meet you again."

"Does that matter?"

"Of course it does. I'm finding it very hard to say good-bye to you."

"Then don't." He smiled. "You're good at writing e-mails and texts. And when you've done what you need to do ... "

"I do happen to know of an apartment on a lovely square in Paris that I've been thinking about renting," she said, wistfully. "Perhaps you'll come for a visit?"

He kissed her waiting lips and turned to go. She called him back. His jacket hung from her hand. "Don't forget this." He dropped it on the floor and wrapped his arms around her, drawing her close. He kissed her mouth and she melted into him, clinging to him, not wanting to let him go.

He slowly pulled away and kissed her closed eyelids. She heard his breathless, hoarse voice saying, "You're wonderful, Marisa." He opened her hand and kissed her palm. "When you finally see that shooting star, reach out with this hand and grab it, and never let it go. It's been waiting for you a long time."

She nodded yes, her eyes still closed. When she opened them, he was at the end of the hallway, a silhouette in the shadows, already slipping away into a corner of her mind.

37

Marisa woke early to pack and join Martin for breakfast. Riding down the elevator she thought back over the days spent planning his tour and how it had eventually unfolded so successfully, quite beyond her expectations. Yes, there'd been a few bumps in the road, there always were. But with the percentages and festival fees she'd handed out the night before, everyone could go home with money in their pockets, including herself. And that didn't happen on many tours.

Martin was waiting for her out on the terrace. It was crowded, but knowing Marisa's fondness for views, he'd found seats at the railing overlooking the Alps and Lake Leman. The Alps were reflected again in the water off the lake. He stood up when she approached.

"I'm going to miss you," she said, hugging him before sitting down, "but what a perfect place to say good-bye, don't you think?" She was trying hard to keep a happy face and turned toward the view.

The waiter took their order for deux petits déjeuners—coffee and croissants. She laughed and reminded him of the first days on tour when he'd demanded an American breakfast with bacon and eggs each morning. It drove the waiters into a frenzy and they usually tried to placate him with one hard-boiled egg.

Now it was Martin's turn to look away.

"Martin? Are you all right? Aren't you pleased with how the tour went?"

"Are you kidding? I'm walking on air. I still can't believe we played Montreux last night! And now I'm going off with the guys to Italy to play jazz gigs. It's awesome."

"Then why the dour face?"

"Because I don't want you to quit. I don't care if you don't remember whether a festival is in The Hague or Rotterdam. How am I going to find anyone else as real as you to manage me? It's pretty scary out here, Marisa."

He looked over at the tables filled with fashion-conscious, self-important music industry types knocking down their double espressos. They were negotiating loudly on their cell phones and didn't mind if everyone could hear. "I need you to maneuver me through this crazy music business. So I'm going to ask you again. Why can't we continue? Is this such a bad life?" He opened his arms to encompass the stunning view.

Marisa felt her eyes stinging but knew she must remain firm. She considered her words carefully. "I deeply appreciate what you're saying, Martin. I really do. I think it's the best offer I've ever gotten and I really believe you're going to be a very successful musician. I just don't think I want this kind of life anymore.

"This tour has made me realize once again that I want to spend the last season of my life being a writer. Of course, there's a chance I'll fail, but I've got to give it a real try. Just imagine how you'd feel if you stopped playing music and took an attractive detour. It may be fine for a while, but you'd be dying to get back to your music, right?"

"Yes, but why couldn't you do both? I understand your wanting to visit your friend and spend some time on your own, but what about after? Couldn't you do both then?"

"I've got to be ruthless about this, Martin, or I won't make the break and do it. I've got to stop trying to give everybody else what they want, as satisfying as that is, and concentrate on what I want. I have lots of ideas I want to explore and I need time and space to do that with no interruptions. I don't want to look in the mirror someday and ask a bitter old woman, why didn't I really give myself a chance?"

They both gazed out at the sailboats bobbing on the lake. "I do understand," said Martin, "but I'm not happy about it." He sighed deeply and his shoulders dropped. "So what do I do now, Marisa? Who else can I trust?"

"Rufus will help you. He believes in you and for that matter so does Philippe. I could tell when you finished your set that he was really pleased. Having those two men in your corner, my dear, is a great beginning." She looked at her watch. "I'm afraid it's time for us to go. You've got a tour van waiting and I have a train to catch."

She walked him outside and, with tears welling in her eyes, she said good-bye to Stuart and Carlos and Damian who were waiting by the van.

"I'm glad you're going with them, Damian. I'll worry a lot less knowing you're there. You're a damn good roadie, or I should say road manager. It was a pleasure working with you."

"It was a pleasure for me, too, Marisa."

"Why thank you, Damian."

Martin stepped forward and gave her one last hug.

They climbed into the van and the Martin Starks Trio headed south for Italy. Marisa watched and waved until the van turned the corner.

Bridget was standing on the platform when the mid-afternoon train pulled into the Montélimar station. Marisa hardly recognized her. The stunning woman looked years younger than her age, fifty-four, and she was glowing. The two women had a deep affection for each other and they wiped tears from their eyes between joyous bursts of laughter. In a mixture of French and English they exchanged heartfelt hellos and hugs. "It's so good to be here," said Marisa, as they left the station arm in arm.

Marisa couldn't wait to find out why her friend looked so exuberant. They sat down at their favorite outdoor café for an apéritif before the hour drive to the small town of Beaulieu.

"You look fantastic, mon amie," she said. "When Jules and I left you at the Lyon airport two summers ago you were pale, depressed, and too thin. I can't believe I'm looking at the same person."

At that point in her life Bridget had good reason to look tired and forlorn. Her husband of thirty years had recently left her for another woman and moved away. He then became seriously ill. The other woman decided to leave him on his own and Bridget was forced to become his caregiver.

"There are three reasons I look different," said Bridget. "One, I quit smoking. Two, I'm in love, and three, I had a face-lift."

Shocked, Marisa took all this in and wondered if she should have a face-lift too. But she believed the glow in Bridget's eyes came from her newfound love and the healing of a broken heart after her husband's betrayal. Bridget said she and her boyfriend were taking it slow, living together on weekends, but soon she would probably move in with him.

Marisa felt very happy for her friend, but nevertheless she was worried about her own situation at Bridget's farmhouse. "Are you selling your farm?" she asked anxiously.

"Mais, non, ma douce!" exclaimed Bridget. "I will always keep it. Your apartment will always be available to you as long as you like, I just won't be there all the time. Why do you look so sad?"

Marisa tried to explain in French by saying, "J'adore la solitude, mais . . ." She wasn't sure Bridget understood. In fact, she wasn't sure she could explain the difference. She loved solitude when her thoughts were her only companion, but she was afraid she'd be lonely when her thoughts were her *only* companion.

Bridget seemed to get the gist of what she was trying to say and said she would be at the farm often. She also reminded Marisa of her other friends in the village and how they were so excited when they heard she was coming back. Already there was a full calendar of dinner invitations.

"And if it's all right with you we want to have a special service for Jules. So many of his friends wanted to come to his funeral. I thought we could do it in my courtyard. Something simple and appropriate. We want it to be a celebration of his life."

Bridget went inside to pay the waiter.

Marisa was suddenly very tired from her journey on the train from Switzerland. She wondered if she'd made the right decision coming to this foreign land without Jules, without the man who had been her constant companion for thirty-five years.

The pastoral views along the one-hour drive to Bridget's farm renewed her spirits. She felt the same childlike wonderment she and Jules had always felt when they returned to what they considered their second home. And she'd arrived at the right time. The lavender fields were bursting in rich violet colors; the fields of mustard-colored sunflowers held their faces upward like turtles enjoying the sun's warmth; and the brilliant red poppies waved at her from golden hayfields. It was like stepping into a Van Gogh painting. Very different from Manhattan's gray asphalt streets and concrete walls, where only privileged penthouse dwellers enjoyed the vast cloudless sky she looked at now.

She and Jules had laid in a field in the sunshine in France under the cobalt blue sky and fallen in love again.

She must have slept for when she opened her eyes, the car was parked and she was looking up at Bridget's farmhouse, an eighteenth century hamlet of buildings melded together over the years. She and Jules had spent their summers in the building in the farthest corner, a refurbished animal barn that once accommodated goats and sheep. Bridget had named the apartment the Salle de Cinema, the movie theater, because it was a long and narrow rectangle.

Marisa stood frozen at the stone stairs that led up to her self-imposed retreat, afraid to take the first step. "Shall I come up with you?" asked Bridget.

"Non, merci, I have to do this on my own."

"There's butter, eggs and jam in the frigo and fresh-baked bread in the basket. If you like, come down this evening and join me for a tisane. I'll be up late."

"Maybe I will . . ." her voice drifted off as Marisa remembered Bridget's healing tea seeped in leaves from the linden trees that grew in nearby fields that she blended with lemon mint from her courtyard.

Bridget walked to the main farmhouse. Marisa had refused her friend's help and now lugged the suitcase up the eighteen stone steps. She rested on the terrace at the top of the steps and breathed in the blushing pink roses next to the doorway that were just opening their petals.

Out on the grass lawn, an ancient walnut tree was proudly showing off its youngest green leaves. The hammock under the tree was swaying in the breeze as if Jules had just gotten up and was coming over to welcome her.

"Jules?" she called out plaintively. She didn't expect an answer, but when she turned the key, squeezed her eyes shut, and pushed open the door she was still hoping he would be there and say, "There you are." Then everything would be all right again. But inside there was only silence. She looked up at the wall clock—2:15. That was the time when she'd removed the clock's battery six years ago. When they first rented Salle de Cinema, she didn't want a ticking clock to disturb the silence.

As she stepped into the apartment, she felt the room tilting and held on to the kitchen counter. An Impressionist art calendar on the wall was open to August. It was a written history in her scribbled hand of their last summer together marked by dinner invitations, shopping days, birthdays, and the night of the full moon drawn with a smiley face.

She slumped into a chair. "I can't do this," she said out loud as she tried to stop the flood of memories and whispering ghosts. "Jules," she cried out. "Where are you? Why aren't you here to meet me?"

She dragged the suitcase to their bedroom. Everything was just as they'd left it. She opened the curtains to let in some sunlight and fresh air. By habit, she left the two top drawers empty for Jules and opened the bottom drawer. The shirts he neatly folded and put away for their next summer were there. She closed it quickly. She'd unpack later.

Summer days were long at Beaulieu, and even though it was seven in the evening, she thought she'd still have time for a hike. She set down her manuscript on a small wooden desk in the living room and put on the hiking shoes she'd left in the closet.

Her metal walking cane was leaning against Jules's wooden walking stick. He found it in the woods and sanded it down to a smooth finish. He wrapped the end with rope to make a comfortable handle.

She wrapped her hand around it and stepped outside.

Just then she heard Jules reminding her to take her phone so they'd be linked. Otherwise he'd worry. She put it in her vest pocket.

Halfway up the paved road she spotted the hiking trail sign and turned off. It felt good to be outdoors where the memories were less suffocating, and she took off on a brisk walk to catch the sun's final rays before it slipped behind the ridge.

Deep in her thoughts, deep in her memories, she didn't pay attention to the direction she took. Why should she? The rains from the past two years had eroded parts of the trail but she'd hiked it countless times before. Reaching the top of a hill with a bird's eye view of Beaulieu down below, she drank some water and noted the time on her phone's screen: 8:00. By then, the sun had slipped behind a ridge and with the drop in temperature she reached for a sweater in her backpack.

She turned and started to make her way back. Thirty minutes later she reached a crossroad that confused her. She didn't remember having to choose between trails but she was sure the trail that led down the hill had to be right. However, after ten minutes of going deeper and deeper into the dense woods she was lost.

She looked around at the approaching darkness and a sudden terror crept up her spine. No one was waiting at home for her. No one would miss her. No one knew she was out there.

Leaning on Jules's cane, she climbed up to another ridge hoping to see the familiar bird's-eye view of the valley below and get her bearings. Beaulieu was nowhere in sight. Her heart thumped. "Where the hell am I?" she cried out.

As she anxiously turned back from another impassable trail, her foot caught under a tree root and letting out a cry she fell down on the rocky path. "Now look what you've done," she moaned, rubbing the pain in her twisted ankle.

The sudden sound of a duck quacking from under a thorny bush turned her fear into laughter. It wasn't a duck quacking, it was her phone! The quacking duck was her ring tone and the phone must have dropped out of her pocket when she fell. But where was it? She crawled around until she found it under the leaves.

"Hello?"

"Mom, is that you?"

"Oh my god, this is incredible. Miles? How did you find me?"

"What? I can't hear you! Speak up."

She was unwilling to admit to anyone but herself that she was lost, so she forced a loud cheery voice. "I can hear you Miles."

"Don't shout, Mom, I can hear you fine. Where are you?"

"You won't believe this but I'm hiking above Beaulieu." She looked up at a few stars in what was now a dusky sky.

"Wow. I was wondering where you were. I was getting worried. You didn't answer my last e-mail. Are you with that guy Serge?"

"No, I'm not," she said, defensively and suddenly wished she were. "Dear, can we talk later? I need to get back to Beaulieu before it gets too dark."

"Okay. I'll be quick. We wanted you to be the first to know. Sheri and I are engaged."

"What?"

He repeated himself, "Sheri and I are engaged."

"Oh! That's wonderful news, Miles." Marisa pulled herself up off the ground with the phone pressed against her ear, stepped down hard on her sprained ankle and moaned.

"Why are you moaning, Mom? I thought you liked Sheri."

"Oh, I do. I do. This is wonderful news. Maybe you two and Camille and Alex can come to Beaulieu for a visit soon and we can celebrate your engagement."

"Does that mean you're planning to stay there for a while?"

"Well, I really don't know, but right now I need to get down off this mountain. It's getting dark."

He must not have heard the panic in her voice.

"Okay. But we need to set a wedding date and need to know when you are coming home."

"I don't know yet. I'm not sure."

There was a long pause on the other end. She figured Miles was trying to decide whether to lecture her on hiking at night or on not having her future plans settled. He touched her heart instead.

"I love you, Mom."

"I love you too, Miles."

After they hung up she took a few baby steps but her ankle folded under her and she fell down again rolling onto her back.

In spite of her fear and pain, she gazed upward at the diamonds in the sky and felt suddenly at peace. She breathed deeply until her heart slowed down and the tension in her body relaxed. Then the completely unexpected happened, she saw her first shooting star race across the sky.

When it dimmed and disappeared like Tinker Bell, she pulled herself off the ground and slowly limped along the trail using Jules's cane for support. She struggled along until she remembered her phone had a flashlight app and then laughed at her good fortune. With the light on she scanned the dark woods and worked her way along the path, until she saw a wooden hiking trail sign nailed to a tree. Beaulieu was carved in yellow paint with an arrow pointing down a path to the right. Several minutes later she saw the lights at the hameau.

"I'm okay now." She stopped to look up at the dazzling night sky. "You don't have to worry about me anymore." She felt Jules's parting caress on her cheek, and pulling herself up as straight as she could, she continued her slow, unsteady walk home.

Exhausted, Marisa didn't even think to brace herself before entering the dark, empty apartment. She shined her flashlight on the wall until she found the switch that flooded the living room in a warm yellow light.

She looked at the manuscript on the desk and felt its magnetic pull. Tomorrow, she thought, there'd be time enough to organize my notes and get to work. She smiled up at the still clock and said, "More time than I've ever known."

Acknowledgments

I could not have finished this book without the help of my husband, Jim Payne, a musician by profession, but one of the best natural editors I've ever encountered. His confidence in my writing was the beam of light I needed when I saw only darkness ahead.

To Steve Lewis, an exceptional writer and editor, I am very grateful for the time he took to offer fastidious feedback as the story continued to evolve.

Fortunately, I have not experienced the overwhelming grief from the loss of a loving partner. My gratitude goes out to writers Joan Didion, Gail Godwin, Dr. Kay Redfield Jamison, Joyce Carol Oates, and Anne Roiphe whose memoirs I plumbed in the making of widow Marisa.

And gratitude to my other sources: George du Maurier's *Trilby*, Ronnie Spector's *Be My Baby*, and Lundy Bancroft's *Why Does He Do That?* Their books gave me insight into the Svengali personality that led to the making of Ryan.

And in writing this book and shepherding it into print, I had the sustainable support of my daughter Amie Ertmoed, who is always my first reader and biggest fan, the Ballantine production team, Webmaster Susan Bancroft, Barbara Bode, Marjorie Bryant, Brisou Buis, Ina Dittke, Julie Evans, Randi Feldman, Patricia Hamilton of Park Place Publications, Kate Hudson, Louise Jones, Jocelyn Kelley and the Kelley & Hall staff, Michael Lydon, Foster Maer, Andrea McCall, Ed McCann, Susan Newton, Tom Nolan, Samuel J.F. Payne, Marcella Silverman, Maria Weisbin, the avid readers of Carmel Valley Book Club, and the Yale Club staff. Plus a special look-in-the-eye toast to the irreplaceable Duckdog Retreat where this novel was conceived, and where I was given the encouragement by my fellow writers to keep going.

To all, my deepest thanks.

About the Author

Joanna FitzPatrick was born in Hollywood, California, and is a graduate of Sarah Lawrence College. She is the author of the historical novel *Katherine Mansfield (1888-1923)* and is married to Jim Payne, a musican. They divide their time between Carmel Valley, California and southern France.

Made in the USA
San Bernardino, CA
15 August 2016